MY NOTRE DAME

MY NOTRE DAME

Memories and Reflections of Sixty Years

THOMAS STRITCH

A NOTRE DAME SESQUICENTENNIAL BOOK

UNIVERSITY OF NOTRE DAME PRESS
NOTRE DAME   LONDON

The author and publisher are grateful to the following sources
for photograhs used in the picture section:
Pages 2, 3, 4, 5, 6, 7 (top), 8, 9, 10, 11 (top), 12, 13, 15: University of
Notre Dame Archives.
Page 7 (bottom): Joe Rudis, Photographic Archives, Vanderbilt
University.
Page 11 (bottom): *South Bend Tribune.*
Page 14 (bottom): *Review of Politics.*
Page 16: *Notre Dame Magazine.*

Library of Congress Cataloging-in-Publication Data

Stritch, Thomas.
    My Notre Dame : memories and reflections of sixty years /
Thomas Stritch.
        p. cm.
    Includes index.
    ISBN 0–268–01396–9
    1. University of Notre Dame—History.   2. Stritch, Thomas.
I. Title.
LD4113.S77 1991
378.772'89–dc20   91–50572
                                                       CIP

To the memory of the Holy Cross Fathers
who engaged and sustained me at Notre Dame:
John Cardinal O'Hara, J. Leonard Carrico,
Leo L. Ward, and Howard Kenna

CONTENTS

Acknowledgments   ix

Prologue   1

1. Notre Dame: A Reflection of Its Presidents   13

2. I Come to Notre Dame   31

3. The Notre Dame I Came to   43

4. Religion   67

5. How I Lived   83

6. I Begin to Teach   99

7. The Bachelor Dons   113

8. Washington Hall   121

9. Sport   133

10. The Arts at Notre Dame   149

11. Reaching Out   167

12. Head, Department of Journalism   185

13. The Making of Modern Notre Dame   199

14. President Hesburgh   213

Epilogue   235

Index   241

ACKNOWLEDGMENTS

Parts of Chapters 1, 4, 7 and 11 first appeared in *Notre Dame Magazine*. I am grateful to its editors for permission to use, in my rewrites, some sections from the originals.

Although written expressly for this book, Chapter 14 on Father Hesburgh was first printed in *Theodore M. Hesburgh: A Bio-Bibliography* (New York: 1989).

Father Marvin O'Connell, of the Notre Dame history faculty, read the entire manuscript in an earlier form and made valuable suggestions for its improvement. Fathers Carl Hager and Anthony Lauck read the portions that concerned their work, as did Professors Thomas Fallon and Robert Schmuhl. I am most grateful for their generosity. But my greatest debt is to my colleague in American Studies, Professor Ronald Weber, whose careful reading and critical acumen helped me to alter and greatly improve large sections of this book.

Former students John J. Powers and Louis Rukavina helped with mechanics. For help with checking and research I am grateful to Wendy Clauson Schlereth and her staff at the Notre Dame Archives and Manuscript Collection, to Father James Connelly and his staff at the Holy Cross Provincial Archives, to James E. Murphy and Professor Edward Fischer, and to Ann Rice of the Notre Dame Press, best of editors.

Finally, warmest thanks to Margaret Jasiewicz and her excellent staff for secretarial help.

PROLOGUE

This book is about the growth of Notre Dame since its diamond jubilee in 1917. That landmark celebration was symbolized by the dedication of the university's first separate library building, still standing on the campus's west side, the lone classical building among the Gothic spires. In 1964 Notre Dame dedicated its present library building, which symbolizes the new Notre Dame, dwarfing in its lofty steel structure the beautiful old campus and trumpeting the contemporary world of numbers, giantism, and computerism.

You might say, stretching things a bit, that I grew up with this new Notre Dame. I missed the start, the surge in the 1920s that brought, to the west end of the campus, new buildings and to the university national recognition. By the time I arrived as a freshman in 1930 every literate American knew about Notre Dame. This was not true in 1917.

But in 1930 the university's academic reputation was low. In certain circles it was thought even inferior to other Catholic centers of learning, notably Georgetown and Holy Cross. The reputable state institutions, still in the grip of pragmatism, were suspicious of anything religious. The private universities, whose origins were nearly all religious, regarded the relics of their founding, the divinity schools still on their campuses, as faintly embarrassing, like poor relations.

All this was to change with World War II. Under the brilliant leadership of Theodore M. Hesburgh, Notre Dame's barque caught the winds of change at their strongest. Hesburgh brought once more to the academic fore talk of values, ethics, character, and justice. In a world floundering for the lack of these he brought Notre Dame to recognition as never before. Under his leadership Notre Dame became a flagship in the search for truth and decency, still under the banner of democracy.

1

This, then, is a story of transition. I came to Notre Dame on a trolley car. As I write this, sixty years later, about half the students have their own automobiles. When I matriculated, the Notre Dame prep school, for years the sturdy underpinning of the entire enterprise, had been gone for ten years, but its mentality still had a strong grip on the Holy Cross community. Now, in the 1990s, the young Holy Cross priests are more in the mold of their great atavar Father John Zahm, the first Holy Cross priest-scholar to bring Notre Dame to the attention of national and international scholarship.

I have lived through this transition. In writing about my experience of it, however, I can't pretend to more than a personal view. The whole story must wait for the competent historian of the future. To his work I feel I can contribute something born of human contact, not documents. The history of a place like Notre Dame, whose principal actors met daily, took their meals and walks together, and conferred informally almost constantly, is made especially difficult by the absence of minutes and notes about most of these. So my modest contribution may have some value. It is what I saw and heard.

One reason why I feel of some use is that my personal history reflects in some sense the same sort of transition. Until I went to high school in 1926 I lived with one foot stuck in a past that's part of American folklore. This is romanticized as the Currier and Ives view of American life, the independent yeomanry of Jefferson's dream, the simple and happy days of a regiment of writers as diverse as James Whitcomb Riley and Mark Twain. I have no nostalgia for it. When asked that favorite question of academics, which period of history would you liked to have been born into, I invariably reply the year air conditioning became commonplace. But let me tell you about it.

My boyhood was spent at 514 Monroe Street in my native city of Nashville, Tennessee. The little section of north Nashville we lived in had formerly been Germantown. Why my grandfather Stritch, Irish to the marrow, settled there I don't know. His next-door neighbors were Stumbs, and across the street lived the Sharenbergers and the Rattermans. Across the street from us were the homes of the Neuhoff brothers, Henry and Lorenz. The spacious home of the virtual founder of the Catholic part of the German colony, John F. Buddeke, was at the other end of the block from Henry Neuhoff's home. The Buddekes were long gone from the neighborhood, their home now the property of the Catholic church just across Seventh Avenue, and other German families were gradually moving to newer and more fashionable neighborhoods. But there were plenty left, Wetteraus and Ritters and Strobels and Brackmans and Floershes and Baltzes and Petres, to name a few who come swiftly to memory. We followed the Neuhoffs to Nashville's west side the year of my boyhood's end, 1926, when I went to a boarding prep school in Dayton, Ohio, just before I turned fourteen.

My north Nashville boyhood was an odd mixture of town and country, old and new, nineteenth and twentieth centuries. The house at 514 Monroe itself is a good case in point. It had no central heating. We were warmed in winter by a big cookstove in the kitchen, a Franklin-type stove in the much-used dining room, and a grate fire in the little-used parlor. The bedrooms also had fireplaces, but these were seldom lighted—ordinarily, only in case of illness. My father's last task at night was to shake down the ashes of the stoves and his first job in the early morning was to dump them in the trash and start the fires anew. As I grew into it, my job was to break up for kindling the boxes he brought home from his place of business, Robert Orr's wholesale grocery, and to keep the coal scuttles filled during the day.

Our house did have indoor plumbing. The house next door, owned and occupied by highly respectable Nashville folk, did not, and I used to note, with a child's absorption, the procession of the numerous occupants to the outdoor privy located just a bit over the fence and away from my favorite perch in a mulberry tree. My mother had told me that silkworms throve on mulberry leaves, so that messy old tree was romantic to my innocent eye.

The bathroom to our house—*to* is proper, for it and its adjoining back porch had been pasted on the main structure much after the event. It was heated in winter by a kerosene contraption which failed to penetrate to the plumbing below, so that my mother and I spent hours in bad weather wrapping rags around the pipes to keep them from freezing and bursting. The porch end of the addition contained a pre-electric refrigerator, for which we bought ice in summer, and a gas stove for summer cooking. One side, looking onto the backyard, was mostly glass swing-out windows with large panes, which my brother and I broke with stupefying regularity as we practiced baseball in our part of the yard. The larger part, the two separated by a grape arbor, was my mother's garden, which I viewed with a jaundiced eye—my brother, three years younger, was never really drawn into its slavery. But I, when my mother could corral me, trained green beans and sweet peas up miles of string, bagged the grape clusters to keep the birds off them, and did other tasks requiring no discrimination, for I was hopeless at weeding, refusing to distinguish the planted from the usurper.

The bathroomless people next door had a backyard about the same size as ours which culminated in a stable complete with horse and buggy. This was firmly off limits to us. Our play yard also culminated in a tumble-down old stable converted to coal storage and other miscellaneous uses. The garden side ended in a little house, which we rented to a fine black couple named Claude and Lizzie Blake and their little child. Lizzie did our washing, along with that of many others, boiling the clothes on fine days in a big black iron kettle heated by a wood fire underneath. Water came from a well whose pump was as cranky as only a well pump can be. The barn also had, oddly, a toilet for the little house. It, too, had an eccentric flushing system, whose water supply was pumped into an overhead tank. Nearly everything mechanical about 514 was problematical. The hot water tank attached to the kitchen stove occasionally roared like a tornado and had to be emptied. You were grateful when the doors and windows operated without complaint. Even the simple front door bell was frequently out of order, its round ring part spun off by a meddlesome child.

My paternal grandmother, who lived in similar but even more primitive circumstances a block away, down the alley to Madison Street, kept chickens and used to pass along to my mother a couple of fryers now and then. It fell to my lot to slaughter these, using the method taught me by my mother, that of grasping the chicken's head and whirling the creature around vigorously till the body flew off and flopped grotesquely into silence. This troubled me less than the next step, one I hated almost as much as I did cracking and picking black walnuts, that of plucking the feathers.

I used to hang around my grandmother's as much as possible, for she was usually good for a nickel, which I instantly squandered on a foot-long stick of hard candy at Mr. Gus Blodau's drugstore halfway home. I struggled vainly against this vice during Lent, fighting my secrecy as much as the vice, for I never told a soul about Grandma's largesse. She also nursed my passion for reading. On Saturday mornings I would go to help her fill her kerosene lamps and trim the wicks. I then would stretch out on the floor with the *Saturday Evening Post*, whose illustrations I loved. I can still recall the work not only of the celebrated Leyendecker, but of May Wilson Preston, Henry Raleigh, and many others. These pictures were the first art I ever liked, and I continue to think well of them. I can't recall anything I read in the magazine, though.

We had gaslight at home, and under its soft glow I read with that total absorption only children know. I don't remember reading books for the very young, but I read hundreds of boys' books, and girls', too—the domain of my older sister Kate—if there was nothing else around. I actually read through a set of the Elsie Dinsmore books we had in the house, possibly before I was old enough to go to the North Nashville branch of the public library. The ladies who ran this were as kind to me as could be, and I record this with the same gratitude I bear for the wise philanthropy of Andrew Carnegie, for I was a shy and sensitive child who, even mildly rebuffed, would have achingly hung around the place afraid to reenter.

Looking back, I sometimes think that I have never been better off than I was at 514 Monroe Street. Everything I wanted was within easy reach. The Carnegie Public Library was only three blocks away up Monroe Street. Grandma's was down Fifth Avenue, a block and a half away, towards downtown. Frequently on my way there I took the shortcut through the alley to stop at Mr. Schott's horseshoeing establishment there. Schott, a muscled and mustached, grizzled old boy didn't mind young visitors who sat quietly and stirred not. Only a foolhardy boy would do otherwise. Speech was impossible through the roar of the bellows and the clang of the hammer shaping the white-hot iron of the shoe. The sparks flew and occasionally had to be stomped out. But the part I liked best was when Mr. Schott took the horse's hoof between his knees, stripped off the old shoe and cut away on the hoof to make a flat surface for the new one. I never saw a horse balk or Mr. Schott nonplussed.

From our house down Monroe Street, the direction away from school, church, and the public library, at the end of our block you ran into Mr. Blodau's drugstore and on two other corners of Fifth and Monroe the notions stores of Mr. Schwartz and Mr. Schatten. Mr. Robert Fehr's grocery store was a baseball throw away across Monroe, and I was constantly being sent on errands to these. In memory I can still hear my mother, "Tom, run down to the dry-goods store and ask Mr. Schwartz to give you a spool of white thread No. 40." Or my father, "Run over to Fehr's and tell Mr. Robert to give you a couple of packages of potato chips." I liked doing these errands; they made me feel important. I did not like scrubbing the kitchen and back porch floors, or bringing in the coal, or the gardening. But I was fascinated by the special tasks of the year's progress, making and storing in the cellar sauerkraut, helping with the Christmas baking, squashing with clean bare feet the grapes for wine, helping with the summer canning, and so on.

However, the true center of our lives was the Church of the Assumption, just a block up Monroe Street. It did not seem so to me then. I liked Assumption School, and I liked going to church, but the influence both exerted on our daily lives was unconscious. No child is aware of his being shaped. I wasn't even aware of the unusual piety of both sides of my family. Each produced an uncle bishop, and my mother's oldest sister was a nun, a member of the Daughters of Charity of St. Vincent de Paul. My mother was very fond of her, and they corresponded regularly. We were frequently visited by Jesuit Fathers Tom and John Stritch, first cousins to my father. We took Catholic magazines. We went to most devotions, May, Lent, and so on. I was a dutiful and biddable, if oversensitive and quick-tempered child; to this day I like to be told which restaurant to go to, which baseball games to try for, and so on. I like order, organization, cooperation. My Catholic upbringing helped.

Our family was poor, but this, too, affects a child but little. I never got the bicycle I yearned for, but I never needed it, either. We were well fed and well clothed and on Sunday afternoons took rides in my father's Model-T Ford. Like all kids we were nuts about cars and knew every model that tooled along newly paved Monroe Street; we watched the paving as we might a circus. This was one of the best attractions to me of 514, especially in retrospect. I felt part of a way of life that was full of interest. We were only a ten-minute walk from the baseball park of the Southern Association Nashville Vols, where I eventually became a box usher. My mother usually took the trolley to town, and we waited for her descent as if she were a messenger from a royal court. I loved the trolleys as much as I did the automobiles. Oddly, I did not hang around the fire engine company, No. 4, just a block further on from Blodau's drugstore. I did accompany my father to the sulphur water springs, again just two blocks north from the drugstore. I thought the water nasty, but Dad thought it good for what ails you, and lots ailed him. He was a pill box.

School, taught by the Sisters of St. Dominic, was old-fashioned rote learning, reading and writing and drill arithmetic. I thought of it as an exciting place to go and yearned to start long before I actually did, since my father had a thing about not forcing the child. Consequently, I could read long before I went to school and was far ahead of my mates in reading and writing. Our school was so small it seemed more like family. There were only three boys in my eighth-grade graduation class. I think the teaching was good, but it was not inspiring. It was learn, recite. I have always had a good memory for school lessons. It's odd. I can't easily remember what I did yesterday and am at a loss to place trips abroad, events at Notre Dame, and birthdays and anniversaries. But I can recall yards of poetry, remember casts of operas heard fifty years ago, long stretches of European and American history, and could always quickly learn enough to pass most exams easily. So I did well in school, academically.

But not socially. I was not really accepted as one of the boys. Part of it was my uncle bishops—my grade-school nickname was Bishop—but most of it was my school smarts. And yet I was seldom teased or bullied, probably because I was fairly big, fairly strong, and a better athlete than most. But mainly that was because the schools I attended were so small. In a larger school I would certainly have been smacked around some, and it would probably have been good for me.

Since we lived so close to the school, we took our midday meal at home. Because my father, a city salesman for the whole-sale grocery company, was on the road he, too, came home for dinner, our principal meal of the day. This was owing in part to the old southern tradition, but there was another reason tied in with the old south as well. In spite of our poverty, we had a servant, a black woman named Florence Swanson, called by us children Tonkey. Tonkey was hired mainly to look after us; I can't recall that she did any cooking, though she did help with the preparations. She was good with children, and we three throve on her kind and generous spirit. My mother and she got along well together. In addition to Tonkey and Lizzie for the washing, we had old Pete, who cut the grass of the front yard with a sickle. There were still plenty of blacks around the alleys, like old Pete. There was a stalwart black woman who roamed the alleys in season with a large round dish on her head, calling out, "Hominy, hominy! Fresh lye hominy!" An-other old gentleman came to sharpen the knives. Still others, white folks, hawked fruits, vegetables, and meats in season; my mother bought much of our provender from these, which meant she didn't have to dress to go to the store. Most of these entrepreneurs, black and white, were well known to the women of the neighborhood, who took a keen interest in them. One of my earliest memories is Miz Josie Rich (my mother's favorite friend, who lived next door) telling Mom how impressed she was at Tonkey's making her daily way to our house in the bitter winter of 1918.

What a curious mixture it all was! All those blacks, living in that peculiar nether world between former agrarian slavery and precarious entry to the new industrial civilization. All those horse-drawn vehicles—the ice wagon, the trash man, the street vendors—spilling manure on our newly paved street. One of my uncles got married in my early childhood, and I remember vividly the gaily decorated horse-drawn landau that drew up to our front door to fetch my parents to the church. All our ill-paid servants, drawn to domestic work partly because the only meat they had on their tables, aside from an occasional ham hock or bacon rind, was what they could tote home from their places of employment, themselves at the fringe of white respectability. And talk of racism! We small urchins used to creep upon the Chinese laundry and yell, "Chink, chink, chink, chink, Chinaman, eat a rat, eat a mouse!" and then run madly away, aglow with our manly adventure. Yet we got along well with the Catholic immigrants, the Italian tailors and fruit wholesalers, the Lebanese grocers, the rare Swiss. There weren't many of these, to be sure, and there was none of the floods of Poles, Hungarians, and Croatians that spilled into the north. Post-Civil War immigration avoided the South. I think this was a pity. Had there been more, we would not have had as much of our sorry Jim Crow history as we did have.

We shared with all American children the childhood diseases that are now only a memory. My sister nearly died of diphtheria and I of scarlatina, and we all suffered through whooping cough, various kinds of measles, and chicken pox. Also only a memory is our restricted diet. In winter we had only the greens that we had canned; commercial canning was still suspect. An orange was a great treat. The meats in the South were mostly inferior. The local beef was poor, and my mother had the usual unfathomable southern prejudice against lamb, so we ate mostly pork in various forms. This we varied with very occasional game, squirrel, quail, and fish. I liked the barbecued kid I had occasionally at big picnics, but my mother avoided it as she would possum. Like most southerners we had lots of biscuits, corn bread and homemade rolls, at which my mother excelled. When I came north to prep school I found the better meats greatly to my taste. I especially recall the first good sirloin steak I ever had. I was about sixteen and from then on became a confirmed, happy carnivore till the sad 1980s when American beef went bad.

My father was not a hunter or a fisherman, and so I did not grow up learning these field sports. And I never really have, despite occasional forays of happy fishing trips. The great boyhood sport in Nashville was baseball. I think I might not have known football at all except that the uncle of our friend Casper Kuhn was quarterback of the Vanderbilt team. Even with this stimulus I recall being uncertain about the rules till I fell in love with the game at prep school. But I did grow up with a love of walking. From 514 Monroe to downtown Nashville was an easy and pleasant walk. In the opposite direction the Cumberland River and its shoreline wilderness were scarcely any further. To be so close to town and equally to genuine pathless uninhabited country was wonderful for a boy—and thoroughly symptomatic of the between-two-worlds condition I am trying to describe. But even in the country, mostly alone, I was basically bookish and priggish. I became less so in the highly organized sports of my prep school, where my comparative size and skill made me among the first to choose or be chosen for pickup games until everyone around me grew bigger. It was the right time of life for this, and it skidded to a close almost as soon as I entered Notre Dame.

My boyhood was ringed round with scads of uncles and aunts, but few cousins. Both my parents came from large but not philoprogenitive families. But I don't want to speculate on heredity versus environment. I feel sure that my bookishness was inherited, and I am grateful for the small-town environment that kept me from growing up in a ghetto. I am especially grateful for the small scale of my early life.

The Notre Dame that I came to in 1930 was also small. All through the 1930s the undergraduate student body was around three thousand. Of these about thirteen hundred were in the College of Arts and Letters, which is, I still think, an optimum size for a college. Of course, I understand that this is no longer possible in our time. Ours is an age of plenitude. But it is also the age of the lonely crowd and the mass man. In this book I write of many individuals, faculty and students. I think that in today's crowded world many, perhaps most, of these would be regarded as cranks and eccentrics. But they wouldn't be possible in today's world.

For its first half-century Notre Dame was the lengthened shadow of one man, Edward Frederick Sorin. Its post–World War II period is dominated by Theodore Martin Hesburgh. Although I conclude with a chapter on Hesburgh, I deal mostly with the period between him and his great predecessor. One good reason for this is that the period between 1900 and 1950 has been largely neglected by Notre Dame historians. But a stronger reason, for me, is that this is my Notre Dame. Mostly my book is based on my observation, my memory, and the memories of colleagues who have passed along to me their recollections and impressions. I have, of course, shored up these memories in our excellent archives, and particularly in Tom

Schlereth's superb pictorial history. But mainly this is the Notre Dame I have experienced in my person and imagination. George Kennan calls one of his volumes of memories *Sketches from a Life*. This has not been my conscious model, but as I try to put this book together I find it more like Kennan's than any other book I know.

This book, then, is not history, though I hope it will be of use to future historians. It's my Notre Dame, not everybody's; vast stretches of history and fact are left untouched because I have no feeling for them. In the chapter that follows this, which is, along with the last chapter, the most history-minded, I give my own impressions of the presidents. I have loved Notre Dame, but I have tried to be honest as well as affectionate. I hope I haven't been dull.

1

NOTRE DAME:
A REFLECTION OF
ITS PRESIDENTS

Edward Frederick Sorin was Notre Dame from his founding of it in 1842 to his death in 1893.

This formidable and willful leader was made of stern and heroic stuff. His name belongs with the other nineteenth-century pioneers in American Catholic history, DeSmet, Lamy, Ireland, and many more. He carved Notre Dame out of the northern Indiana wilderness and by sheer strength of character made it go. He built and rebuilt, recruited students where he could, and gradually began the unique image Notre Dame still enjoys. In a college or university reputation is everything. Somehow Sorin developed a favorable one for Notre Dame, one that reverberated throughout the American Catholic world, the Eastern Seaboard as well as the Midwest. Long before football was invented, Notre Dame caught the imagination of American Catholics.

Sorin was lucky in that the railroads, just beginning to penetrate the Midwest when he arrived on the scene, made South Bend easily accessible to the growing Catholic population of the Great Lakes cities. But he was not lucky in everything. Some of his educational ventures elsewhere failed. At home his principal enemy was fire. The worst of these, in the April of 1879, shows Sorin at his best. Called back to the campus from beginning a trip abroad, Sorin found rebuilding well advanced under the vigorous leadership of President Corby. Sorin leaped into the work, and somehow he got the enormous present Main Building up in time for the fall term. Not quite all of it, but enough to live and work in.

Sorin also grew powerful in the development of the Holy Cross community and eventually tried to run it. Here he had a fitful temporary success, full of tension and struggle and misunderstanding. But he foresaw that the future of the community lay with the New World. It was a world he had come to admire and love. He certainly left his mark on it.

The presidents of Notre Dame who succeeded Sorin during the founder's lifetime were all, with the possible exception of Father Thomas Walsh who died at forty, dominated by Sorin. After Sorin's death the conservative Father Andrew Morrissey took over as president. His twelve years in that office were years of neglect of the university. His heart, and above all mind, were with the prep school. He thought of Notre Dame as a boys' boarding school and did his best to make and keep it so. Thanks to strong community opposition, led by Fathers John Zahm and James Burns, he did not quite succeed. But he did delay the rise of the university side of Notre Dame, not least in the legacy he left his successor.

This was the legendary Father John William Cavanaugh, a robust and larger-than-life character who became president, like Theodore Hesburgh a half-century later, at the age of thirty-five. Notre Dame history has an odd touch of presidents with the same name: two Cavanaughs, two Walshes, two O'Donnells; no kin, and little in common besides their brotherhood in Holy Cross. I knew them all except the first Father Walsh, Thomas. The second Walsh, Matthew, followed the brief term of James Burns, who succeeded the first Cavanaugh. Then came the first O'Donnell, Charles; then John O'Hara, and the second O'Donnell, Hugh, followed by the second Cavanaugh, John J.

John W. Cavanaugh was the first president of Notre Dame I ever saw. This was on Easter Sunday, 1927, in old St. Francis Cathedral in Toledo, Ohio, where my Uncle Sam was bishop. I had come up from my prep school in Dayton to spend the Easter holidays with him and in his shadow attended the Holy Week services climaxed by the solemn mass on Easter Day with a sermon by the former President Cavanaugh of Notre Dame. I greatly enjoyed this and the subsequent Easters in Toledo; I even enjoyed the churchgoing because of the beautiful music. The Toledo cathedral had an excellent choir, conducted, I am pleased to recall, by tasteful Father Ignatius Kelly. He gave the singers, including a well-trained complement of boy sopranos, the great music of the Church to sing, the medieval plainchant and Renaissance polyphony. I can hear the boys now, in musical memory stretching back well over sixty years, singing the beautiful Gregorian setting of "O Redemptor, sume carmen, temet concinentium" on Holy Thursday.

I can also hear Father Cavanaugh preaching his lengthy Easter sermon, but I hear him in memory as I heard the choir, as music, not as discourse. His mellifluous voice rose and fell like an organ prelude. He was an imposing figure in the pulpit, now some eight years away from his tenure as president of Notre Dame but still in vigorous middle age. It was common in those days for cathedrals and other big congregations to invite a distinguished academic figure to give the Easter sermon. It was an agreeable practice except that the invited speakers, wishing to earn their honoraria, tended to go on and on. This was nothing new to my uncle. At his consecration, six years before in this same cathedral church, his predecessor, Bishop Joseph Schrembs, preached for nearly two hours. I was an altar boy at the consecration. My honor was saved by a sympathetic young priest who slipped me out of the sanctuary into the sacristy during Schrembs's vasty periods and showed me, a timid nine-year-old who wouldn't have dared to ask, where the plumbing was. I still in memory bless his understanding heart.

Of course I hadn't a clue as to what Schrembs was talking about. And now, six years later, I still found Cavanaugh's Easter message incomprehensible. My uncle, however, thought highly of it. "What a phrasemaker Cavanaugh is," he said in the car coming home. He quoted, "On Good Friday, the Church with its mangled services and mutilated rites" — here my uncle broke off, saying, "There's a sermon in just that phrase."

Neither then nor later at Notre Dame did I hear the famous Cavanaugh conversation. Everyone who was exposed to it spoke of its charm, and the pleasure he took in exercising it was plain. He loved to preach, but he loved meeting people just as much. During his presidency, from 1905 to 1918, he knew every denizen of Notre Dame, lay and clerical. He loved talking to them, just as he loved talking to the great and the near-great he invited constantly to the campus for lectures. Both faculty and students, expected to attend these talkfests, became bored and irritated at the constant intrusions into their class schedules, even though the speaker might be Vice-President Tom Marshall or Henry James.

But not Cavanaugh. He loved meeting these famous people, loved stories about them, loved the chaffing and the camaraderie, the genial repartee, the sentimental indulgences, the whole ambience of good fellowship. It may be that this charm of manner was his undoing. In his youth he was identified with the liberal, anti-Morrissey wing of the Holy Cross community, and I think that's where his sympathies lay. But, succeeding Morrissey, he made no waves, started no innovations, proposed no programs. Not only did he coast along the well-traveled Morrissey ruts, he actually deepened them. It is a strange paradox. Cavanaugh seemed unable to translate his sympathies into programs. Behind his genial and courtly manner was a genuinely high-minded person, in maturity with rhetorical flourishes, in youth with a touch of priggishness. Here is a sample of the young Cavanaugh writing in the *Scholastic* in 1887:

> One of the evils of the day is the mania of the student for athletic sports. A student should positively be a man of thought and mental application and, in an education, the diligent pursuit of learning should be the paramount idea. Nothing renders a man so unfit for study as excessive exercise. It strains every muscle and exhausts every particle of mental energy, thus excluding study from the mind of the wretched enthusiast. The number of those who can confine themselves within the proper limits in athletic sports is small indeed; and the college man who is at once a dunce and a baseball fiend is a standing disgrace to the college world.

What a surprise to learn, in the last sentence, that the indignant writer is writing about — baseball! By 1887 baseball had taken hold of the American sporting imagination, but the football legend had not yet got underway. Notre Dame had by then played only one football game, a loss to mighty Michigan. Certainly Cavanaugh was not troubled by football. When Coach Jess Harper resigned and recommended Knute Rockne as his successor, Cavanaugh agreed, much as if he were agreeing to an appointment to teach — indeed, it *was* that in a sense, since

Rockne was also teaching chemistry. The Great Awakening to football had not yet come.

Cavanaugh's charm, love of talk, and contentment with the sentimental Catholic provincialism so prevalent in his time led him to develop the character of a prep school headmaster rather than a university president. Cavanaugh's Notre Dame was a small, cozy enclave ruled imperiously by him — and him only. He did everything. He recruited students and awarded scholarships like a benevolent uncle giving his nephews a little spending money. He made just about every decision, major or minor, that had to be made, excepting only some purely academic ones. These, beyond his ken, he left to his able academic chief, Father Matthew Schumacher. And woe betide anyone who opposed the Boss. The Cavanaugh charm could turn to wrath as swiftly as a Notre Dame weather change. Yet Cavanaugh did not challenge his peers. He got along well enough with his provincial superior, Father Morrissey, even though Morrissey openly disliked Cavanaugh's courtly manners and flowery rhetoric. Perhaps Morrissey half-intimidated him, for Cavanaugh kept on as president much as Morrissey had before him. In a community showdown, Morrissey would almost certainly have won. So it may have been the only course left for Cavanaugh. In any case, very little of the progressive spirit seething in the priests' community spilled over into presidential action.

Yet, in his defense, Cavanaugh had been left alone. The men who had led the progressive forces had departed from Notre Dame. Something of their spirit survived in their friends and disciples, but their drive had been, temporarily at least, blunted. However, it was too strong and true to die out. It had been growing, especially on the science side, for many years. When Fathers John A. Zahm and James A. Burns came along to give it strong leadership, in the last quarter of the nineteenth century, it grew into a movement demanding scholarship, higher learning, and real university work and status instead of Morrissey's complacent prep school.

Zahm was a marvel and a wonder. Both he and his remarkable brother Albert came to Notre Dame around 1870 from a northern Indiana farm: no one knows whence their talent or why they came. Both took the normal classical course. But both were fascinated by science. Polymath John took on half a dozen of them, physics, chemistry, audiology, and biology among them. He learned them much on his own. Albert was all his long scholarly life devoted to the emerging technology of aviation. He was a pioneer in several aviation areas. He had a distinguished career, first academe, then government.

John decided on the priesthood and Holy Cross. Still in his twenties, he became a well-known professor of science, a writer, lecturer, almost a savant, and a vital force in the Holy Cross community. He was an instant pet of old Sorin, who took him traveling to the Holy Land in 1888. He also deeply impressed Father Gilbert Français, Sorin's successor as superior general of the Holy Cross community. Français authorized a pet Zahm project, a new Holy Cross theologate on the perimeter of the Catholic University in Washington.

Picked to run this institution was Zahm's fervent co-worker Father James A. Burns. Burns had come to Notre Dame as a student in the Manual Labor School, one of those projects dear to the heart of the Morrissey contingent. Morrissey's backbone of support in the community was the Holy Cross Brothers, who were naturals for this sort of instruction. But Burns soon found his way into Zahm's chemistry laboratory. Here he discovered the real meaning of scholarship and higher learning. It was Cavanaugh's fatal flaw that he never did. As time went on Burns left physical science for social studies and took his doctorate in the fledgling field of education. With his usual thoroughness he became the foremost expert in the country on Catholic education, still much quoted by scholars and historians. Along with Zahm and the younger Julius A. Nieuwland, these three made a stunning trio of Holy Cross priest-scholars.

From 1904, when he moved to Washington, until 1919, when he became president of Notre Dame, Burns lived in Washington as superior of the Holy Cross School of Theology. But he did much to shape the future Notre Dame there. He sought out the best and the brightest of the students preparing for the priesthood and urged them on to advanced studies. Most of the deans, department chairs, and leading priest-scholars at Notre Dame after World War I were schooled by Burns in Washington. His touch was lighter than Sorin's and his style more enigmatical than enthusiastic. Above all, he knew how to accommodate. He was flexible and patient. And he was not in the least vain.

Many years before this Zahm was continuing his brilliant career. As time went on he became more interested in biology and anthropology in order to further his professional ecclesiastical mission, as he saw it, to reconcile faith and science. It was an agonizing time for literal interpreters of the Bible, who saw, in the theories of Darwin and the spreading evolutionists, a fatal challenge to religious orthodoxy. Zahm contended that proper interpretation of the Bible was consonant with evolution. He startled the conservatives in the Church as well as those embroiled in the controversy outside it. In his writings on evolution he did the Church a service invaluable in the long run. His daring views were, however, questioned in Rome.

His career in the community was less fortunate. Appointed procurator-general of the community with residence in Rome, Zahm became embroiled in projects and politics outside the interests of Holy Cross, making conservative enemies left and right as he drove ahead. Elected provincial superior, he returned to Notre Dame somewhat reluctantly; he had loved the cosmopolitanism and sweep of life in Rome. But he worked hard at his increasingly ambitious plans for the community. He was tumbled from power by the election in 1906 of his archenemy, Andrew Morrissey, to succeed him as provincial.

Zahm was bound to fall. His lordly ways finally lost him the support of wise old Français, who had seen him through the Rome questioning of his views on evolution. Zahm was a notorious spendthrift: this was Morrissey's constant charge against him. He was nervous, driving, impatient. While Burns adjusted, Zahm flouted. His very brilliance did him in. After his defeat in the election of 1906, he departed for Washington, there to live at Holy Cross House, to write his brilliant books, to travel, to hobnob with Theodore Roosevelt and other bigwigs, but to have nothing more to do with the Congregation of Holy Cross except to retain a nominal membership in it. He never returned to Notre Dame. Burns put it best: "He [Zahm] is too far in advance of the men among whom he is living. He is a man of the twentieth century, and we are still, I believe, living in the nineteenth."

Both Burns and Cavanaugh were still young men when Zahm went into eclipse, Cavanaugh thirty-six, Burns thirty-nine. By an odd, ironic stroke, Cavanaugh became president the same year Zahm retired, 1906. The succeeding years, till World War I, saw Burns biding his patient time in Washington, molding the young students as best he could into would-be scholars. Cavanaugh meanwhile ruled the roost at Notre Dame. Prompted by Father Burns, he made some gestures at money raising, without success. Cavanaugh was no Morrissey intellectually. He genuinely wished to improve Notre Dame education, but he did not seem to know how to formulate programs and put them over. His brilliant and cultivated man in academics, Father Matthew Schumacher, was full of plans and programs. He was the one member of his administration to whom Cavanaugh deferred, but even he could not persuade the president to order and seemliness. Cavanaugh's Notre Dame was like one of those enormous house parties described in novels of the same period about imperial Russia. There was an air of geniality about, but all concerned knew anything they did might at no notice at all be overturned by a whim of the master.

The master himself was overturned by an odd stroke of fate. In 1918 the Catholic Church put into operation a new code of canon law, which limited the term of office for superiors of religious communities to six years. This rule, still in effect, meant the end of the reign of John Cavanaugh the First, for the president of Notre Dame was also the religious superior, and it was generally thought had to be, till Hesburgh's time. In any case Cavanaugh, still on the sunny side of fifty, did go. And like Zahm he drifted into the shadows. Both Morrissey and Zahm died in 1921, but Cavanaugh lived on till 1935, writing a little and occasionally preaching, as I discovered him doing in Toledo.

Cavanaugh, who had an occasional spell of modesty, said when made president that the office should have gone to Father Burns. It now did. The provincial council chose him to succeed Cavanaugh. Burns's presidency presents a paradox. He was unquestionably the greatest president Notre Dame has had, barring Sorin and Hesburgh. But he thought himself a failure, and in some sense he was.

Burns's first job was to clean up the academic muddle. The reform plan was basically Schumacher's, who had probably been urging it on the vacillating Cavanaugh for some time. But it took Burns's influence and prestige to make it work. Under

Cavanaugh there was, really, no organization. Programs of study came and went, living and dying on the drive of their makers. There were no clear requirements for graduation. Credits were like a Chinese puzzle. Some were fractional, one and a half, three and a quarter, and so on. Burns swept out this trash and installed the present system, still creakily operating after seventy years: colleges, deans, chairpersons, order, system. He also closed out the prep school, the pride of Morrissey, to concentrate on the university. He raised the salaries and dignity of the lay professors.

Above all, he recognized the need for raising money. He got grants, the first of their kind, from the Carnegie and Rockefeller Foundations to help him raise a million dollars. He then set out to raise another. He failed at this, largely, I think, because the Catholics of that time who wished to support Notre Dame — remember, there were very few alumni — simply did not have that kind of money.

Burns also failed of reelection to the presidency after his first three-year term was over. The reasons for this are not clear. Speculation is endless. The failure of his money raising may have been a factor; he kept on at that after he left the presidency. But my personal guess is that he was defeated by a lingering relic of the Morrissey era. The Holy Cross Brothers who supported Morrissey were not disposed to follow a program like Burns's. They had disliked and fought Zahm; Burns was only marginally better. In a General Chapter of the community, like the one that unseated Burns in 1922, the race is rarely to the best or the brightest.

Burns had now lost two battles. But he won the war. The cadre of priest-scholars he had trained in Washington were now running Notre Dame. Add to them a sizable number of lay professors who were grateful to Burns for improving their status but who also recognized the worth of his programs.

The next president, whose term of office was roughly the 1920s, was Father Matthew Walsh. Father Walsh is the first of the presidents who would recognize me on the campus. My name would bring recognition from Cavanaugh and Burns, but not my face alone. For my part I was intrigued by both these emeriti presidents and studied them shyly, from a distance. Father Cavanaugh was around a good deal, especially in the library.

I tried without success to bum a ticket from him in the lobby of the Auditorium Hotel in Chicago for the 1930 Northwestern game I eventually crashed, and I saw him on a few other occasions when I was reporting for the *South Bend Tribune*. He was a big man, round in person and orotund in address. He looked like the actor Sidney Greenstreet, though there was warmth in his eyes and manner. Burns was wholly different. Physically he was all angles, tall and thin, his long nose adorned with pince-nez glasses. He was both handsome and distinguished looking. He was grave, distant, and courteous in manner; his closest associates loved him for his wry humor and devotion to duty. But he had little crowd charisma. He was an ineffective public speaker and inconspicuous in large gatherings. But tête-á-tête he was impressive.

Father Walsh, who had been a community *wunderkind*, and had served as vice-president to both Fathers Cavanaugh and Burns, had more than a little of Burns's dignity and style. Like Burns he was also reserved and quiet. I find him the most enigmatic of the presidents I knew. He was greatly liked and admired by many of his fellow priests. The student body also respected him, and those who came to know him found him warm and pleasant, as I did. But there was something impenetrable about him.

The Walsh years were a time of tumultuous growth. After World War I Notre Dame, like just about every other American university, was flooded with students. But, at Notre Dame, there was no place to put them. Walsh threw up two barrackslike temporary structures to house some of them, old Freshman and Sophomore Halls. But many were forced to live off-campus and, try as they did, the administration could not get a firm hold on them.

It wasn't easy. The roaring twenties were nowhere more uproarious than among the young, and the new Domers were a far cry from the docile collegians of the Cavanaugh era. They were a lively, zesty lot. They broke out in a rash of clubs of all sorts, went mad about their great football teams, roistered around South Bend, invaded Chicago and New York, unabashedly wrote reams of verse and fiction, founded an excellent humor magazine and a good literary one, rejuvenated the ancient *Scholastic* and supported for a couple of years a daily newspaper, shook up their old professors and challenged the new ones.

In many ways the Walsh administration was a high point, perhaps the highest, in the Notre Dame modern history. It was certainly highest in the arts. John Becker in music, Ernest Thompson in the visual arts, and Father James Connerton's choir in Sacred Heart Church were a trio of distinction. Everything seemed new-minted. The Burns reorganization worked well; the new deans and department chairs waxed strong in their new powers. They were mostly Burns-trained, in Washington, and college-minded. The swarms of students forced the hiring of new young professors, mostly Notre Dame graduates; the faculty was very inbred. This had its obvious dangers, but also obvious advantages. Apologists for the inbreeding were fond of saying that Notre Dame was like West Point: where else could the faculty come from?

The new and predominantly young faculty brought a spirit of adventure to the campus. There was a sense of freedom. If Jim Withey wanted to section the incoming freshmen into the College of Arts and Letters into three groups based on ability tested in an opening day exam, why let him. A daily newspaper, proposed by John Cooney and his bright students? Sure. A national tour for the Glee Club? Well, anyhow, not quite to the West Coast, but go to it! A student-written and produced musical, with real live girls on the Washington Hall stage? A trip to the Rose Bowl? Yes indeed. And so on and on.

Underpinning all this was the religious spirit fostered by prefect of religion Father John O'Hara. He was himself a new breed; the piety he promoted was anything but the traditional hearts-and-flowers variety. Frequent communion and loyalty to Church was manly — that was his message. Most of the faculty, lay and clerical, went along with O'Hara. At worst it was a help to discipline. It was noisy, unintellectual religion, but it worked.

Walsh was faced with the necessity of building. He turned for its design to his own Department of Architecture. The first job its chair, Francis Kervick, did for him was the charming Memorial Door to the east transept of Sacred Heart Church. Here Kervick showed his mastery of his beloved Gothic by taking some imaginative liberties with it. This may have won him and his associate, Vincent Fagan, the design of the new west side dormitories, Howard, Morrissey, and Lyons. They were the first since Walsh Hall was built in 1909 and remain the best. As the building demand went on, two of Kervick's mentors and models were engaged, Ralph Adams Cram for the dining hall and Maginnis and Walsh for the other buildings along the new mall. Most of these were built after Matthew Walsh left office, in the administration of Father Charles O'Donnell, but they were planned by Walsh and his advisors. Thus Walsh pioneered the enormous physical development of modern Notre Dame.

Walsh seems to have had a hands-off attitude toward the academic side of Notre Dame, leaving it to the new administrators who were finding their independent ways. I have no idea how deliberate this was. It may be that he played a more decisive hand than appears at first, although a long look suggests the contrary. There is nowhere, during or after his turn of office — he lived another twenty-five years after leaving it — any writing or address of his on education, or even a memory of those who knew him best, about educational theory. When I came to Notre Dame he was teaching history, but it was more Catholic apologetics than the real thing, which I doubt he had much interest in. Still, it's not clear. I repeat, of the presidents I knew he is the most enigmatic.

Walsh was succeeded, after his canonical six-year term, by Father Charles Leo O'Donnell. O'Donnell had a rare talent for poetry, not the perfunctory verse tossed off by every ambitious seminarian and undergraduate in the college, but the real thing. Here is a poem of his youth.

After the Christmas

Snowed over with the moonlight
  Or turning back the noon light
  Down through the grooves of space
Earth swung its old slow way.
  But thronging the rim of heaven
    Angels from morn to even
    Watched earth with reverent pace
Silent its orbit trace
Cradle wherein God lay.

Talent like this is rare, and O'Donnell went on to become the poet laureate of the Holy Cross community. In his published works the level of taste and fine feeling for language is uniformly high, that of inspiration somewhat uneven. He was a well-remembered professor of English from 1910, when he was ordained, to 1917, when he departed to be a chaplain in World War I. From then on it was administration, not teaching, for him, though he wrote and polished verse to the end of his days.

Unlike most poets he wrote prose well. From France he wrote charming letters to Father Burns and others, later printed. His letters as president as well as his official statements often come close to good art, as in the eloquent tribute to John F. Cushing in the lobby of the Engineering building. But his poetical temperament sometimes got the better of him and he would rage at some criticism of the university more wisely ignored, or dress down some erring student in language better suited to Coriolanus. At the other end of his lengthy emotional range he sometimes let his enthusiasms slip perilously close to bathos, as in his funeral eulogy of Rockne. I once heard him preach a May sermon in Sacred Heart Church in which he called upon Our Lady to perform a miracle on the Notre Dame campus. His emotional, and no doubt deeply felt devotion, edged toward demand rather than prayer.

Yet the presidential tenure of Charles O'Donnell is a brief time of great importance. The new building program gave the campus a different look and a different feeling. O'Donnell bridged the gap between the vigor of the twenties and the Great Depression. G. K. Chesterton came and Knute Rockne died. The dynamic center of the campus shifted from the Main Building to the new Kervick mall flanking the new dining halls.

In 1931 O'Donnell's health began to fail, and for the last year of his life, 1934, he was unable to function at all. Father Burns, who had returned to Notre Dame as provincial superior in 1927, with unerring wisdom appointed Father John F. O'Hara as his successor.

O'Hara had become nationally famous as the dynamic prefect of religion during the 1920s. His powerful advocacy of frequent holy communion, which could be received at most any hour of the morning, made Notre Dame into his cherished "City of the Blessed Sacrament." He was easily the best-known figure on the campus when he was made acting president in 1934, but, like his predecessor, he was not thought of as an administrator. Students and alumni who knew him as a pastor were surprised when he was named president, forgetting that he had been the founder and first dean of the College of Commerce.

Although O'Hara was, again like his predecessor, a native of Indiana, he had an exotic background. His father was in the consular service in South America, and the young John had spent three years there. From there he came to Notre Dame to study for the priesthood. He never said why. It is interesting to speculate whether his acquaintance with Charles O'Donnell and his family in Kokomo, Indiana, whom he met visiting his Kokomo grandmother, may have slanted him toward Notre Dame, but it is odd that, like Zahm and many others, it's simply not known. But come he did, age twenty, and did well enough in his studies at Notre Dame and Washington to be invited by Peter Guilday, the great Church historian, to stay on at Catholic University and work with him. But O'Hara had always had Notre Dame in his mind and heart and Father Burns, whom he had come to admire and love, at his back.

O'Hara was no intellectual. He was even suspicious of intellectualism as dangerous to faith and morals. He wanted no truck with abstractions, had small use for philosophy, thought of theology almost wholly in terms of apologetics, and was utterly indifferent to art. He was devoted to business. Although Notre Dame was teaching some business skills, it was O'Hara who developed these into the College of Foreign and Domestic Commerce, as it used to be rather grandiosely called. But there was nothing grandiose about O'Hara. He was plain, direct, forthright, simple to the point of naivete in some ways, fond of stats and numbers, interested in whatever was practical and could be tested by practical means.

He had, to an unusual degree, the virtues that go with this character. Practical English is journalism, and O'Hara was as good a journalist as ever covered the Notre Dame campus. He was no stylist, but he got to the heart of the matter with a surgeon's neat touch. He was no theorist, either. But he was efficient and systematic. So far as internal administration goes, he was probably the best president Notre Dame has ever had. He reorganized the business side of the university and engaged a professional to run it. The depression had shrunk the student body to where it could be accommodated on the campus, and O'Hara eventually shooed just about all of them onto it, building Cavanaugh, Zahm, and Breen-Phillips Halls to house them. The smaller student body enabled him to enforce the strictest discipline since the 1910's but the quiet mood of the depression made this comparatively easy. The depression sobered O'Hara, but it did not frighten him. Not only did he continue to build, he dropped not a single lay professor from the payroll.

However, the greatest achievement of the O'Hara administration was academic. This is strange indeed, considering his anti-intellectualism. Almost any charge usually leveled against this class can be made against him. He banned books from the university library he thought dangerous to morals and banned *Time* magazine from the university newsstands. He was a censorious prude, one with the popularly caricatured nuns of Catholic schooling. But they were teaching grade and high school, and O'Hara was supposed to be a university man.

He was, as it turned out. This same John O'Hara founded the Graduate School at Notre Dame and named a worshipper of academic scholarship, Father Philip Moore, to run it. He invited a group of English and Irish scholars to teach as visiting professors, Christopher Hollis, Shane Leslie, Desmond Fitzgerald, and Arnold Lunn among them. These were not basically academics, nor did they come to stay. O'Hara also invited a sizable group of refugees from central Europe, fleeing Hitler and his anticulture. These did come to stay, and they were a distinguished lot: Waldemar Gurian, Karl Menger, Emil Artin, Arthur Haas, F. A. Hermens, and from France, Yves Simon. These became luminaries of the permanent faculty. Only one of them, Eugene Guth, was solidly Jewish. Most were Catholics who despised Nazism.

O'Hara authorized Gurian, Hermens, and homegrown faculty stars like Father Leo R. Ward and Frank O'Malley to found the *Review of Politics*. He agreed to the many scholarly meetings and conferences Gurian and Menger loved to sponsor, which brought such famous men as Canon LeMaitre, Jacques Maritain, Kurt Gödel, and many others to spark a Notre Dame faculty sprouting new scholarship of their own. O'Hara, in brief, founded the *University* of Notre Dame. There is no doubt in my mind that he did so in concert with Father Burns, whose foresight in training Notre Dame priests who would welcome the new intellectual life kept him steady to the goal of Notre Dame leading American Catholic intellectual excellence. It was a wonderful and exciting time, and it put Notre Dame on the map of academic achievement.

As if to make up for the year he was acting president while Father Charles O'Donnell was ill, O'Hara left his office a year before his term was out, in 1939, and went on to a distinguished ecclesiastical career, first as bishop to the military chaplains of World War II, then as bishop of Buffalo, New York, and finally as cardinal archbishop of Philadelphia. He was succeeded at Notre Dame by his vice-president, Father J. Hugh O'Donnell.

Taking office in mid-1939, O'Donnell was scarcely comfortable in it when World War II became inevitable. By early 1942 the students and faculty had largely departed and military units took over the university. It is greatly to O'Donnell's credit that he saw this coming and cooperated with the military to their satisfaction, but they, not he, ran the place.

O'Donnell the Younger's nickname was Pepper. He had been varsity center on the football team and retained something of the blustery athlete in his makeup. He was an active prefect of discipline during the turbulent 1920s before becoming president of St. Edward University in Texas, another Holy Cross fief. He returned to Notre Dame in 1934 as O'Hara's vice-president, and did his work in that role and as president with all his good heart. He lasted only a little beyond the war, dying the year after his term ended, in 1947.

He was succeeded by the most charming and likable of men, Father John Joseph Cavanaugh, President Cavanaugh the Second. John the Second had been a student secretary of John the First while attending Notre Dame. The two became firm friends but, Irish-like, were wary of each other's wit and will. When young John, after a stint working at Studebaker's, decided he wanted to become a Holy Cross priest, John the Elder said to him, "Now remember, you are *joining* a religious community, not *founding* one." Clever, but misleading: Young John was the most modest of men.

And one of the ablest. Hand-picked by O'Hara as his successor as prefect of religion, Cavanaugh liked the job and gradually developed his own style in it. But when O'Donnell became president, he chose Cavanaugh as vice-president, and Cavanaugh got valuable experience for his own presidency. In the top office he was innovative and creative. He was the virtual founder of the Notre Dame Foundation, then the University's fund-raising arm, and spent many a weary hour tracking down prospects, among them the Kennedy family. Father John became virtually the Kennedy family chaplain, somewhat to his dismay, for the Kennedys gave nothing to Notre Dame. Others did, however, and the groundwork was laid for the successful Hesburgh fund drives. Cavanaugh also reorganized the university administration into the form it still largely rests on.

But perhaps his most notable achievement was simply that he led Notre Dame into the twentieth century. Both the great wars of this century were followed by great increases in the Notre Dame student body. Burns had modernized the curriculum but not student life. Cavanaugh realized that the veterans attending college on the GI Bill of Rights required a new approach. Not so much by code as by attitude Cavanaugh created a new mode of association between faculty and administration, on the one hand, and the student body on the other, one marked by greater equality, tolerance, and accommodation.

Nothing illustrates this better than the decline of O'Hara's office of prefect of religion. After Cavanaugh it fell off sharply in student respect; to the veterans it was childish and irrelevant. Out of inertia it lasted too long. Theodore Hesburgh inadvertently helped to kill it by his new style as veterans chaplain, one that had Cavanaugh's full approval. I think Cavanaugh himself, however, would choose as his outstanding accomplishment the establishment of the General Program of Liberal Studies, based on the great books of Western civilization. He fell in love with this program; it became, in his own view, his real education, and he ardently hoped it would infect the entire university. To some extent it has, and that would please him. But he would be unhappy that it has not seized the collective Notre Dame academic imagination as fully as he wished it to, although characteristically he did not impose it on the College of Arts and Letters, as his close friend Robert Maynard Hutchins did at the University of Chicago.

Cavanaugh had a great gift of friendship. One of his best achievements was the establishment of closer ties with the South

Bend community. With some periods of exception, Notre Dame and South Bend had stayed aloof from each other. Cavanaugh changed all that. He beamed that wonderful smile on the city, and the effect was like the conversion of Clovis and his army.

But it was left to Theodore Martin Hesburgh, Notre Dame's fifteenth president, to realize fully the Cavanaugh promise. Hesburgh's achievement was like the mustard seed of the biblical parable. He took the seed that Cavanaugh had so carefully nurtured and made it grow into the tremendous tree of contemporary Notre Dame. His accomplishments are of a magnitude none of his predecessors would have dreamed of.

My closest friend in the Holy Cross community was Father Howard Kenna, who, as provincial superior for fourteen of the Hesburgh years, was Maecenas to Hesburgh's Virgil. It is impossible to write about the Notre Dame presidents without including their provincial superiors. Zahm and Burns are, willy-nilly, among the heroes of this story. Kenna, worthy to stand with them in the history of Holy Cross in the United States, found in the success of Theodore Hesburgh the greatest satisfaction of his career. Nothing could please Hesburgh more than that.

2

I COME TO NOTRE DAME

It was midway in the presidency of Father Charles O'Donnell when I came to Notre Dame. I was seventeen, eighteen come November, on that hot September day in 1930 when I trudged, suitcase in hand, from the Notre Dame streetcar terminus to the Main Building. I was a day late and more troubled by that than excited by the prospect of college.

I was late because, at his direction, I came from a visit to my uncle Samuel Stritch in Toledo, Ohio, where he was bishop. He was young for a bishop, only just over forty, and his youthful ardor was most attractive to me. Unobtrusively he taught me manners, taste, and poise, and I knew lessons from him would be better than anything I could get in college. When I came of high-school age he relieved my parents of the burden of educating me and sent me, in 1926, to the tutelage of the Brothers of Mary at the University of Dayton Preparatory School. He chose Notre Dame for my college. I would no more have thought of questioning these choices than I would have of doubting the sunrise.

All my life I have shuttled up and down mid-United States (suitcase in hand). My prep-school shuttle had been Nashville, Cincinnati, Dayton, Toledo. Since my uncle was made archbishop of Milwaukee shortly after I came to Notre Dame, my next shuttle became South Bend, Chicago, Milwaukee, and Nashville. After he moved to Chicago in 1940 as its archbishop I virtually lived with him, stowing my few chattels in his house while I was in World War II and often popping in from South Bend after returning to teach at Notre Dame once more after the war. Himself a thwarted teacher, Cardinal Stritch took a great interest in my modest career.

Uncle Sam admired the Holy Cross Fathers of Notre Dame. I had encountered more than one of them in Toledo and had grown up with the *Ave Maria*, the national Catholic weekly they published at Notre Dame. For years the back cover read, "For further information write to the Reverend Daniel E. Hudson, C.S.C." Father Hudson, the long-time editor of the *Ave* and maker of its high reputation, became in my childish imagination a figure of legend, like Father Damien of Molokai.

Approaching eighteen, I was only marginally wiser. I had drifted through four years of prep school as thoughtless as a dog. In some ways I loved Dayton Prep. The classes were dismally bad, but I never learned much in a classroom anyhow. The boys were as fine a lot as could be found anywhere, decent and manly. They nearly all also meant to be good and kept me on that side of the ledger, who would cheerfully have fallen, like Miniver Cheevy, with the slightest encouragement. But the good life was dreary. We were bright enough, but we were not challenged. The curriculum was Dullsville. There was no exposure to art, or music, or even typing, and the conventional subjects were ill taught by untrained and uninspired teachers. In this way four impressionable years sped by in the worst of the Catholic tradition—that is, little exposure to evil but little to positive good, either. The curse of the Catholic schooling of my youth was not mainly a priggishness about sex so simple-minded as to be inhuman—ordinary courtship, as J. M. Cameron has so neatly said, was like making one's way through a minefield. But bad as this was, especially in girls' schools, the dullness was worse. There was not a flicker of interest in or excitement about the life of the mind. The intellect was simply shut out officially. On their own the boys occasionally flashed a spark of life, rarely encouraged or nourished by the faculty.

I was the beneficiary of one such. In my freshman year I made a good friend of a sophomore. We became chums in the old boys' books sense, took long walks together, had our private rituals and jokes. Since we both were better than average athletes, we could flaunt our intimacy unmolested. But nothing could have been more innocent than our friendship.

My friend Joe had a taste for literature and aspired to a level higher than Zane Gray. We talked often of books and authors. "Swinburne," he said to me one day, "that's the one for poetry. He's the best." God only knows where Joe picked up this critical intelligence, but it fired my simple soul. I swooped off to the library and found Swinburne all right; to this day I can rattle off yards of anapests from the choruses of *Atalanta in Calydon*. I loved the music of them, and if the words often made little sense, what of that? I was well acquainted with literary puzzlement. I had read what our home library afforded, *David Copperfield*, *The Last Days of Pompeii*, *Ivanhoe*, and other books of that kidney, between the rounds with my boys' books. I didn't understand them very well, of course, but I enjoyed even the puzzlements. I think it does a grave disservice to the young to write down to them, to emphasize grasp of meaning as the only end of discourse. Something of Swinburne's onrushing rhythms, something of Dickens's mastery of language, seeped into my soul, there to stay.

Alas, illness took Joe from our school after his sophomore year, and I retreated into solitary reading and fantasy. It is odd how little the world impinged on our almost monastic prep-school lives. We had very little freedom in which to pursue our natural interest in girls, though we made the most of what we did have. Although keenly interested in sports we rarely read the daily papers and so were reduced to childish arguments, like could Strangler Lewis, the world's foremost wrestler, beat Jack Dempsey, the celebrated pugilist? Even the Lindbergh flight failed to kindle my imagination. Although I was by no means the brightest boy in the class, I was the most sophisticated and its leader, but I got no kick out of it. Indeed, I resolved never again to try for school office. I mention this to show that I was no shrinking violet, wasting its sweetness on secret dreams of power and place. I think I was a cheerful and lively boy, but I was almost totally undeveloped.

Upon my astonished and delighted and empty little head the Notre Dame of 1930 burst like fireworks, shooting sparks in every direction, casting off cascades of color, brilliance, and wonder. I had gone that first day to the Main Building to see about my room. It was on the fourth and top floor of Howard Hall. My roommate, from Dayton, was already established in it, and I soon took shelter under its dormer angles. In a few days I met most of the hall's residents, basically much like the Daytonians but much more lively and varied. I quickly settled in, bought the standard yellow cord trousers, and began to talk.

Talk is the heart of education. Much else is necessary, especially reading and writing. But talk is the solid, steady undercurrent of college life. Not wild talk and certainly not dirty talk. You can get those anywhere, in an army barracks or any leisure-time hangout. The best college talk is high-minded, in the midnight hours, searching, groping, for goals and God, seeking "that selfless self of self, most strange, most still, fast-furled and all foredrawn to no or yes." I found that kind of talk abundant at Notre Dame. Perhaps I was just then ready for it, as I might not have been in prep school—I know I was unready then for such an insightful line as Hopkins's about the self. Early in my freshman year I found talk at its best in two friends, Joe Carroll and Frank Sullivan.

Joe and I were in the same freshman English class, but I forget whether the remarkable teacher of that class, James A. Withey, brought us together. Whatever, we became firm friends, despite Joe's being streets ahead of me in knowledge and sophistication. He was a West Side Chicagoan, a graduate of St. Ignatius Academy, a Jesuit showcase. He made me realize what I had missed at Dayton Prep.

There were also many upperclassmen from St. Ignatius. The literati among them were known to Joe, and he brought me into their circle. Brought up to believe that freshmen were to upperclassmen as peasants to overlords, I was astonished at their kindness and generosity. From the first I loved Notre Dame for its canon of equality among students. All were on the same footing. Any distinction had to be earned at Notre Dame; you could bring none with you. Academically we were strictly classified: all classes were for freshmen only, and this rule was only slightly relaxed for upperclassmen. But outside of class equality reigned.

The group of upperclassmen Joe introduced me to were interested in literature and writing. Joe and I had both been part of our high-school literary establishments, but mine was a much more modest niche than Joe's. To the best of my recollection I never tried to imitate Swinburne or any other poet I read. It never occurred to me to write verse. But it had occurred to Joe, and he practiced his craft steadily. Here is a poem he published during our freshman year in *Scrip*, the Notre Dame student literary magazine.

Song for a Girl Asleep

Oh girl, let your eyes be blind:
There is little enough to see,
And little enough to find
In knowing the sight of me.
Better you hide me away,
Lovely and pure and wise,
Out of the night and the day
Under the lids of your eyes.
Better you see my face
Not in the great sun's sight,
But dim in that holy place,
In your kindly candlelight.
Better I be concealed
Under your own dream heap,
In the starred and dream-strewn field
In the secret way of sleep.
In your eyelids, O holy and fair,
More than I am you will find:
Better to look for me there.
Girl, let your eyes be blind.

I thought then, and still do, that this was a lovely and remarkable poem, and not just from an eighteen-year-old but from
anyone. It is fresh and original in conception, even though its
imagery owes a little to the English Georgian poets Joe and I
were then reading—"Great sun" and "secret way" are reminiscent of de la Mare and Watson.

Joe also loved the poetry of William Butler Yeats. Neither
he nor I knew then that Yeats had visited Notre Dame much
earlier, in 1904, speaking on Irish literature and folklore. In my
senior year of 1934 he returned, speaking on the same subjects. I
vividly remember listening to his high, thin voice in Washington
Hall, but I couldn't follow what he said very well. I also recall
meeting him, but I don't recall how. Would I, I wonder, have
had enough temerity to barge in on him and ask him to sign a
book of his poems—one had just come out—for Joe Carroll, long
gone from Notre Dame but not from my life? I still wonder, but
I recall Yeats's long, thin frame resting in a long, thin chair in
one of those warren rooms behind the stage in old Washington

Hall. He was then seventy, five years away from his death in 1939.

Carroll and I also shared an interest in the theater. We both tried to act. He was better than I but still no threat to a Barrymore. We both had clear, resonant voices, and that was about it. Still, we loved it. We read plays, together and separately—as with poetry, it had previously not occurred to my simple mind that contemporary plays, pleasant and unpleasant, were printed.

My sorry lack of development is nicely illustrated in my lowbrow taste for vaudeville. I went as often as I could to the Dayton vaudeville house, and my trips back to Nashville were made into delight if I could get to one of the Cincinnati houses when I changed trains there. The vaudeville houses were then beginning to show films, too, but I much preferred Will Mahoney live to Norma Talmadge on the screen and much preferred the vaudeville dancing and knockabout comedy to such high falutin' films as *Ben Hur* and *Camille*. I did love the Marx Brothers' movies; they are vaudeville writ gloriously large.

All this changed as I accompanied Carroll to the live Chicago theater. There were many houses lighted up for the season: the Grand, the Erlanger, the Harris, the Selwyn, the Blackstone, the Schubert, the Auditorium. We saw Katharine Cornell, Maurice Evans, Walter Hampden, Ina Claire, Eva LeGallienne. We saw the Abbey Theater from Dublin in its repertory of the great Irish plays, such as *Playboy* and *Juno and the Paycock*, with actors like Barry Fitzgerald and Sara Allgood. We went to the really good Shakespeare repertory Fritz Leiber ran, with such stars as Helen Mencken and Tyrone Power, Senior. (Junior had been at Dayton Prep with me.) Oh, it was a golden time for me.

Golden, too, was the Notre Dame football team of the fall of 1930. Big-time football was not new to me, as the theater was. But I loved our games that freshman year when we dedicated our stadium after finally managing, the week before, the defeat of a surprisingly good Southern Methodist team with its charming jazz band. I also managed to crash Dyche Stadium, along with about three thousand other youngsters milling around its open end, to see us beat another good team, Northwestern, in Evanston. These and the other games that second consecutive national championship season are the more memorable to me because this was my only year in the student section of the stadium. In the following season of 1931 I moved into the press box, where I stayed for the next forty seasons, minus the World War II years. At first I did various jobs, some for money, some to help my friend Joe Petritz, the press box boss and my good friend these nearly sixty years. Later on old student Charlie Callahan and old friend Roger Valdisseri, Joe's successors, franked me, as chair of our journalism department.

I loved the games, but, before and after them, South Bend was no Chicago. The Chicago of the 1930s was to me as glamorous as Xanadu. Joe Carroll and I wandered all over its downtown streets and along the lake front. We had very little spending money, far too little for dates with girls, but we had youth, energy, stout legs, and cheap streetcars. Even the train that took us to and from the city was like a streetcar: the South Shore Line of those days ran every hour on the hour, with many a stop. The city had so much to offer penniless youngsters—museums, parks with their free summer music, inexpensive dance halls, free university events, the zoo, wonderful walks. When tired we would drink coffee and eat snacks at Harding's or Toffenetti's excellent cheap restaurants. Many a waitress must have scowled at our retreating backs after a long stay and a short tip. I loved it all and began in that wonderful freshman year a pleasure in visiting Chicago, so happily nearby, that has lasted me a lifetime. I suppose that, in actual fact, I went seldom in that freshman year, far less than I did later on when music and opera replaced the dying theater in my affections. But the early years were the eye-openers.

The other great friend of my freshman year was Frank Sullivan, another Jesuit product, from faraway Denver, Colorado. Frank also became a good friend of Carroll and, like me, a visitor to the Carroll home on Chicago's West Side. Sullivan must have felt at home in that Catholic enclave–there seemed to me to have been a Catholic church, a huge one, about every five blocks in any direction. These were so close together that Catholics placed new acquaintances by parish, not subdivision. Sullivan was devoutly religious, in youth and age. Carroll was a rather perfunctory Catholic, I a rather rebellious one. But Sullivan was ardent, strong in faith, devout in practice.

Though a faithful altar boy, Sullivan was no prig. He was free and easy in all he did—he was the first man I ever saw kiss a nun. He was attractive to girls, while Joe and I were rather diffident and shy. But we were only eighteen. Neither Carroll nor Sullivan returned to Notre Dame after their freshman year. Depression finances bit deep into both. Carroll finished at Loyola Chicago, Sullivan at Denver Regis. I kept in touch with both by mail and visits, frequent to Chicago, rare from Denver, till I broke with Carroll over his membership in the Communist party. I met a good many of his Communist cell and took a keen interest in their talk. But this was not the soaring, midnight college talk. It was of tactics and strategy in acts designed to embarrass the capitalist establishment. In the end I could subscribe neither to their doctrine nor especially to their ethics. Compounded with all this was Joe's developing alcoholism. Years later, after many a sea change, he ended up, of all things, as copy editor for *Sports Illustrated* magazine. He made several signals from there to renew our acquaintance before he died in the 1970s, but I am a convinced adherent of the you-can't-go-home-again faith and stayed aloof.

With Sullivan things were different. He and I were both good students, and we both were encouraged to academic careers. I stayed on at Notre Dame, but Sullivan went to St. Louis University. He was then, of course, much closer, and we saw much more of one another. After he got his doctorate at Yale I was instrumental in having him offered a place here, but he went instead to Loyola of Los Angeles, where his family had migrated from Denver. There his success at teaching and his rather flamboyant personality made him into a legend. I kept on seeing him occasionally, delighted as ever by his disarming simplicity and generosity.

I don't know whether Sullivan was tempted to enlist under the Marx-Lenin banner or not. He was an extremely liberal Democrat, active in ADA and similar liberal enterprises. I don't know how far these were tied into his deeply felt Catholicism, but he subscribed, I feel sure, to the denunciation of atheistic communism, as was the official Catholic line. No official line on most anything has ever been my line; what turned me against communism was watching the lying, deceit, and provocation of the Communists I knew. Nevertheless, to be or not to be

Communist was the great issue among young people of the late 1930s. It certainly jerked me into the twentieth century.

Oddly, this had nothing to do with Notre Dame—or with Loyola of Chicago either. Intelligent youth is frequently, perhaps usually, somewhat radical, but our radicalism did not center on our universities. This seems strange, when one considers the ruckuses and riots of students for the last thirty years. But we did not encounter radical ideas in college. For us, college still meant classicism, Latin, Greek, Shakespeare, and Moliere. For Catholics, college was Aquinas, not Marx. My friend Don Price, the dean emeritus of the Graduate School of Government at Harvard, once wondered aloud to me whether he had ever heard any discussion of Marx during his undergraduate days at Vanderbilt. I can recall none at Notre Dame.

But I heard plenty in Chicago, and some, though much less, in Nashville. It was pure chance that led me, through Carroll, into a Communist would-be Catholicism rather than the group of young Catholic social reformers who congregated around Bishop Bernard Sheil—good-hearted and devout devotees of Monsignor John A. Ryan, the papal social encyclicals, and organized labor. I did not know the bishop, but I knew and liked a good many of his followers.

Why these Marxist or liberal ideas filtered so little into our college curricula I don't know. Part of it was simply stodgy tradition. But I am grateful for one aspect of it. It kept the radical young teachers from making the classroom merely a platform for their own programs. I thoroughly disapprove of using one's classroom captive audience as receptors of one's own prejudices and personal opinions. I have always disliked teachers who announce at their first classes, you won't leave this class still believing in matrimony, or Catholicism, or liberalism, or whatever. This is propaganda, not instruction, and I think implicitly ruled out by the nature of the teacher's case: callow youth at the mercy of older sophistication. To be sure, one's own convictions will show through, but one should not flaunt them.

My own youthful radicalism had as its starting point southern agrarianism, in which I grew up, in a manner of speaking. I was working on the *Nashville Banner* in 1930, the year that the agrarian manifesto, *I'll Take My Stand*, was published. At the next desk that summer was the man who was to become my best friend for the rest of his life, Robert West. West was a year or so out of Vanderbilt, where he had come to know, as teachers and acquaintances, several of the contributors to the book, and there were two or three others on the paper's staff who knew many of them and had participated in their talks. Through them I came to know one or two and, as time went on, more. I even eventually met Sidney Hirsch, the guru who brought the fugitives together originally. West himself went on to a distinguished career as a specialist in English Renaissance literature.

I brought a special dimension to the agrarian case, that of my Catholicism. Almost from the first I have maintained that the true implications of the Nashville agrarians were religious and that many of them would find the answers to their quest in Catholicism. There was much sympathy for their position at Notre Dame, which strengthened my attachment. But, although they were constantly debating politics and social policy, the real case of the agrarians was for education. As Louis Rubin put it, "It [*I'll Take My Stand*] is a rebuke to materialism, a corrective to the worship of progress, and a reaffirmation of man's spiritual and esthetic needs." After sixty-odd years, I'll still take my stand on that.

Thus far I have been writing about the intellectual and esthetic interests that absorbed me in college. This is in seeming contradiction to the life of rules and regulations so many students in the 1930s found harsh and stifling. And there is some truth in this. Along with the set patterns of living at Notre Dame went a strong streak of philistinism in the place, a disdain of learning, a passion for blood sports, a fellowship of hearties. This strain found some official recognition in the Blue Circle, student guardians of the so-called Notre Dame traditions, which basically meant pressure to cheer for the football team. I don't think there were many pure representatives of this breed. Most of those who joined in the rousing of their dorms to meet the team, or dunk in the lake someone who didn't, were decent men at bottom, slipping into that barbarism the young fall into so readily when caught up in the vortex of mass action.

This herd behavior of the young male is still with us and probably always will be; it is the sorry underside of youthful idealism. But if my experience of it at Notre Dame is set alongside the atrocities of hazing in some of the Greek-letter fraternities at other universities, especially back in the 1930s, it seems little enough.

And, to me, less than that. I was simply untouched by it. I certainly did not trouble to conceal my intellectual pursuits, nor did those I shared them with. Nobody ever interrupted our Shakespeare readings, or made fun of my efforts in the University Theater, or derided my position of class poet—discounting, of course, the good-natured ribbing of my friends. Just about every step of the college experience of youth independent for the first time is fraught with tremulous uncertainty, but no mistake of mine brought much obloquy upon my head. All my days at Notre Dame have been lived on the bounty of the generous and the warm-hearted student body.

This sounds, I know, like Rebecca of Sunnybrook Farm. And everybody over the age of sixteen knows that life ain't like that. Of course I had fits of anger, resentment, and, alas, even malice. I suppose I griped as much as most about the food, lights-out at eleven, and so on. Yet I don't remember my college days as harsh or restrictive. I think of them as genuinely educative.

But it must be remembered that times were hard. Those whose families were hit hard by the depression, like Carroll's and Sullivan's and indeed, my own, had no money for wild oats and little enough for oatmeal. Notre Dame's rules prescribed a life I would have had to live anyhow and made it easier for me to give up dating and dancing and dining out. True, I was in worse case than that; I often did not have a nickel for a newspaper, fifteen cents for cigarettes or a coke in the caf. I owed Harvey Rockwell seven cents for tea for several embarrassed months. My penury was mostly my fault. I had plenty of chances to earn some spending money, and did earn some, but left more chances either unrecognized or unexploited. Like Russell Baker, whose delightful *Growing Up* has many echoes of my own, I was no salesman and could not bring myself to try the hard sell. In the dawn hours of truth I used to accuse myself of indolence, and this was partially true. But I also inherited a defect of energy which has plagued me all my life. I had to go through a couple of youthful breakdowns before I faced that fact without feeling I was making excuses.

Virtual confinement to the campus made us more aware of it. And coming to know some other university campuses made me appreciate our own the more. Was it vision or just plain old French thrift that made the Holy Cross Fathers hold on to their ample acres? We know that Father Sorin himself was mainly responsible for the layout of the beautiful main quad and its buildings, so charming in architecture and so ambitious for the future. I more and more came to love the campus, to walk its many walks, swim and skate its lakes, and loiter in its woods. It may be that the march of progress is slowly eating away the beauty and the charm. The new campus to the east has the feeling of an airport rather than a university. In 1990 my walks seldom take that direction; I follow Thoreau's famous dictum, "Eastward I go by force, westward I go free."

3

THE NOTRE DAME I CAME TO

The Notre Dame I came to was catching up after a breathless decade of growth. Its compass needle pointed southwest from the Main Building, slowly moving eastward. A badly needed new mall was re-orienting student life. If the statue of Father Sorin could turn its head, it could survey the new axis left and right, one suspects with pleasure. In 1930 it was busily a-building.

Howard Hall was five years old when I moved into it as a freshman. In my sophomore year I moved next door to Morrissey, a year younger. But for my junior year I moved into the almost new Alumni Hall. My first floor room faced the Law Building. I had a class in it that year with Father Pete Hebert, well-known for taking leaves of absence from class as the spirit moved him. I had a classmate who waved a handkerchief to me out the window when Father Pete was on hand; I could make it to class in seconds.

All these halls were new. They were anchored on the east by the Engineering Building, which took the place of the old one, razed to build Alumni and Dillon. The old Engineering Hall, in its last phase—it had suffered many a sea change—was as vernacular as Notre Dame gets, plain local buff brick and little more. But the buildings that replaced it were very fancy, the last gasp of American building handicraft, replete with niches for sculpture, outdoor pulpits, and carvings of student life. They were nothing like as well designed for student comfort as my senior year hall, Sorin, as quiet as Alumni was noisy. The final building of this phase was the new football stadium, dedicated in the fall of my freshman year. It is by all odds the best stadium for viewing a football game I ever saw, and its parking facilities were the best I've seen on a campus. No wonder it's been a football Mecca for Notre Dame fans.

From my quarters in the new dorms—I had private rooms for my last three years—I sallied forth to classes, mostly in Main, or old Science, but with an occasional foray into Law or Commerce. Uneven is the word for my classes, all through college. The faculty had a few great teachers and more than a few competent ones. But it also had more than its share of incompetents. These included Holy Cross priests who should never have been assigned to a classroom, lay teachers who were their relations or connected somehow to someone with clout, and more than a few who were hired because they happened to be on the spot and were making gestures at teaching while waiting, like Mr. Micawber, for something to turn up. Only a few of these took teaching seriously, studied it as one would study any other occupation to find one's way in it, and recognized the students as paying customers, not audiences to boost their own egos.

The students themselves were less varied, in part because of their youth. There were some first-rate minds among them, as likely to have been schooled in Tulsa as Chicago. There was a foggy bottom of sons of the pious, sons of alumni, sons of football fans, and other sorts of sons. And there was the dutiful middle, uninterested and unimaginative. These, then as now, preferred clear organization to charm or brilliance in their teachers. But too often they got none of these. Many older professors, trained in the rhetoric of public address, lectured in the old tradition, full of fake drama and windy anecdote. They had become by my time sad figures of fun, at Notre Dame and elsewhere, made obsolete by Sinclair Lewis and his followers in satiric fiction, by the growing informality of manners, and perhaps most of all by the cozy intimacy of radio.

The intellectual temper of the Notre Dame student body is hard to judge. For me, it was stimulating and exciting in my freshman year, and continued to be so thereafter, though with steadily diminished ardor. This was in part because I became caught up in journalism, which had been my natural bent since prep school. But I had another side, a literary and speculative one, which went relatively uncultivated at Notre Dame. That part of me was more stimulated by Nashville. I don't want to suggest I had hidden, unexplored depths. Mine is not a first-rate mind. I do want to suggest that a good education needs more than one source and that I was lucky to have another at home. Most of my friends there were connected to Vanderbilt University, and I owe a great deal to that splendid institution.

The Notre Dame curriculum was rigid, old-fashioned, and standard. By the time I arrived on the scene, however, Greek had gone out of the window. Latin emphatically remained and kept many of us bound to that cheerless language when we would have been much better off learning a modern one. I studied Latin in schools for one year of grade school, four years of prep school, and three of college. Much of this was wasted time. However, my own feeling is that the study of any other language besides one's native tongue is vastly overrated. I see nothing wrong with taking an interest in French or German literature, but I see nothing salvationist in it, either. I know this is a highly controversial position and that there are all sorts of grounds for disagreement about it. My friend Eric Voegelin, the most learned person I ever knew, believed that what was wrong with American scholarship in the humanities was its lack of command of languages. Voegelin knew a half dozen or so, and learned a new one when he needed to. But he couldn't write well in any of them. Is there a connection between these two attitudes? I wish I knew. Cardinal Newman, who certainly could write English superbly, refused to learn French well for fear it would get in the way of his writing English. If I am on his side, it is for the more modest reason that the study of different ways of naming things bores me. I know that the secret of humanity lies buried in the mystery of language and the way children learn it. But I don't believe that learning different ones unravels the mystery.

In any case, my Latin at Notre Dame was farcical. A full half dozen of the boys in my freshman Latin class knew more than the teacher, who had obviously been pressed into service at the last minute. Jack Turley, who took on the sophomores, knew Latin well but had sense enough to see the class was uninterested and so taught us a little Roman law and history instead. Father Hebert taught botany, bridge, movies, anything but the infinitely boring texts from the Latin fathers. At just this time I was reading Thackeray and some more recent chroniclers of English school life and never ceased to wonder at how the English schoolboys kept at the Latin and Greek, which seemed to me to make up at least half their curricula, without revolt.

More than any other subject language raises the question of the content of higher education. It seems to me undeniable that a must subject is the study of English, both composition and literature. Notre Dame agreed, and the courses in English were the best we had. I also think history a necessary subject, but the Notre Dame courses in history were among the worst we had. They were nothing but pious mouthings in praise of Catholicism and Americanism, in that order. This began to change the year I graduated, with the coming of James A. Corbett, who was followed by M. A. Fitzsimons and William O. Shanahan, the nucleus of the brilliant faculty Father Thomas T. McAvoy built onto when he became chairperson in 1939. It is now perhaps the best of the humanities departments.

McAvoy's counterpart in sociology came on the scene earlier, in 1927. This was Father Raymond Murray. Both Murray and his predecessor, Father John McGinn—it was largely a one- or two-man department—had been trained under the able Father William Kerby at Catholic University. But McGinn, a man of exceptional talents, drifted into other occupations, and it was left to Murray to become the real founder and mainstay of the department. Murray's teaching was an odd combination of standard content and fabricated pedagogy, but he was an able scholar devoted to his work and writing.

Economics and politics were joined in a single department until 1936. In my time it was headed by Father William Bolger, whose background was in still a third subject, public address and debate. Both economics and politics, as well as sociology, were required in the curriculum and the courses I had, with Paul Bartholomew and Joe Apodaca, were solid. But, as with history, the development into genuine college departments lay in the future.

My freshman year saw yet another attempt at courses in education, an academic discipline which, despite intelligent efforts, has never taken root at Notre Dame. This development created a required course for freshmen called College Orientation. The course didn't last long in the curriculum, but I lasted even less long. The teacher got me aside one day early on in the course and told me that if I refrained from coming to class he would give me a grade of 90. I joyfully accepted the proposition, but I have no idea why it was made. I can't think it was because I was a class nuisance, for in that case he would need to have simply told me to shut up, or whatever, and I would have totally obeyed; I was drilled to obedience. I rather think it was because he saw I had been through, in prep school and family, much of his message. As a teacher I have occasionally done the same thing, but usually with some compensating outside work—and a grade higher than 90.

The subjects which were supposed to unite all the students in Catholic universities and give them a special stance are, of course, religion and philosophy. Yet, strange to say, religion was not taught in the classroom at Notre Dame till the early 1920s. This may be one reason why the religion courses were so bad. Students solidly agreed that the required courses in religion were a waste of time and that the staff of the department was as motley a collection of misfits as could be found this side of the French Foreign Legion. Real religion was much better taught in the philosophy department, which had a large and very uneven faculty. There were a few brilliant teachers, there were dull perfunctory teachers, there were old-fashioned Thomists with their charts, new-fangled psychologists and axiologists. I was an undergraduate major in philosophy. What I mainly remember is that there was a hell of a lot of it. My transcript lists an incredible fifty-two credits in my major subject. This would have been too many in a department which made a point of teaching differing philosophic views. In a department with only one, Thomism, it was repetitious and numbing.

English was usually thought of as the intellectual's major, and the English major student was often caricatured as a rather pretentious ass, spouting polysyllables and reading cabalistic lore. This was nonsense, of course; most were like everybody else, though they were a cliquish lot. I should have been one of them but majored in philosophy to please the uncle who was paying for my education. It did, and that was enough for me.

The courses in science touched me very little; the curriculum requirement was mercifully slight. I admired Arthur Reyniers, who taught me my semester of biology, for his excellent organization and clear exposition, but the subject matter did not excite my languid spleen. I suppose I ought to be grateful that I was exposed to no more. Although I did well in my prep-school science courses, anything beyond the elementary is hard for me. And this is, of course, the biggest stumbling block for Notre Dame freshmen and the best reason for a separate freshman year. Most bright youngsters like their high-school science courses. They are fresh, generally well taught, and they are taught as exact sciences. Students can learn them. So they come to college determined to major in math, or chemistry, or biology, or what not. There a good percentage, I'd guess a third, learn that they are not really meant to be scientists. It's no use trying to tell them beforehand; I have tried again and again. They have to learn this lesson themselves, and learn it they do. For most it is a useful lesson, very educative, though at some cost to the grade average.

Of course, all this ought to take place within the college, which means no separate freshman year of studies. Why Notre Dame has, uniquely so far as I can ascertain, a separate College of Science is not wholly mysterious to me. Why they have kept it all these years is.

The historical heart of academic Notre Dame has lain with the sciences. The early faculty scholars were mostly in the sciences: from Father Carrier on through the Zahms, Nieuwland, and on down into my own time of Wenninger, Just, Collins, and Coomes, plus many another. The scientists stood for the *university*, for high standards of scholarship, for national recognition. By comparison the arts and belles lettres slid into mediocrity until the 1920s.

I think the main reason for this is the low standards of Catholic literature and indeed the genteel tradition of American literature generally. One of the sillier incidents in Father Finn's book for boys, *Claude Lightfoot*, has the hero reciting to an awed audience of his peers(!) a poem by Thomas Buchanan Reid which begins "My soul today/Is far away/Sailing the Vesuvian Bay." On and on went Claude, quoting the long whole of Reid's "beautiful poem," says Finn. This trivial incident suggests what was wrong. Reid, and Thomas Bailey Aldrich—they went in for three names—were among the host of minor poets who set the tone. Notre Dame's Charles Warren Stoddard was one of them, as was his successor as star of the English department, Maurice

Francis Egan. Holy Cross Father Charles O'Donnell was a wide cut above these, but at his worst, as in the forced occasional verse, he shared its bathos. So, to be among the best in poetry, in history, anywhere in the humanities, was to be genteel rather than imaginative or forceful. This was the tradition that H. L. Mencken fought so valiantly. The Catholic version of it was especially mushy.

Another reason is the texts used for college courses. At Notre Dame most courses simply ploughed through a single text. Occasionally some outside reading was required, in material placed on reserve in the library, but this was rare because dozens of copies were needed for classes of normal size, and even so it was hard to answer the student who insisted the copies were all in use when he asked for them. Theft and despoiling were too common to ignore. So, most courses in literature used anthologies. History and the social sciences usually relied on a single textbook.

So, of course, did math and the physical sciences. But in these one text is enough. Master that text and you've mastered the course. But this is pathetically untrue of the humanities, no matter how good the text. It is hard to realize now what a difference cheap paperbacks made to collegiate education, especially when they *were* cheap, in the 1950s. I took a course in 1933 from the admirable John Frederick in modern fiction. It was a large class, and providing books for it was very difficult, even with Frederick's wide-ranging reading list. But when Sy Gross taught the same course in the 1950s he simply assigned a paperback a week. Students could afford these, and they were easy to get from the publishers.

However, neither of these reasons explains the separation of the sciences from the arts. Other universities had the same tension, but founded no separate undergraduate colleges of science. I spent the last years of the Hesburgh administration hoping he would effect the merger into a single College of Arts and Sciences. In Fred Crosson we would have had an ideal first dean. I still hope it will be done. But 1930 would also have been a good year for the merger. Professors in the sciences were only then becoming specialists; John Zahm taught all the sciences, under the umbrella of "natural philosophy." The same was true of the humanities. Take the case of Father Lawrence V. Broughal,

who taught English, philosophy, and religion during a long
Notre Dame career. The prep-school teachers of the time also
taught everything. I can easily imagine Father Broughal turning
to math.

I knew Father Broughal very well. He was intelligent and
cultivated, very much the well-groomed, shoes-shined gentleman cleric. In addition to his many-faceted teaching, he was
secretary to the Building Committee, and a tasteful consultant
to the architects. He designed, with their help, the beautiful
chairs and tables whose basic pattern still serves the noble South
Dining Hall. He was the active supervisor of the sweep-out-
the-trash remodeling of Sacred Heart Church which architect
Wilfrid Anthony so successfully undertook in 1933. He was a
thorough individualist, autocratic and cranky. He was kind to
the students he singled out to improve and refine. These came
mostly from the literary set; he was for years faculty overseer of
publications, and a good one. Of course he was not much use
to the typical student journalist passionately seeking some way
to insert some salacity into his publication, but he helped with
writing and story ideas and stood behind his chosen ones firmly.
The best thing about him in many ways was his constant elegance. Not for a moment did he get down on all fours with his
students. But he was garrulous and demanding. Frank O'Malley
and I devised many unworkable strategies for avoiding him.

Father Frederick McKeon was attracted to the religious-
minded. His academics were a little less mixed than Broughal's,
Spanish and religion, plus a little administration. Both McKeon
and Broughal were forbidding in manner; I doubt that more
than a mumble ever passed between them. But both knew how
to net their possible disciples. McKeon was a devoted confessor,
to many more than students, and had very strong ideas about
prayer and worship. Now that I think back on it, it seems to me
that the Church of that time was more tolerant than it is now.

Perhaps the most eccentric of all was Father Peter E. Hebert.
He was by trade a classicist. He taught the required Latin to
hundreds of undergraduates, but they were much more likely
to learn how to lead from an interior sequence in bridge, or
how to tell a white oak from a red one. This latter was his
real passion. As a student in the early 1900s he fell under the
spell of the great Julius Nieuwland, then in his botany phase.

I often wondered why Hebert didn't turn into a botanist himself. He did become a devoted amateur. He spent every afternoon he could roaming the campus, collecting specimens for the herbarium he treasured. Nieuwland had persuaded the well-known Edward Lee Greene, his mentor at the Smithsonian in Washington, to give Notre Dame his herbarium, and Hebert assisted the botany staff in increasing its holdings. He became a friend of Joseph Oliver, a rich South Bender who had a herbarium of his own in his home, now the Copshaholm Museum. Hebert hoped that Oliver would finance the university herbarium. But he only joined a long list of those who failed to get money out of close-fisted Joe.

A life in the Notre Dame woods may have helped Hebert to good health. He lived to be eighty-eight, roaming the fields almost to the last. Toward the end of his life he produced a spiral-bound mimeographed book of seventy-eight pages entitled *Trees, Shrubs and Vines on Notre Dame Campus*. This has given me more pleasure than I can describe, for I, too, caught a touch of the Hebert interest in campus planting. I didn't bother with botanical classifications and names, but what I did get from the book added much pleasure to my daily (when possible) walks. Only *Seeing Stars*, a tiny little book from the old five-and-dime store, is comparable, but it has been useless for some years now. Population growth has made it close to impossible for professional astronomers to locate new observatories. It (and mugging) have also written finis to us night strollers watching the stars come and go. I used to gaze for long from the first tee of the Notre Dame golf course, or in Nashville's Centennial Park. Now I have to go to northern New Mexico. From here to there the night skies are lighted up from below.

Father Hebert went his own way. He loved the movies as much as he did bridge but was a typical "Isn't she beautiful?" fan with no interest in the cinema art. Without either scorn or rue, in my time he blandly ignored community and academic affairs; I think he loved a life in which he didn't have to think about food, clothing, shelter, or schedules, content to have all these done for him. Of course he retained the Domer's God-given privilege of complaining, but he never did anything beyond an occasional utterance. He was a teacher of extreme latitudinarian practice; his pedagogy consisted entirely of the

exposure of young unformed minds to his beautifully enunci-
ated pleasures and prejudices. I have no idea whether he agreed
with me that required Latin was a waste of time, but I am
grateful to him for letting me join his walks now and then instead of doing any serious work in his courses.

It is interesting to imagine a conversation between Hebert
and Father Thomas Crumley. Each of them was disconcertingly
unconventional. "Speak to your girl in French, a musical language," Hebert used to admonish his classes. "The trouble with
my students," Father Crumley once said at a faculty meeting,
"is that they don't know the meanings of words." "Look at that
shadow," he said to a companion and myself one late afternoon
in the fall. "What color is it?" "Purple," said my sharp friend,
while I gaped foolishly. "Right," said Father Crumley. My friend
had the advantage of having had Crumley as a teacher, which I
unfortunately hadn't—one more stupidity among many in my
academic career. Those I knew who did take his courses greatly
enjoyed the experience, the slow pace of his talk, so that the listeners could get "the meaning of the words," the sardonic wit,
the unexpected questions. All this in my time came in the only
two courses he had kept on teaching after a long career in several branches of philosophy and English. These were Inductive
Logic and Deductive Logic. It was those titles that kept me on
the sidelines.

But here the Hebert comparison stops. Crumley was a man
of affairs in the Holy Cross community. Highly esteemed by
his colleagues, he had been both vice-president and director of
studies. He was a stalwart in the camp of Father John Zahm,
outspokenly progressive, brutally direct. He was especially vir-
ulent against the continuation of the brothers as an integral part
of the Holy Cross community. Many of the best minds in the
community had argued for separation for years. Crumley became their leader. His 1932 petition, signed by ninety-six priests
in the American Province, to dissolve the partnership foundered
in the General Chapter of that year, and Crumley was exiled to
a chaplaincy in Anderson, Indiana, for the rest of his life. His
was the lone purge, but his also was the lone courage to assume
the leadership of a widely believed cause.

In time Crumley was vindicated: the brothers became a separate province in 1946. In 1958, however, some brothers who

wished it were admitted once more to the priests, Indiana Province. The long controversy, however, lost its edge as vocations
to both declined. But the brothers historically have had a hard
time of it. Originally they taught grade school. Then the sisters
took these over, and the brothers were not prepared to teach
the boys' high schools they began to be in demand for. They
rightly complained that the priests were not responsive to their
needs. When Zahm was the provincial he finally lent them a
helping hand, but the brothers thought this late and grudging.
Most of the priests were on the side of division, but they also
did not wish to be uncharitable toward the humble brothers,
who historically, from Sorin on, had played such an important
role at Notre Dame.

Among these priests were two who had dominant roles in
making the Burns-Schumacher academic revolution of 1920
work. These were Fathers J. Leonard Carrico and Charles C.
Miltner. Carrico ran the large and influential English department while Miltner headed philosophy. In 1922 Miltner became
the dean of the College of Arts and Letters. Carrico became director of studies in 1930.

The two men were very dissimilar. Carrico was a southerner,
dignified, courteous, fastidious. His prose style, immaculate and
accurate, had a touch of Johnsonian elegance, very much a part
of his character. "In the interest of a desirable uniformity," he
instructed the faculty, "the academic mortarboard should be
removed only during the consecration of the mass." In the university bulletin, which he wrote and rewrote in its entirety for
all of the 1930s, he described the campus as "1700 acres of
wooded park." Elsewhere the bulletin states: "The University
believes that a system of education which gives little attention to
the development of moral character is pernicious. Accordingly,
certain regulations, shown by experience to be salutary, are
enforced."

Carrico's teaching in the English department was mainly variations on his central theme of "Practical English," by which
he mostly meant good usage. Through the years he accumulated literally thousands of examples of "Sentences Faulty as
to Taste," "Sentences Faulty as to Ease," "Sentences Faulty as
to Euphony," and so on. He took keen pleasure in collecting
these. I once asked him to pass on a M.A. essay in the field of

his interest. He did so promptly and efficiently, but also furnished me (and himself) with two pages of faulty sentences he had culled from the opus. And I once saw a letter from him to a student—I worked in his office for a time—which dealt neatly with the matter of the student's letter, but had a last paragraph which ran something like this: "I note you use in your letter the word *thusly*. Thus is an adverb and only an adverb. The *-ly* is superfluous. Constructions like *thus-ly* are called by English grammarians barbarisms."

Carrico was a much loved teacher but a highly personal and eccentric one. Although as director of studies he urged professors to teach hard from bell to bell, he himself never arrived at a class on time. He would come in ten or fifteen minutes late, usually pushing before him a cart of mimeographed materials. Rather than lecture, he seemed to talk to himself, a mannerism one of his favorite students, James Withey, appropriated. His turns of language were often delightful. He had a wry and understated sense of humor as well, which he reserved for class and conversations with good friends. It never appeared in his numerous official documents. His usual manner was avuncular, so much so that his nickname was Daddy. Although he had a pet hate or so, he was anything but mean-spirited; he usually projected amiable goodwill. He was, perhaps, overfond of the academic regulations he had worked on so long and phrased so inimitably, but on the whole he presided over the faculty with good sense and good judgment. As time went on he stayed somewhat behind, becoming less sympathetic and more eccentric.

I came to know Father Miltner when I was an undergraduate. I believe this was rather unusual; he certainly did not court student popularity. His official manner, as dean, was coolly objective, yet many of us found him more willing to say yes to our requests than his assistant, Professor Paul Fenlon, who did court student popularity. Like most of the priest faculty till Corby Hall was reclaimed for a priests' residence in 1937, Miltner lived and prefected in student dormitories, mine among them in junior year. The few of us who breached his studied indifference found in him a wise, charming, and amusing companion. I continued to find him so, on through his last illness in the community infirmary, Holy Cross House, in 1966.

Miltner was brilliantly intelligent and marked as such from his earliest days at Notre Dame. He came from the simplest of backgrounds in rural Michigan and never aspired to the polish of a Carrico or a Broughal. His was a slightly delayed vocation; he did not come to Notre Dame till he was twenty-one, in 1907. In 1911 he was sent to Rome, but World War I transferred him to Quebec, where he completed his studies in 1916. He returned to Notre Dame that year for his ordination and began teaching in 1918. In 1940 he left Notre Dame to become the president of the University of Portland.

Many thought he should have become the president of Notre Dame when Father John O'Hara departed in 1941, but if he thought so I never ran across a trace of it. As teacher and administrator he performed with solid integrity. He was an excellent teacher, interesting, nimble-witted, and personal. As a philosopher he was, as befits his training at the Gregorian in Rome and Laval in Quebec, conventional and old-fashioned, somewhat unimaginative. As a writer he was clear but lusterless. In personality he was somewhat forbidding, but he had a character of noble dignity and modesty.

Because both were of German extraction, Miltner's name is sometimes coupled with that of Father Francis Wenninger. There is reason for this: both were captains in the Burns revolution, and both became deans at about the same time. Both were about the same age, both were impatient, neither suffered fools gladly, both had the reputation of being undeviatingly humorless. But Miltner had a lighter side. If Wenninger did, I have run across no record of it. In his Notre Dame history Father Hope speaks of him as "terrifyingly serious." He must have been deeply committed to his work to have done the unusual thing of taking leave of his College of Science deanship in mid-career to get his doctorate at the University of Vienna. My only personal recollection of Father Wenninger is his iron-handed conduct of his perennial job as master of ceremonies at important liturgies in Sacred Heart Church.

Wenninger's predecessor as dean was the celebrated Father Julius A. Nieuwland, the most distinguished scientist Holy Cross has produced. Nieuwland, a South Bender of Belgian extraction, started off in chemistry under John Zahm. He then veered off into botany, establishing, along with Hebert's beloved herbarium, the *American Midland Naturalist*, Notre Dame's long-running botanical journal which continues to this day. Nieuwland then went back to chemistry, where he made a distinguished record as a researcher, eventually creating the solidest early department of graduate study in Notre Dame's academic history. He had the reputation of being a poor teacher of undergraduates, but I suspect he was merely an uninterested one. I knew him slightly. Because of a balky digestion he often took his meals in the cafeteria rather than the dining hall, and so did I, because of my newspaper work. He was to me a welcome companion, an amusing and easy talker, a cultivated gentleman. He now reminds me a little of other distinguished scholars I have known, Waldemar Gurian and Eric Voegelin among them. There was about all three a certain courtliness I found attractive, although my acquaintance with Nieuwland was very slight.

The English department had historically close ties with the *Ave Maria*, the well-regarded Catholic weekly. It had been founded by Father Sorin and came to national prominence in the long editorship (1875–1929) of Father Daniel Hudson. Apprenticeship to Hudson was a standard part of the training of many Holy Cross fathers who taught English. This, to the few best teachers, polished off training in writing English begun on the *Scholastic*, the lively student weekly partially masterminded by the English department professors, who fed it the work of their best students.

In 1884 Father Hudson, in cahoots with President Walsh, invited a leading literary light of the last quarter of the nineteenth century, Charles Warren Stoddard, to fill the post of "Professor of Belles Lettres," which was to stimulate literary activity on the campus. Stoddard's precious temperament didn't flourish in northern Indiana, however, and he soon departed. He was succeeded by another Hudson connection, Maurice Francis Egan.

Stoddard's reputation had been made on the West Coast, but Egan was a well-known literary figure in the East. President Thomas Walsh built him a house near the campus that is still standing on Notre Dame Avenue. Egan called it "The Lilacs," and solicited plants of that hardy and lovely bush from his friends. I remember that Aubrey de Vere sent him one, but I don't remember whether Egan's close friend, the distinguished critic James Huneker, did. Huneker's firm place in the history of American letters rests on his bringing to American attention the French avant-garde in the arts of the turn of the century, most notably Debussy. Nothing could have been further from the concerns of Egan. To us he seemed arty, precious, self-consciously a "character," rhetorical, almost false.

But to his contemporaries he was a cultivated gentleman. He had edited the *Freeman's Journal*, the outstanding Catholic paper of the era of independent Catholic journalism before the bishops took over the papers. After he left Notre Dame for the Catholic University, he became well enough thought of in Washington to be appointed minister to Denmark. Today we find his genteel novels and verse unreadable, much like the pulpit oratory of his time. Egan's autobiography, *Recollections of a Happy Life*, is full of revealing details that give us insights into his tastes. One I recall is the satisfaction he took in discovering, at his daughter's wedding, as he watched the young couple kneeling before the alter, that the soles of the groom's shoes were "decorously black." But before we snort, we should remember Evelyn Waugh's outrage when the guests at his daughter's wedding showed up in black, not white, ties. Black mischief indeed.

The star of the English department in my time was Charles Phillips. President Matthew Walsh had met Charlie, as he was universally known, when both were caught up in World War I, Walsh as chaplain, Charlie with the Knights of Columbus field service. Phillips had been, like Stoddard and Egan, a novelist and a poet, as well as a free-lance journalist. The odd thing is that, a generation later, his work was very like theirs, a footnote testifying to the strength of the genteel tradition. At Walsh's invitation he came to Notre Dame in 1924. A widower, he lived in Sorin Hall, where he became a much-loved figure. As a teacher he was an old-fashioned enthusiast, but he was an ardent member of the Notre Dame community, helping out in all sorts of endeavors, literary or not. He died suddenly during the Christmas vacation of my senior year.

Other fiction writers on the faculty were Father Patrick Carroll and the long-time head of journalism at Notre Dame, John M. Cooney. Cooney's subject was the rural Kentucky he came from and where he had been president of a small college as well as a newspaperman. Carroll's subject was Ireland. A small-ish, witty Hudson assistant on the *Ave Maria* for many years, he taught English and produced an endless stream of stories, long and short, which sentimentalized life in Ireland.

The key word here is sentimental. The writers of the genteel tradition had no hesitation in falsifying experience to teach some moral lesson. They meant to edify their readers and lead them to a better way of life. Catholic literature was especially soggy with this well-meant hypocrisy. Pious stories of heroic priests, self-sacrificing sisters, and saintly lay folks filled the Catholic magazines of the time and often flowered into books. I was keenly aware of the style at the early age of ten or so. My cousin, Florence Moran, was secretary to the premier writer of boys' books for Catholics. This was Father Francis J. Finn, S.J., who wrote of life at fictional St. Maure's boarding school, as well as about boys in parishes. Dear Florence Moran fed me a steady stream of Finn's output. Without any prompting (if there was any, it would surely have gone in the other direction) I found myself repelled by the arch cuteness even of the titles— Percy Wynne (he was a sissy), Tom Playfair (he was a hero), Harry Dee (he was mischievous). I feel sure I decided against this diet by comparing Finn's books with the better ones I'd been reading, books by Ralph Henry Barbour, Mark Hellinger, and Clarence Buddington Kelland.

The fiction for adults was well above this level. Isabel C. Clarke, F. Marion Crawford, Monsignor Robert Hugh Benson, wrote well—Benson is to this day readable. True, they were romantically melodramatic, like a Puccini opera. So were their secular counterparts, John Fox, Jr., Peter B. Kyne, Rex Beach. But both these groups were a long way from the new fiction that was beginning to emerge in the wake of Twain and Howells. Stephen Crane, Hamlin Garland, Ellen Glasgow, Theodore Dreiser, Frank Norris, and Ring Lardner were bringing realism to American literature. Some of the older Notre Dame English faculty ignored the new realism and derided it when they no longer could ignore it. Their leader was crusty old Henry Staunton, who taught his subject as if it were tracts of the Ethical Culture Society. "I can't see that there is anything prophylactic about Shakespeare," I once heard him say.

But the winds of change were blowing, softly but firmly. This was the way of the unlikely leader of the change, Father Leo L. Ward. Where and how Leo Ward learned his impeccable taste and style I'll never know. He came from rural Indiana, wrote about it, and cherished it. But he saw it with the eyes of sincerity and truth. At almost the same time, around 1927, another Leo Ward was beginning his long and fruitful career in philosophy. What an odd coincidence, two of the same name. Their middle names were different. The English teacher's middle name was Lewis, and so his nickname became Literature; Philosophy Ward's middle name was Richard, and so he came to be known as Rational. But this was only for explanatory purposes. To his friends L. R. Ward was always known as Dick. Literature Ward stayed with Leo. In character and temperament they were rather similar. Both were quiet and reticent, both free from ambition and vanity. Together they made a wholesome revolution in the Notre Dame humanities. They helped to kill the genteel tradition.

Leo L. Ward joined the faculty in 1927 and straightaway began to teach writing. He was totally innocent of classroom pedagogy, but he was a superb critic. His tutelage consisted of long-ish and courteous criticism of student papers, that and little more. He inherited Father Carrico's course for the English majors, but the distance between the two was astral. With freshmen as with the majors, Ward aimed at the same thing, which might roughly be called art. He worked on and with the creative powers of the students: first the tone, then the music, as music teachers sometimes say. He wanted the tone of elevated ordinary speech, emanating from an organic whole. Almost at once he began to develop good student writers, Louis Brennan, Louis Hasley, Richard Sullivan, Harry Sylvester. He published some of his own stories in the then prestigious *Midland* magazine and in that way came to know its editor, John Towner Frederick.

Frederick was another farm boy, but he came from a family of some distinction. His uncle Towner was a well-known jurist and was for a time governor of Puerto Rico—young John visited him there. From teaching rural country school John went on to Iowa University. While still an undergraduate (albeit somewhat older than the norm), he began to plan the *Midland*. Its first issue appeared in January 1915, the year Frederick graduated, and was handsome in design and superior in content, which was mostly short fiction. It retained these features till its end in depression-raddled 1933.

During all these years Frederick *was* the *Midland*, editor, publisher and owner. With the help of his intelligent and devoted wife, Esther Paulus, another Iowa undergraduate, he did it all. He enlisted some capable readers, but his was the decisive and guiding hand. His greatest achievement, besides keeping the admirable enterprise afloat, was in developing young writers. In this he was, as one of them put it, "as patient as Griselda, and as hopeful as Penthesilea," writing back and forth to them again and again, suggesting, encouraging. The writers he published, many for the first time, are a prestigious group. Their listing in Milton M. Reigelman's excellent history of the *Midland* covers fourteen pages. But writers Frederick didn't publish often praised his painstaking help. For its first ten years of publication the *Midland* used no rejection slips; all was personal, demanding, and time-consuming.

Largely because of this Frederick neglected his own academic career. He did not finish his M.A. at Iowa till 1917. He then took a teaching post at Moorhead, Minnesota, for two years but left it to live with his father in Glennie, Michigan, where they had brought fourteen hundred acres of land for about a dollar an acre. Together they cleared and farmed some of the land, and John had time to write two excellent novels of his own.

The *Midland* was still being published in Iowa City, and John accepted an offer to join its English faculty with time off to edit his magazine in 1921. There he stayed till he moved himself and the magazine to Chicago in 1930, except for one year at the University of Pittsburgh. In Chicago he changed the scope of the magazine from regional to national, hopeful that its mid-1920s mild prosperity—it actually almost paid for itself then–would continue. But the depression ruined all his hopes. When the *Midland* ceased publication in 1933 Frederick busied himself with teaching at Northwestern and Notre Dame. He kept on some outside interests, a book column in the *Rotarian* magazine and a literary radio program, "Of Men and Books," aired by WBBM in Chicago. Very gradually he shifted to Notre Dame as his major teaching concern, returning to Glennie for the holidays.

I became very close to Frederick in the 1930s when he com-
muted to Notre Dame from Chicago. He lived next door to me
in Lyons Hall. He had been a favorite teacher of mine, one of
the best classroom lecturers I ever heard, and we had mutual
interest in agrarianism as well as literature. I often stayed with
him and his family in his Chicago apartment and became very
friendly with his wife and two boys. Our friendship deepened
when he came to teach full time at Notre Dame, ending eventually as chair of the English department and my office neighbor.
Though not a Catholic, Frederick was deeply religious and fitted
in beautifully at Notre Dame. I once said to him at the beginning of a fall term, "John, don't you love this time of new starts,
when everyone is full of good intentions?" "I do here at Notre
Dame," he replied promptly.

In 1936 Father Ward brought his and Frederick's former student, Richard Sullivan, to teach and practice creative writing
at Notre Dame. Sullivan became a beloved and tasteful teacher,
but more than his teaching was the influence of his well-
wrought novels. Somehow, the note of wide popular approval
escaped him. In a time when John O'Hara was setting the pace
in fiction in the United States, Sullivan was only a little ways
behind—a little less sharp, a little less energetic. Still, as with his
great friend Frederick, his work deserved greater success than
it achieved.

Ward, Frederick, and Sullivan established good fiction as a
part of Notre Dame literary education. Around the same time
Ward brought to the Notre Dame faculty two poets who belong
almost in the top echelon of poets of their time. These were John
Frederick Nims and Earnest Sandeen. Nims went on to become
editor of *Poetry* magazine. Another editor of that famous journal
was Henry Rago, a graduate student in philosophy here during
Ward's heyday. During the late 1930s Notre Dame welcomed
a great many refugees from Hitler's Europe to strengthen its
academic side. But there were also homegrown movements like
Ward's in English. Others in philosophy, physics, mathematics,
and biology joined with the refugees to make the Hesburgh
Notre Dame. This was a real intellectual revolution, swinging
Notre Dame away from the genteel tradition in literature and
writing, and bringing it into the mainstream of American higher
education in other branches of learning.

Ward had one failure. He wanted deeply to improve the drama department. An excellent theater man himself, he produced and directed plays at Moreau Seminary, where he lived and taught, superior to anything on the university stage. He engaged the distinguished English actor and writer Robert Speaight to do an outdoor *Midsummer Night's Dream* in 1939 that would have done credit to any professional theater in the country. But the then president, Father Hugh O'Donnell, was impervious to the Ward-Speaight demonstration, and no offer of a faculty position was made to Speaight. In spite of the superb acoustics of Washington Hall and its central position on the campus, drama at Notre Dame had only one or two sporadic moments of excellence until Father Arthur Harvey stabilized it in the 1950s.

Meanwhile Father Leo Richard Ward was developing his career in the philosophy department. L. R. Ward was a rare combination of teacher and scholar. He was, so far as I can tell, largely a self-made scholar, though he was a devoted disciple of his Catholic University graduate school mentor, Monsignor E. A. Pace. But I doubt Pace had much to do with Ward's wide reading in contemporary philosophy. A faithful founding member of the American Catholic Philosophical Association, he also belonged to the secular American Philosophy group. He read widely in the publications of this society, John Dewey, Wilbur Urban, R. B. Perry, the elder Sellars, many more, and was welcomed by them to their meetings. He corresponded with them and introduced his students to their thought. He was ecumenical before the word was generally used.

But his deepest commitment was to Aristotle, whom he revered all his career as *the* philosopher. He taught himself Greek because he wanted to know Aristotle plain. He also taught himself French so as to get more nearly to the thought of his friend Jacques Maritain, the great contemporary exponent of Aristotle and St. Thomas. These marks of his commitment to scholarship, rare in the Notre Dame of his time, brought him into close association with medievalist Father Philip Moore, the bustling dean of the Graduate School. Moore, who pioneered in several new Ph.D. programs, wanted Ward to start one in philosophy. He got President O'Hara to suggest it to Ward. "For that," Ward said, "you'll have to get a first-rate new man." "Well, go and find one," said forthright O'Hara. Ward did just that, engaging the estimable Yves Simon. Between them they got the program off to a fine start, one which has become outstanding in the United States.

Ward used to say that the most neglected figure in the modern history of Notre Dame was Father Moore. There is some truth in that. But a better case could be made for Ward himself. I hope that his biography will someday be written. A dedicated member of the Congregation of Holy Cross, he was also a Vatican II priest, breaking new ground but cherishing tradition. At Notre Dame he was a bridge between the old and the new. The new professional philosophers, specialist to the core, found him a sympathetic and knowledgable colleague, and we older ones loved him as the wisest and best of friends.

As a teacher, Ward was simply himself. His classes had no design. He just stood there and talked to himself, in winter hunched over a radiator in that most cheerless of classroom buildings, old Science, and, patting his hand up and down, would grapple with an idea, tossing it back and forth and up and down like a dog with a bone. He was utterly undramatic. By no criterion should he have been a successful classroom teacher, but he was very popular in the 1930s. By the 1950s his approach to philosophy had become less singular and his appeal diminished. But for the previous twenty-five years he was something of a master teacher.

This was in some part owing to his approach. For at least twenty-five years before his Notre Dame days, Catholic philosophy in the United States had become a dead language. Not for everybody in it, to be sure; an occasional maverick, likely to turn up anywhere, breathed a little life into the corpse. But for most, philosophy was an enterprise that was finished, all solved and done, tricked up in little aphorisms and distributed to docile students like pills. Ward shied away from this approach. He stressed that philosophy was, above all, inquiry. He was wary of providing pat answers. Toward the end of a course I took with him he distributed a sheet headed, "The following propositions are suggested as defensible."

Ward was a genial and lovable person, a great favorite in Notre Dame society. He loved to play cards, at which he was a whiz, loved to visit and talk and laugh. He had some acerbic disdain for the pretentious, but to all others he was brother and friend. And above all to his former students, who wanted him to witness their marriages, baptize their children, and come to see them. He was without a doubt the best man I ever knew, yet his deliberate simplicities were such as to make me feel that the desirable life for him would be rather dull for me, not unlike those proposed by H. G. Wells and, in our time, B. F. Skinner. Still, of all the professors I have known his was perhaps the most useful life. It was happily a long one; he lived into his nineties, in them as sharp as ever. In old age he turned to writing verse, spare, homely, and compassionate, like his noble self.

I was a devoted friend to both Father Wards. Father Leo L. Ward became chair of the English department early on in my teaching career and sustained me with advice, encouragement, and the best of companionship. At some point in the late 1930s Big Mac, the maxi-size Dean McCarthy of the then College of Commerce, asked me to teach his freshmen, offering to winnow out the best for me. I wanted to do this, but Father Ward nixed the deal, and I now thank him for it. McCarthy's proposal would surely have lasted no longer than he did and would in any case have become a dead end for me. Most of all, it would have estranged me to some extent from my natural friends in Arts and Letters, Sullivan, O'Malley, Fitzsimons, et al. When, after World War II, I returned as chair of journalism, Father Ward and I planned an office suite with a common secretary for our adjoining offices in the new O'Shaughnessy Building. But Ward died, at the age of fifty-five, before we moved in. I have been lucky in friendship all my life and even luckier in working for men and women I have rejoiced to work with and for. On both counts Leo L. Ward is tops.

The main accomplishments of the Fathers Ward were intellectual. Leo L. refashioned the English department, making Frank O'Malley its center and showpiece. The important thing is that he encouraged Frank to center on religion. This was a rather dangerous thing to do, because after all Catholicism is not the mainstream of English literature, but Catholic traces remained, and it was a wholesome thing to recall these to the minds of Catholic students. Perhaps Frank overshot the mark, finding in Blake almost a Catholic instead of simply a deeply religious person, disparaging the great nineteenth-century novelists for their sentimental humanism, despising the rationalism of Johnson as well as that of Wells. But it is also right to remember that Johnson was also deeply religious, that Newman reawakened the religious spirit of England for nearly the whole of his century, and that Hopkins deserved the rank of a great poet. Rufus Rauch was O'Malley's able partner in this venture, working the less popular early centuries but again emphasizing the religious spirit of the Renaissance dramatists and the metaphysical poets. Yes, it was dangerous. Literature, no less than history, should never be made merely confessional. And certainly Frank overvalued the specifically Catholic writers he dealt with: Blois, Peguy, Mauriac, Claudel, and others. Nevertheless, it was a danger worth risking, at the passionate and brilliant O'Malley level. And it certainly worked to excite the minds and hearts of Notre Dame students.

To me personally Ward's other work for contemporary literature was immensely vital. To steer the concerns of Notre Dame students away from the sorry sentimental Catholic literature of the time into interest in what was rapidly becoming the mainstream of realistic American literature and vernacular American writing was part of my own work, part of what I wanted to do in teaching. The new depression literature was pretty awful, but we still basked in the afterglow of the 1920s, relishing Sinclair Lewis, John Dos Passos, Edith Wharton, Scott Fitzgerald, Ernest Hemingway, even to some extent Henry James. Not only did Ward in this way stimulate us to the present, but he pointed the way to a future in fiction which Notre Dame has kept up to this day. It is a modest but honest achievement, far beyond the earlier standards. This is worth remembering.

These were the bright stars of my early days at Notre Dame, those who changed the course of our thinking and doing. There were many more, of course, who didn't, but who taught and thought memorably. There was dear Fred Myers, a beloved teacher of post-Restoration English literature, and with him in the department were Andy Smithberger, Frank Moran, Norb Engels, and twinkling Father James H. McDonald. There was John Scannell, who for many years ran the physical education department with astute efficiency. There were scientists who touched us, Regidius Kaczmarek, Edward Maurus, Daniel Hull. In law, there were Clarence Manion, John Whitman, Eldon

Richter, and Homer Earl. In business, there were Stan Price, Clet Chizek, Lee Flatley, Wes Bender, Gene Payton, and Herb Bott. I wish that each of these colleges and even departments had its own historian. I name only those who came to my attention. As I do so, I reflect on how few had doctorates. Of the major figures I deal with only a few C.S.C. priests, mostly proteges of Father Burns at Catholic University. There were even fewer Ph.D.'s among my Nashville agrarian mentors. Many, perhaps most, of the best minds in both Nashville and Notre Dame not only did not go on for their doctorates but actively opposed the national professional stampede for the degree. John Frederick was one of these, I another. The main reason Frederick left Iowa for Chicago in 1930 was the turn there toward German-inspired scholarship as the only criterion for place and preferment in the English department. John felt that this sort of thing, enshrined in the Modern Language Association (whose meetings he occasionally attended in a mocking spirit), turned literature into a phony science and inspiration into a Freudian slip. Anyone who has followed the proceedings of the MLA since his time, or the more recent arguments over course content in language departments in the universities, will recognize how well-grounded were Frederick's fears.

John and his allies did not despise good scholarship. He did pioneering research in early American magazines, in cooperation with his close friend Frank Luther Mott, the author of what is still the standard work in the field. Donald Davidson at Vanderbilt was a pioneer in collecting and studying the balladry of the Appalachian mountain region of the South. In literary criticism the Vanderbilt group largely reshaped its entire course in the English-speaking world.

It would be strange indeed if I had not been drawn into this on the side of my mentors. I did not try for my Ph.D. when it would have been comparatively easy, on the GI Bill after World War II. I thought, with spurts even of passion, that Notre Dame was for its undergraduates and unsuited to most graduate work, and that its mission was to educate its undergraduates and through them the Catholics of the United States. And I believe I was right, at least till the Hesburgh regime drowned us all in money. But that, and its aftermath, are shrouded in the future.

4

RELIGION

At the heart, the core, the center, and central nervous system of the Notre Dame I came to was religion. It was, of course, the Roman Catholic religion, based on the Apostles' Creed and the organization maintaining it of pope, bishops, and clergy. But it had a different flavor from, say, the Church in France, or Florence or Fusan.

Ours was the Irish-American Catholic Church. There were plenty of German-American Notre Dame students, not to forget the French, Poles, Italians, Lebanese, Latinos, Slavs, Croatians, and still others. But the dominant tone was set by the Irish Americans. The French element, which founded Notre Dame and colored the early American Church everywhere, was swamped by the Irish immigrants who took over in the decade between 1830 and 1840 and continued their domination till Vatican II in the 1960s. I don't know why the Irish became so dominant. Part of the complex of reasons was, of course, language. Another part was that Ireland exported clergy as well as laity in far greater numbers than any other country. Perhaps the most important reason was the seeming natural affinity of the Irish for the American system. They got on better here than in any other country they immigrated to in considerable numbers.

The mother Church in Ireland was at that time deeply influenced by Jansenism, which is basically Puritanism. Although H. L. Mencken oversimplified when he said that a puritan was a person who couldn't bear the thought that someone somewhere was having a good time, the saying does suggest the austerity and severity of the sect. Of French origin, it had deeply affected the French clergy who came to the United States as refugees from the French Revolution. Many of these, like Father Stephen

67

Badin, the founder of Notre Dame's landholdings, were more austere than the Irish who succeeded them.

The Holy Cross community does not seem much touched by Jansenism. Certainly Sorin was not. His deep piety and faith were combined with traits that now seem very American. He took chances, he tried much and failed often, he fought and won and fought and lost, but he never lost his drive and his optimism. It's true that his school was merely a school, and I think he cherished its inbred schoolishness, although he encouraged Zahm and others with a university point of view.

Sorin's domination gave way, after his death, to that of Father Andrew Morrissey. Morrissey would probably be puzzled to hear himself described as an Irish Jansenist, but I rather think he was, down to the last detail of his birth in Ireland. His struggles to retain his leadership, and the compromises he was forced to make with his antagonists, give some indication that the spirit of Notre Dame was not exclusively Jansenist. Nevertheless, he did retain, however uneasily, his leadership of the Holy Cross community at Notre Dame until World War I.

If I think Father Morrissey would be puzzled at my calling him a Jansenist, I wonder what Father, later Cardinal Archbishop, John Francis O'Hara would think. His mind did not dwell on such matters. He came to Notre Dame thinking not of Jansen or his most famous disciple, Blaise Pascal, but of his dream of a College of Foreign Commerce he hoped to develop out of the one Father Schumacher had started in 1916. This ambition was a result of his spending some years with his family in South America, where his father was a member of the consular service. But once in the arena at Notre Dame, O'Hara, with his strong sense of realism, saw that his dream was too grandiose. Working with the simpler scheme of Schumacher, he became the real founder of the College of Commerce and its first dean. Along with this he got the job of prefect of religion when Father Charles O'Donnell went off to World War I as a chaplain. At that time, however, the job description of prefect of religion was merely a simple scheme for encouraging boys to daily Communion as a means to a better, certainly a quieter life, an additional duty post not unlike that of confessor to the sisters. It was neither difficult nor demanding.

But by 1922 O'Hara's zeal had made it both. He relinquished his deanship to James E. McCarthy and devoted his full time— to O'Hara twenty-four hours a day—to being prefect of religion. There were only two "prefects" in the Notre Dame administration. The other was prefect of discipline. Both were unfortunate titles, I think. The job of prefect of discipline was easy to rename "dean of students," but O'Hara's job would be difficult to rename. "Chaplain" is too slight, "pastor" misleading. Looking back, most students would think of it as simply O'Hara's post. He made it important. It was little when he took it, and it did not long survive his leaving it.

To his enormous clientele O'Hara seemed sempiternal, in office since time began and his leaving it unthinkable. But in fact his sway was a brief decade. It was 1924 before he got a full head of steam, and he left it in 1934 when he became president. But during that decade O'Hara did more to fix the character of Notre Dame than anyone else. It was a time of growth, both in number of students and in national reputation. Most Americans thought of Notre Dame as the home of masculine Catholicism. It was a macho image, of good boys becoming good men, appealing to high-school teachers all over the Catholic world who followed O'Hara's lead as well as to the boys themselves who, if they could not play for her, at least wanted to cheer, cheer for old Notre Dame on the home grounds.

O'Hara's crusade was for daily Holy Communion, or at least frequent reception of the Blessed Sacrament. This devotion was instilled in him when a young man looking for a job in Indianapolis after some years in South America. Bishop Joseph Chartrand, then the rector of the Indianapolis cathedral, was his mentor. Chartrand spent all morning in the cathedral, hearing confessions and distributing Holy Communion. His main target was the young men working in nearby downtown Indianapolis. He cultivated them, gave them the little blue prayerbooks O'Hara also used, advised and helped them. Chartrand openly and firmly did not believe Holy Communion should be only a part of mass. Nor did he believe that Communion outside of mass should be exceptional. O'Hara absorbed all this and remained in touch with Chartrand, who lived on as bishop of Indianapolis till 1933.

O'Hara's job was different, to be sure. His young men were already in the churchyard, so to speak. His job was to get their attention. Once he had that, he could teach them the lessons of practical goodness. There was nothing theological, and little doctrinal, about O'Hara's message. It was simple: join with me in making Notre Dame "the City of the Blessed Sacrament" by receiving Communion frequently, and you will be better men, better students, and better athletes. One of O'Hara's main targets was the football players. He accompanied them as chaplain on their one and only trip to the Rose Bowl in 1925. He knew their example would mean more to younger boys than all his preaching.

The chief means he chose, or perhaps stumbled upon is the better phrase, for getting the attention of the collegians was the *Religious Bulletin*. At first this one-page collection of church notices, advice, and other short squibs was simply posted on the bulletin board outside O'Hara's Sorin Hall office. When it elicited comment it was also posted elsewhere. Finally it was slipped under the door of every dormitory room on the campus and made widely available to off-campus readers by mail or just by picking one up in Sorin.

O'Hara was a born journalist. His style was short, snappy, and trenchant. He knew the bulletin was in demand. Early in my freshman year of 1930 he wrote, "The standard complaints are coming in that the *Bulletin* snatchers are getting in their dirty work. From one bulletin board or another the copies are disappearing before the day is over. That is as dumb as it is selfish. There is hardly a student on the campus who does not pass Sorin Hall at some hour. If he wants a bulletin all he has to do is drop in at 141 and help himself."

Everybody read the *Bulletin*. "A pious tradition at Notre Dame," he wrote on October 3, 1930, "is the remembrance of the team in Holy Communion on the morning of every game. Most of the members of the squad have already started daily Communion; even those who have not done so will appreciate your prayers. We want no accidents to mar the season." Religion and football, the nun and the radio of Hemingway's story. O'Hara deliberately fostered the connection. I doubt he understood the game any better than the nun in the story, but he was ahead of his time in knowing the ways of publicity.

One of O'Hara's favorite subjects was "Objections to Daily Communion Answered." Here is a sample: "I am too lazy to go daily." *Ans*: "Which means you are probably in college only because you are too lazy to go to work. There are such people, but we don't envy their ambition." Another: "Nobody gets me up in the morning." *Ans*: "That can be arranged. What's your room number?" And so it went. He returned again and again to his theme of frequent Communion. One of his telling bulletins of 1930 was headed, "It Looks Like an Old Settlers' Picnic," which notes that all sorts of faces not seen all fall were going to Communion in preparation for the semester exams. "It looks like a League of Nations," O'Hara exclaimed. "Belgians and Bavarians, Prussians and Frenchmen, Irish and English, Poles and Italians, Lithuanians and Greeks, Slavs and Czechs," and from a long similar list of places they come "to the heavenly banquet, travelers long lost in the desert, stray sheep caught in the brambles, lost goats found only by diligent searching, one by one they come for their wedding garments. Will their Faith perish, their Hope dissolve, their Charity vanish when exams are over? History answers Yes; Hope answers No."

But the *Bulletin* pursued other subjects. As the depression came on, "The other day some over-fed freshmen amused themselves by throwing oranges at one another. Those of them who looked out the window later felt chagrined when they saw ill-clad, pinched children picking up the fragments of those oranges." For Lent, "The stupid sin—Pride. The miserable sin—Avarice. The pitiful sin—Lust. The outrageous sin—Anger. The despicable sin—Envy. The sordid sin—Gluttony. The contemptible sin—Sloth." For Mother's Day, "If you cannot afford to buy the card for Mother's Day the Prefect of Religion will supply one for you." And every *Bulletin* ended with requests for prayers, reminiscent of O'Hara's Sunday performance at all the student masses. He would duck out of his confessional in the west transept after the gospel, and, standing at the altar rail, deliver in the clearest, most audible voice I ever heard, the announcements for the week, which always ended with requests for prayers, and this always ended "and six special intentions," or however many. He did all this from memory. The sermon that followed was anticlimatic.

But Sunday was perhaps his easiest day. The last student mass was at nine. Part of the Jansenist creed was the erroneous connection between dawn and virtue. Since mass was Sunday's law, he did not hear confessions or distribute Communion in Sorin and so had the late morning and afternoon to himself. Sunday evening was a favorite time for meeting students individually. You didn't make appointments with O'Hara. You simply waited till he was free, improving the time by browsing through the collection of pamphlets in his waiting room. His manner in consultation was as terse as his bulletin and Sunday announcements. Yet he was oddly comforting. He made you feel that you were not a lost sheep but an integral part of his flock. Frequently he would quietly don his stole at the end of a talk and say, "Now, regard this as your confession." His memory for names and faces was prodigious.

After graduation, when I got to know him better, I thought his judgment sound. "Oh, never mind about so and so," he once wrote me, "he's all right. He'll come round." And he did. Or, "He's just going through a phase. Underneath he's sound." In consultation he was serious. He was not without humor, but he did not indulge in it in these talks with students. He did not ramble, he was never personal, he was really almost machine-like. But he was also never mean-spirited, never vindictive, and, however stern his principles, knew to temper the wind to the shorn lamb. He neither praised nor blamed. In his *Bulletin* he was prodigal of both, but not to the boys who sought his advice. He was a strict minder of his own business.

This may be a reason why he had such solid support from the Holy Cross priests at Notre Dame. There must have been some, as certainly there were some lay professors, who doubted his methods, questioned his deft-handed advice, and wondered about his theology. But I never heard such disagreement publicly expressed, and I saw how many priests of varied styles cooperated with O'Hara.

He needed such. Not all was centered on his Sorin headquarters. Each hall had its own active chapel—my freshman hall, Howard, had two—and the rectors and prefects worked with O'Hara, counting Communions, noting absences and nonparticipants, and passed their tallies along to Sorin Hall. O'Hara loved surveys and counts and polls. This may have been his

college-of-commerce background showing; he was always practical, never speculative. During the summers he worked up a
volume of statistics, results of surveys, and review of the year's
religious activities. This was widely circulated throughout the
United States. O'Hara was becoming known, like Father Daniel
Lord among the Catholic high-schoolers and Monsignor Fulton
J. Sheen among the adults.

O'Hara placed great faith in the missions he began each
school year with, the first for freshmen, the second for upperclassmen. During these he exhorted all to a new clean slate for
the coming year and set out his plan for keeping it so through
daily Holy Communion. As supports for this he backed strongly
half hours of adoration before the exposed Blessed Sacrament
each day during Lent and on other special days, like First Fri-
days and Corpus Christi. He knew that zeal evaporated with
time and pressured backsliders relentlessly. I must confess I
found the pressure somewhat uncomfortable. I was once reluctantly taken, by a devoted disciple, to Communion well after
midnight so we could eat, in those days of the Communion fast.
There was something fanatical to me about the whole O'Hara
mission. Yet frankly it didn't touch me much or deeply. Male
students are deeply involved with grades, games, and girls.
Most Notre Damers were as little troubled by O'Hara as they
were by the disciplinary system. It was easy, and indeed normal, to steer by both without any danger of shipwreck. For most
of us O'Hara was there to consult, if we needed him, about the
very normal, practical matters that concerned us: masturbation,
petting, petty theft, drinking, vandalism, lying, the gamut of
adolescent falls from grace.

I came to know O'Hara rather better than most only after he
became president. I had often wondered at his incredible energy, and he told me he needed to take cold showers now and
then to stay awake in the afternoons. He was a water bug, loved
swimming and sunning, and could be quite chatty and companionable while taking his ease. I think he liked my student
journalism and thought me "all right," his favorite commenda-
tion. Although I never broached the matter to him, I privately
used to wonder about him, wondered if he ever saw anything
incongruous in his cost-accounting methods of cultivating religious sensibility. Even more, I wondered if he ever reflected

on what he was doing, or whether, as it seemed from watching his instant decision making as president and his steady adherence to a coherent program of action, he simply acted from instinct, like a bee in the hive. I even wondered what he really thought about Notre Dame. He spent almost as many years as a bishop away from Notre Dame as he did as a priest at the university. I saw him only briefly two or three times after his consecration. I have the feeling that his conservatism, or what I have hesitantly called his Jansenism, continued and hardened in his episcopal career. His devotion to Catholic education did not abate; in both Buffalo and Philadelphia his principal activity was planning and building schools. But the interest in intellectual development which marked his Notre Dame presidency seems to have vanished. One wonders whether his building schools was designed to shield Catholic youth from education rather than encourage it. As a bishop, he clearly returned to his natural anti-intellectual bent.

Although the O'Hara brand of Catholicism was dominant at Notre Dame, there were some other aspects of religious life he did not touch. One was the liturgy itself. High mass on Sundays was celebrated with taste and reverence. The music of the Moreau Seminary Choir was devotional, the attention to liturgical detail meticulous. Great feasts were done with similar eclat, and when the Moreau Choir was elsewhere engaged the Dujarie Hall brothers were more than adequate substitutes. Holy Week was particularly memorable, with evening tenebrae on Wednesday, Thursday, and Friday, and the morning services, especially on Good Friday, impressive. These were all community affairs, of course, though all were invited. I never missed.

I doubt whether the college boys were attracted by this display of liturgical splendor. I used to feel that O'Hara was one with the boys in insensitivity to liturgical esthetics. The typical Irish-American Catholics of the O'Hara era were totally loyal to the Church, but liked services to be swift and succinct. They admired a good old-fashioned fire and brimstone sermon and enjoyed whatever else they could grin at from the pulpit, but the actual words of the mass were incomprehensible to them and their significance a matter of catechism belief, no more. Because of this I have long been an advocate of the vernacular liturgy.

Even as an undergraduate, influenced in part by the very devout Jim Withey and also by some like-minded friends, I became interested in the liturgy. I became a reader of *Worship*, a fan of Father H. A. Reinhold, and even wrote and lectured on the need for good idiomatic English to replace the sentimental Italian prayers then in common use. How many now remember the dreadful Litany of the Sacred Heart? The numbing prayer to St. Joseph? The prescribed prayers at the foot of the altar after low mass set the tone. I for one was glad to see them go.

I welcomed the Vatican II decision to replace Latin by the vernacular, and saw in it a chance to enable English-speaking Catholics to pray in decent English. So I wrote to George Shuster, then the Notre Dame president's adviser on grants and projects, pointing out that two widely praised translators were Catholics with Notre Dame connections. They were Robert Fitzgerald, the much honored translator of Homer and Virgil, and John Frederick Nims, a Notre Dame graduate and former professor. I suggested to Shuster that Notre Dame engage these good friends to translate the Bible into a Notre Dame English edition, in the hope that it would be adopted by the official Church for daily use. I should, of course, have known better. The shameful neglect of the excellent translation of fifteen years before by Monsignor Ronald Knox, abandoned by the very English bishops who commissioned it and now unobtainable, should have been warning enough. But I needn't have worried about that. Shuster was unimpressed. And we got the insipid translation that now troubles my prayers, and I hope those of many. I refuse to say, "The Lord is my shepherd, there is nothing I shall want," or go on to the verdant repose. Ugh. Even these tasteless translators cannot quite ruin the beautiful Lenten collects, and it is a minor miracle that the canon of the mass turned out passable—better, indeed, than the lusterless Latin of the old days. But there is scarcely a single prayer of my childhood that I care to repeat, saving only Our Father and the Hail Mary.

Even as an undergraduate, then, I was pursuing different paths in religious practice from those laid down by O'Hara. I continued my esthetic interests by studying *Liturgical Arts*, a tastefully edited journal run by Maurice Levanoux. This acquainted me with good modern work being done in Europe as well as the United States and whetted my desire to travel. I was just then reaching out in travel a little, though sticking to the United States east of the Mississippi. I was continuously dismayed by the poor quality of Catholic building. The ubiquitous Jesuits were the worst offenders, though some of the religious orders of women came a close second. The Dominicans were best; I regret they were so small in number. I was immensely proud of the work of my Uncle Sam. I think his Cathedral of the Holy Rosary in Toledo a very beautiful church, and his remodeling of the fire-damaged cathedral in Milwaukee was the making of that church, producing an apse to match its exquisite frontal spire. He was that singular figure, a bishop not enslaved by the Roman baroque of his seminary days.

It was not until I came to write this book that I learned that Father Sorin had discarded the grandiose Roman baroque plans that the celebrated architect of so many Catholic churches in the United States, Patrick Keeley, drew up for his Sacred Heart Church at Notre Dame. Sorin himself, working with Brother Charles Harding, then designed the present structure. Its Gothic ascent into the heavens seems to me very appropriate for a college church; it is surely the noblest of the old Notre Dame buildings, as Cram's South Dining Hall the best of the newer. Although the church is not very large, it has a wonderful sense of space: the arches, the ample space around the main altar, the lofty transepts, the choir seats, above all perhaps the succession of apsidal chapels culminating in the Lady Chapel.

When I came to Notre Dame the interior was out of key with the plain and well-proportioned exterior. The proportions, happily, couldn't be altered, and the space was still expressive. But the decoration was baroque-awful, tasteless, and dishonest. The main altar was full of excrescences, curlicues, and ribbons in every shape that metal could be hammered into. Even worse were the piled-on jigsaw ornamentations of the chapel altars; Father Broughal, who supervised the renovation of 1933, said to me during it, "You'd be surprised to see what good wood there is underneath all that trash." I was, and pleased to see it. But even more pleased to see the fake marbling of the pillars disappear, along with the garish bare-bulb lighting on the ribs of the ceiling vaults. Architect Wilfrid Anthony, who designed the beautiful chapel that graced the Holy Cross House of Studies in Washington, presided over this tasteful remodeling of 1933, while I was still an undergraduate. It is by far the best of the three or four I have seen.

One of the great charms of the church to me is the bell tower, so graceful and elegant. Those who live near them can come to hate the bells at night, but I love them, especially the carillon, one of the oldest in the United States. My friendship with Professor Willard Groom of the music department led to my occasional playing the carillon, done by leaping with cupped hands on levers marked as music notes, while Groom counted time. It was very hard work. Even then they were played electrically most of the time, but Groom liked to vary the hymns with the liturgical seasons.

When Alumni and Dillon halls went up, O'Hara moved his operations to Dillon, as being nearer the dining hall. It didn't seem the same to many of us. The fancy, and correct, Gothic ornamentation of new architects Maginnis and Walsh simply does not have the warmth of the Kervick-Fagan chapels in the Howard group. Sorin, heaven knows, was no architectural gem, but it had a pleasant north light and a homey atmosphere, made in part by O'Hara's yelling out from his adjacent office, "Be right with you!" In Alumni he was farther away, across the corridor, and seemed to many of us ill-at-ease. It is pleasant to record that the Sorin chapel underwent a tasteful renovation in 1988 as a memorial to its long-time resident, Professor Paul Fenlon, a worthy one with beautiful stained-glass windows designed by Professor Robert Leader. No other hall chapel is worth a second glance architecturally. And the renovation of the crypt of Sacred Heart Church is no better, with poor lighting, coloring reminiscent of a bus station waiting room, and a drafty heating and cooling system which has driven many a worshipper, myself among them, elsewhere.

But in fact, in 1990 as I write this, campus religious life is standing with reluctant feet on the threshold of the unknown. The uncertain future of women in the liturgy leaves much up in the air. No men's college which has lately admitted women has quite absorbed them into its once masculine ethos, and Notre Dame, with its special religious tradition, is rather worse off in this respect than most. The Judeo-Christian attitude toward women was anything but generous, although the Jews, in or out of the synagogue, were far worse than the Christians. In spite of the cult of Our Lady, joyfully emphasizing the feminine maternal principle as well as the male one, the Christian churches were, except for a few minor sects, dominated by males. The education of the Catholic clergy for the last three hundred years emphasized lack of contact with women. This resulted in an unreasonable fear of the sex by far too many priests and religious men, and a frequently unwholesome brand of masculinity in schools and religious houses.

There was plenty of this at Notre Dame in the past. Yet it was not true of any student body I knew from 1930 on. Even back in the nineteenth century, though there was more isolation, I do not get a feeling of misogyny as I read the old *Scholastics* or page through the old yearbooks. The presence of St. Mary's College helped some, though not nearly as much as it should have, owing to the mutual suspicion of both institutions. Both suffered from isolationism to the point of absurdity. For example, in theatrical productions both scorned each other and went in for a transvestism morally as well as dramatically mistaken. A theatrical production needs both sexes. A course in Latin grammar does not.

I speak here of morality. I do not think coeducation immoral, as so many older priests and nuns did, as, I think, Cardinal O'Hara did. Indeed, I think it the only way in our society. In a more stable society than ours, in which young men and women meet in normal ways at homes, in social engagements, church functions, and such like, I prefer single-sex education. Coeducation, I think, coarsens the relations between the sexes and breeds a familiarity which does not necessarily mean contempt, but something even worse, a loss of decency and mutual respect, a lessening of both manhood and womanhood. But in our restless society, where one neighbor rarely knows another, where a family may move three or four times during their offsprings' schooling, and where family roots and branches are unknowable, coeducation is socially necessary for most.

It is morally in many ways an improvement on the single-sex education it has largely replaced. Its commonsensical recognition of the world we live in is preferable to the impossible standards of religious who saw, apparently, something questionable in God's own creation of Eve.

Most Notre Dame undergraduates certainly did not. Most were consciously headed for marriage; the "Marriage Institute," a series of lectures on practical aspects of this future, was one of the most popular events of the senior spring in the 1950s.

Even more significant, to my way of thinking, was the popularity of such lay apostles as Frank Sheed. Sheed came to Notre Dame and St. Mary's often. He was welcomed by a large set of friends and admirers on both campuses. But his effect on the big audiences of undergraduates who came to hear his inimitable lectures was astonishing. He was the best lecturer I ever heard. Better than anyone I ever experienced he had the knack of catching his audience almost immediately, and he held them longer than you'd think possible. His intelligent common sense and his reverent irreverence was especially pleasing to the young. Unlike C. S. Lewis, whom he resembles in many ways, he talked better than he wrote, though Lewis was an effective lecturer. I have often thought that men like Lewis and Sheed, in the wake of the great Chesterton, did more for religion than all the earnest mission preachers put together. Maisie Ward Sheed was also a good talker, though she and Frank had the good sense not to appear together. But unfortunately they left no model for the future, unlike the founders of religious orders.

Dorothy Day and Peter Maurin did, of course. Their Catholic Worker example, has been, I think, highly instrumental in the development of the hundreds of soup kitchens and parish shelters for the homeless that are such outstanding marks of contemporary Catholic charity. Although she came to Notre Dame for talks, I did not get to know Dorothy Day. I greatly admired her work and recall with pleasure the admiration Hannah Arendt had for her. She had many friends and not a few followers here.

Peter Maurin I did get to know. He often showed up at Notre Dame talking fifteen to the dozen. When I lived in Lyons Hall Annex I appropriated a large storeroom for my use, and, inter plenty alia, had a bed for guests in it. Peter occupied this a time or two, still talking as he slid under the covers. I had great admiration and affection for this old dear, who radiated charity and good will. Since I had to help out at home, there could be no question of my following his or anyone else's lead. As a matter of fact I had, in the 1930s, with my fifty dollars a week salary plus a little from free-lance journalism, more income than many of my classmates. My trouble was that it never got much better, while they later rode the high waves of Eisenhower prosperity.

Much as I admired the Catholic Worker leaders, I found little to admire in the social consciousness that flowed through the Church of the 1960s. This seemed to me dripping with sentimentality, as disorderly as it was frequently misplaced. The Catholic theology that developed in that dismal decade still strikes me as sentimental mush, with its constant emphasis on us-ness and abandonment of personal responsibility. The phrase, "People of God," raises my hackles almost as high as "Have a nice day." I am alarmed at the total catholicism the new theology seems to foster, as well as at the intolerance of a differing viewpoint. In a curious way it seems a throwback to the O'Hara ways of thinking about the Church, with its tunnel vision and Feeneyesque exclusiveness. I firmly believe that true freedom can be had only upon a foundation of religious commitment, but I also agree with Flannery O'Connor, that "Freedom cannot be conceived simply. Free will does not mean one will, but many wills conflicting in one man. It is a mystery." That is the human condition. It is what Notre Dame is supposed to study.

I suppose it does, in the highly visible religious studies developed at Notre Dame since World War II. O'Hara would be shocked at their breadth; even the most ecumenical of Catholics might lift an eyebrow at certain courses, and only a short few years ago one could wonder whether the non-Catholic faculty would come to dominate the confused Catholics. This O'Hara would think incredible. It does pose some key considerations.

One is, just how much do religious studies influence belief and behavior? Almost none, O'Hara thought. I think him more nearly right than wrong, but who knows? Other observers besides myself feel an increase of religious spirit among undergraduates of the 70s and 80s after the upheavals of the 60s. But it is inchoate and wordless. I often wonder whether the liturgy brings the young such keen pleasure as I found in it long ago. Since I dislike the new so much I am no doubt a poor judge, but I can't help feeling that today's church is no place for a lover of music or language. The new music is to me mostly banal, the constant sermonizing mostly boring, and the atmosphere, I repeat, one of cloying sentimentality. But if it brings the young to the good and the true, even if not the beautiful, let it be.

Another knotty consideration is, how catholic can a modern university be? I don't mean the stupid old Bernard Shaw argument. Belief has nothing to do with the troubles I see. Every man sees, deduces, and judges from some point of view. The Catholic one makes more sense to me than any other I've encountered. To choose none, as Shaw implies, is to choose just the confusion and contradictions that beset Shaw's own strange intellection.

No, I don't mean Catholicism is incompatible with modern science. On the contrary. Modern physics and mathematics have opened the modern mind to the deep mysteries of matter, just as the failure of social engineering is now opening the modern mind to the mystery of behavior. The religious spirit is attuned to mystery. That's not what makes it hard for today's Notre Dame to be Catholic. It is simply the complexity of the contemporary great university, the new and defining institution of Western civilization. The intellectual life that flows into and out of the university is so various and so unconnected that it can have no effective center. O'Hara's Notre Dame, small, nearly all undergraduate, and committed in every detail to its organizing religion, could have a faculty nearly 100 percent Catholic in the humanities and cherish the informing spirit of the Church most everywhere. Frank O'Malley's classes in English, Joe Evans's in philosophy, Bowyer Campbell's in history, did more for the religious understanding of the students than all the formal religious studies then or now. That's what being Catholic means. It can't be done now. The modern university, like the modern democracy it serves, has to be all things to all men. In such a system the campus ministry, at Notre Dame or Southern Methodist as well as Illinois or Oklahoma, cannot serve as a unifying force. I incline to think it has yet to find just what it can do.

However, I am firmly convinced that the most important thing in education, in any school anywhere, is its moral tone. You can't have anything without that. This is true of society in general, and its absence is what makes contemporary society so rotten. But it is even more important in education. I was raised to think even entering a Protestant church questionable, perhaps a sign of approaching loss of faith. I now am at the opposite pole, believing any Christian sect admirable, useful in forming good men and women, providing as only religion can the moral base of society. A sure way to cripple this base is to enforce a moral code too rigidly, to legalize its every movement, to make all hew to an arbitrary and inhuman standard. Toleration ought not to be incompatible with orthodoxy.

5

HOW I LIVED

I have before me the 1930 edition of the Notre Dame catalog. Like all such it gives no idea of what life was like at Notre Dame in 1930. It merely furnishes the cold facts of it.

The financial facts are fascinating. Memory tells me that my bills at the university ran around $650 a year. But that must have been for my senior year; rooms were cheaper in Sorin than Howard, where I lived that first year. Anyhow, the bulletin tells me I paid $729 for the first year, broken down as follows: tuition, $200; room, $134; board, $375; fees (library and entertainment, $10, athletic $10), $20.

Even then I thought we got our money's worth. Low tuition excused much poor instruction. Rooms were cheaper than most city rents. But the real bargain was the food. Most students carped incessantly about it, but after the austerities of my prep school I thought it good. It wasn't, of course; to this day I have not looked mashed potatoes in the eye, and it was some time before I discovered that not all restaurant chicken was like the albatross Sundays brought to the dining halls. But as institutional cooking goes it was very good, the breads and other baked goods especially.

Because I had learned at my prep school to try anything, I was over the squeamishness of childhood. There were some like me and some not. Food tastes are the most erratic thing I know of, and the American taste surely the worst of all the countries of the West. As I write scarcely anyone has noticed that Ralph Nader and his disciples in the Washington bureaucracy have ruined the taste of meat in this fair republic, and the erosion of its memory in the fast food arcades goes on apace. Anyhow, when I began teaching, I noticed that, like the food or not, the average freshman gained twenty to thirty pounds during the school year. Regularity of sleep and mealtimes had much to do with this, of course, but the calories came from Cram's beautiful halls.

Meals there were sit-down, and you did well to get there early. My arrival on the scene as a freshman a day late placed me at a table in the corner, the last to be filled. It was a lucky accident. Other latecomers were a lawyer or so, several seniors, and only one other freshman. The older men treated us freshmen with kindness and, yes, politeness, a rare commodity in those halls. Our waiter was another freshman, Ed Krause, who mowed down the other waiters to bring us the best-looking dishes. He was also aware of the unusual tone of our table and matched his own somewhat to it, without losing his dash. Krause was also in a couple of my classes and has remained a good friend through the years. At the end of the semester, he and the elders at the table proposed we return as a group. We two idiotic freshmen thought we should join with our fellows. Later on in the spring term we would get together in mutual regret. Our fellows turned out to be a mixture of hogs, sadists, and exhibitionists when it came to mealtimes. We longed for the good old days.

In the fall of my sophomore year I became the campus correspondent of the *South Bend Tribune* and wangled my way into the university cafeteria for meals at irregular intervals, depending on the demands of my job and the mood of the prefect of discipline. There the food was really excellent. For the entire decade the posted menu for the evening meal led off with "Roast Prime Ribs of Beef 30." Thirty *cents*, that is. The little steak, grilled to order, was 35 cents. Both the roast and the steaks were far superior to anything obtainable today for $15. The other dishes were also good; I recall with especial pleasure the lamb shanks and the fresh vegetables in season, like corn on the cob and asparagus.

The only illustration in the 1930 bulletin is a diagram in heavy black and white of the campus buildings. I count twenty-one major structures, grouped as they still are today. The earliest loss came soon after I arrived, when Engineering went down to make way for the dormitories east of the dining halls. I can barely remember its razing. The loss of Freshman and Sophomore dormitories was a similar victory for esthetics. They had all the charm of big chicken coops. Freshman was razed in 1932, but Sophomore lived on, renamed Freshman, till Zahm and Cavanaugh took its place, in 1939.

By then the building of the Rockne gymnasium had replaced the old natatorium, directly behind the Main Building, but the building itself stayed on till the 1960s, the private demesne of Father Bernard H. B. Lange, billed as the fourth strongest man in the world. Under Lange the place became a gym for body builders. I swam in the little nat pool as a student once or twice, and under Lange's aegis a time or two. The Lord knows I was no body builder, but I was intrigued by Lange, who tolerated me. In one respect alone he was like Father Hebert: going his own way without let or hindrance. But, if it comes to that, his was also something like the career of Father Zahm. Although a Ph.D. in biology, Lange taught not, neither did he lab. He simply rolled into his natatorium building (to which he alone had the keys) after breakfast and stayed on till the shades of even fell. He was tutor to many earnest body builders and occasionally let some small boys who hung around into his swimming pool. I admired the Holy Cross community for its tolerance of eccentrics but couldn't help wondering where "community" went.

Most freshmen literally lived in dormitories, big sleeping rooms with their serried ranks of white-curtained cubicles in the upper reaches of the Main Building. On the first floor were equally large study halls with *their* serried ranks of desks with lift-up lids and oddly comfortable movable chairs. Washrooms, coruscating with water droplets and splotchy with rust spots, were in the basement, where the toothbrushes never dried in the ancient little black lockers. Showers were in the natatorium. Missing were adequate lounges and recreation space; that in the basement of Washington Hall was insufficient and uncomfortable. These dorms, in the wings of the Main Building, were named Carroll and Brownson Halls, presided over by tradition and practice by brothers, and suggestive of the prep-school presence that still lurked in the minds of the local council. After all, what would you do with the huge Main Building?

Freshman Hall, with four to a room, was really a long row of mini-dorms, in each room of which there were washbasins and steel lockers for closets. Having gone through both dorm and mini-dorm in four years of prep school, I was glad to escape to the relative luxury of Howard Hall. But many dorm residents loved that freshman year. It was sort of like advanced camping and boy scouting, its austerities more like play than real, its forced study times wryly welcomed. These zealots had only a year of it, of course; they then went on to single and double rooms, shifting from hall to hall for each year. There were plenty of single rooms, a rare luxury since 1950. I went from a freshman double to singles for the next three years, though I was never much of a housekeeper. Some students dressed up their rooms with easy chairs, a decent floor covering, and often other amenities such as fish tanks and clothes hampers. My rooms were minimum; to this day they are little better. However, they were fairly neat, even in college. Though I declined luxury I disliked squalor. Unnatural boy.

In yet another respect the upperclassmen were well served. This was our maid service. A Notre Dame housekeeping supervisor once told me how easy his job was compared to his opposite numbers at most places. South Bend then and now, though less so now, had a large pool of middle-aged women, mostly of Polish and Hungarian extraction, who were pleased to pick up some extra money working as Notre Dame maids. These could, especially after World War II, have found better-paying jobs as maids in homes; this they disdained not only as servant status but because of the more desirable hours. They arrived in droves at seven and departed at two, usually very companionable in small groups, laughing and chattering more often in English than in their native languages. They were usually good at their jobs, tolerant of the sleeping boys who upset their morning routine, cluck-clucking their way throughout midden heaps of college-boy junk. Particularly for the permanent residents, the priests and campus resident lay faculty, they were often helpful beyond the call of duty, providing a little touch of the missing femininity. I am embarrassed to recall how readily I took them for granted.

I am not embarrassed, only somewhat puzzled, to recall how little the hall administration impinged on me. Through a mutual interest in music I did come to know my freshman rector, Father James Connerton, but I have no recollection of our floor prefect. I assume we had one: Notre Dame tried hard to live up to its "*in loco parentis*" ideal. Not only can I not recall him, I can't recall any other floor prefect. I can recall other rectors, Father James Stack in Morrissey and the legendary Pop Farley in Sorin, but the Alumni Hall rector is a blank. Of course I could look it up, but my point here is how little the system meant to me. I spent four years as an undergraduate at Notre Dame without ever encountering the famous disciplinary system that was supposed to be choking us to lifelessness. I was aware of its existence, hearing of it with bitterness from my less fortunate mates. But if I had any unpleasantness from it the occasion has slipped my memory, and I think most of my friends would say the same. Of course I had other friends whose temperaments kept them daring the system. One or two were caught and suspended for a semester. But the two most notorious, Dave Froelich and Bob Jaynes, dodging many a bullet as they flashed dolphinlike through their four happy years, graduated with the rest of us and, like all of Peck's bad boys, ended up pious conservative citizens of self-conscious rectitude. So much for Sandford and Merton.

Indeed, on the few occasions when I successfully dared the system, I found myself rather at a loss in an indifferent South Bend. On the loose, we went to the dime-a-dance places, drank wine in the dingy kitchens of our furtive bootleggers, and hung around the few spots where poor jazz was poorly played. Of the real South Bend we knew nothing, nor cared to. The iron curtain dividing South Bend from Notre Dame was firmly drawn to. I don't know how it came to be built. From older friends like Pat Manion and Paul Fenlon I knew it wasn't there in the 1920s. These two, and many more, were very much a part of the city, often marrying and settling there, like Pat Manion and Big Mac McCarthy, and becoming, like them, conspicuous on the social scene. On the other hand, many lay faculty, especially after World War II, who made their homes in South Bend might as well have been tourists. Focused on Notre Dame, they gave little thought to the city. They had a better idea than the students did of its essentially industrial culture, and many concluded that this consorted ill with the higher learning.

When I became a faculty member I often speculated on this iron curtain. It was not successfully breached till the administration of Father John J. Cavanaugh right after World War II. Cavanaugh had worked for Studebaker before joining Holy

Cross and knew the city was far from being Ninevah or Sodom, as some of the older priests seemed to think. The influx of married veterans in his administration helped him to get rid of the iron curtain, though mostly it was his abundant Irish charm.

Already initiated into city circles through my newspaper work and believing in principle the town-gown separation bad for both, I plunged into the life of South Bend after World War II with both feet. I became involved with politics, the Press Club, the Art Association, the Community Fund, and such like. I'm glad for the experience; it was certainly good for me. But I am bound to note that my Notre Dame circle and my South Bend one did indeed "consort ill," and still do. Our situation is somewhat similar to that of Cambridge, where Harvard and the town are poles apart. On the other hand, in my native city of Nashville, Vanderbilt and the city are so closely intertwined that I have frequently thought it a positive disadvantage to go to college elsewhere.

As an undergraduate, my town life set me a little apart from my peers. While they stormed the Notre Dame streetcars, faking fares, smoking, exuding vitality as only the young can, I was often the lone passenger going downtown to work in the late afternoon. I became friendly with some of the motormen, simple pleasant fellows one-on-one, some of whom allowed me to drive the car till we met other passengers. I was still boy enough to enjoy this hugely and came to have a sneaking affection for these bare, ugly old cars with their long yellow rattan seats facing one another across wide aisles. The cars swayed wildly when empty and accelerated wheezily, like an old horse. All us students rode them often. We were forbidden automobiles— not that I could have afforded one in any case. Students who could often kept cars circumspectly in the city in rented garages, using them sparingly. I can recall shivering in the rumble seat of a Model A Ford belonging to J. Walter Kennedy, later the professional basketball czar, ever the entrepreneur.

The no-car rule helped bind us to a campus admittedly short on social life and amenities: one more holdover from the prep boarding school mentality in the community. We had many more opportunities to meet girls in my Dayton prep school than we did at Notre Dame. The administration of our neighboring women's college, St. Mary's, was if anything stricter than Notre

Dame's, and, owing to the smaller student body, better policed. Even so, some contact was possible. It was then and now a great puzzle to me why there wasn't more. There was at Notre Dame a stupid prejudice against the St. Mary's girls. Anyone would think they had all been imported from some Eurasian orphanage, when, in fact, they were exactly like the Notre Dame men, from the same families and backgrounds, and similar schools. Yet most Notre Damers, dreaming dreams of fairer and freer women, foolishly shunned St. Mary's at least for normal everyday contacts.

Nor for dances. All through my college years (plus prep-school senior year only) the great social events of the year were the class dances—Freshman Formal, Sophomore Cotillion, Junior Prom, Senior Ball. These were planned and replanned, fussed and fought over for months before and after the event. They were dressy affairs. Girls wore the long dresses of the depression years. The college girls, St. Mary's not excepted, were more stylish than the hometown imports—that much at least they learned from college. The men often wore full evening dress, tails, white waistcoat, and top hats, usually opera, but sometimes a genuine silk one. We were a dressy lot for dates, too. Dark suits set off shirts with highly starched colored fronts. Pearl gray spats were common, as were derby hats. Around the campus we wore cords, of course, but nearly always with shirts, and often suit coats.

My college years were a watershed time for men's clothes. The revolution was technological, not mere fashion. Gas and oil heat controlled by thermostats began to make central heating reliable. No longer did we have to dress as we did in grade school. Those costumes were ugly but very efficient for the 1920s, when central heating was not laid on, as at my house, or fitful, as in our school. We were dressed for all occasions. Next to our skins we wore long yellow underwear. Over it came the one dumb article, shirts with no tails, complete with ties. We wore long black stockings, wool knickers, and stout shoes, often with uppers, like old men. Mostly we wore Norfolk-style jackets rather than sweaters, though these were becoming more and more popular.

In this costume we could climb trees, play football or baseball, go to church and school, scrub the front porch, indeed do most anything we had or ought to do. In the Nashville of my nonage organized sport for grade school was unheard of. To play our pickup games we simply took off our shirts, and for basketball changed shoes as well—we wore Keds in the summer anyhow. When the weather became warm, we swapped the wool knickers for khaki ones and left off the stockings and long underwear.

Between 1926 and 1930 all this became slowly obsolete. The long underwear departed permanently with better central heating. It, and the one-piece BVDs, were replaced by the present two-piece shorts and tops. Knickers gave way to long trousers, and the wool caps of grade school disappeared. Nobody wore head covering. To this day I can remember how the water I used to tame my unruly hair would freeze in the winter and my alarm and half-amused fright at feeling the icicles in my hair. All through college the pace of change was slow. The one-piece bathing suits of my grade school and camp very gradually gave way to trunks only. The war made some difference. The Navy introduced shorts as regular uniform in warm climates, and this helped the very slow trend to shorts practically the year round. The T-shirt, an old Navy invention, also became standard during World War II.

In my senior year in high school I wrote an article prophesying the future dress at my school. This was a mildly dressier type of ski suit. Along with my forecast of victory for Truman in 1948, this is one of the few insights into the future I can boast of. The costume I foresaw is now vulgarly called sweats, but that will change; they are beginning to be worn everywhere. I accurately foresaw a lessening of distinction between sportswear and daily wear, but even my mighty powers of futurity did not foresee the rejection of leather for shoes nor the vanishing gym locker room. Students nowadays change in their rooms before playing some game and return there to shower. The only gym lockers in steady use at present at Notre Dame are the faculty and staff ones, not the students. Not true of varsity, of course.

The unisex movement in clothes did not hit the campuses strongly till the 1960s. Long before that girls had been using boys' shirts, but pants did not take over, so to speak, till the flower children moved in. I wish I could comment on the changes in women's wear. They were very similar to those of men, but I simply don't know enough to document the shifts.

Not shown on my bulletin campus map, but very vivid to my memory, are the play spaces. Boys will play anywhere, but the broad acres of Notre Dame were especially hospitable to so many Notre Dame boys who came from inner-city high schools. In these, play space was often a concrete-paved court-yard scarcely big enough to accommodate the student body. A pity, for play is almost as important to adolescent boys as it is to children. I recall my first day at prep school. After the evening meal the boys hung around the playground, silent, awkward, timid. Then Bob Quinn, a Chicago sophisticate, yelled out, "Let's play Pom-Pom-Pull-Away." Half of us had never heard of this game, but it sounded as simple as it is, and shed-ding our suit coats and risking our Sunday trousers we roared into the contest. When it was time for study hall the game broke up in a chorus of laughter and chatter, of friendly arms around each other, of beginning friendships, but above all of ease succeeding the distasteful unease before the game. Games are above all competitive. But they also are rituals of fellow-ship, festivals of unity, testing grounds of manhood. Not for nothing were the games of primitives, like the Greek Olympics, conspicuously a part of the tribal religion.

Most of the schools I know with ample play space try to shoo playing into official spaces well removed from the rounds of daily life. I wonder if any of them are successful. Notre Dame certainly hasn't been. I lived in Howard Hall as a freshman, and from my window I could look down on a little space framed by the east chapel wall of Morrissey and its northeast wing. There was nearly always a touch football game going on there in the fall, and a baseball pepper game in the spring. I was always tempted to join either. If age is the time when a man sees a game going on and doesn't want to join it, my youth lasted till I was almost fifty.

When the Morrissey corner was choked, we drifted over to the well-named Badin bog, whose stretch between that hall and Walsh was larger but was filled with cross-campus traf-fic and preempted by the two halls defining it. The official play spaces were north of Sophomore Hall, where the interhall foot-ball games took place, and east of Freshman, across Eddy Road. We were a good deal more law-abiding than the present stu-dents, who will play anywhere. A year or so ago, as I walked in front of the Architecture Building (formerly the library), the Bookstore Basketball tournament was going on to my left. But I noticed to my right, through the big window of the drafting room, a basketball game going on inside, too, doubtless inspired by the bookstore extravaganza. As I was saying, you know you are old when you don't care to join the game, or don't feel an urge to travel when you hear a train whistle in the night.

Present-day students often dress for these pickup games. We never did. Bookstore basketball now involves deals for good players to live and practice together. It is in danger of tumbling the good player, too short and slight to make a varsity team, those for whom the tournament was originally meant, out of contention. It's the times, of course. These boys and girls have been brought up on teams from age six on. They have been encouraged at home and coached abroad. They have done soccer and Little League baseball and every other sport known to our culture. They have spent hours pumping iron. They are very narcissistic, happy in their glowing muscle tone.

I don't believe we played as much, or as seriously, as college boys and girls do today. We had no cult of the body, as they do. We were smaller and more spontaneous. In most sports, aside from the varsity teams, we had no coaching and what we did have was often ignorant and amateurish. We simply thrashed around and learned from one another. Some of those old cartoons of farm boys awkwardly diving into a swimming hole, arms and legs every which way, have vanished from the suburban scene of kids gracefully diving into elaborate swimming pools—in art, a difference neatly illustrated by Thomas Eakins and David Hockney. Almost as far removed are the kids playing tennis using the correct form, as opposed to those in our day holding the racquet parallel to one's face, like an engraving screen.

Much of this is owing to film and TV. We had no models. A kid today watching a tennis or golf match on television gets more good coaching than we did in a career. Coaches themselves live by film. On my high-school football team the quarterback knew far more than the coach about the way the linemen were blocking. Who could, watching from the sidelines? Telephonic communication with the press box was unknown—indeed, I wonder who started it. And as for the conventional wisdom, we'd have been far better off without any. The incredible prohibition of drinking water during football practice, for example, or the heavy ingestion of salt tablets during a long, hot tennis match were fair examples of our almanac-type maxims. But the engineers were another matter. The improvement of every material aspect of sport is astonishing. Tracks are much faster, poles for vaulting vastly superior, football-field drainage more efficient, golf-course maintenance practically a new profession, football uniforms, especially helmets, way, way better, and so on.

It is impossible for me to say which is the better time, our simpler and more spontaneous play, or that of today, where boys and girls are coached for uniformed sports practically from infancy. However, I will set out an allegory. When I was about twelve I was sent to Camp St. Francis up in east Tennessee on the Clinch River. I loved it. I learned to swim, and played baseball the day long—I should note that baseball is the only game we did have models for, from watching our hometown teams, and was by all odds the game we played best. However, what I liked best about the camp was a wheezy old wind-up victrola with its small batch of classical records, singing by Luisa Tetrazini, Geraldine Farrar, Enrico Caruso, John McCormack, and some others of that glorious stature. I played and replayed these records. I don't recall that anyone told me not to, or derided my taste. But the allegory is this: I plainly had enough leisure to discover these records and play them. I can't imagine a contemporary camp leaving a boy that much time in his daily schedule. St. Francis was certainly not an ideal camp. We had no archery, no horseback riding, no explorations into the wilderness. But we did have something far more precious and far more beneficial for me, those wonderful phonograph records. I won't say they changed my life, because my mother began to buy the same sort for herself and us at about the same time. But still, it's an odd way to remember camp. Whether good or bad, I don't know. Would I be a better man if I could shoot arrows into targets?

As for indoor amusements, once again I feel the outsider. For it was mainly reading, for me. I read to the detriment of my sports, my studies, my social life, my very sense of reality. And I read with almost total lack of discrimination. Well, not altogether. I never succumbed, even as a young man, to the best-sellers. I discovered early that they were nearly all calculated mixtures of hot air, sentimentality, cagey promotion, and indifferent writing. I read enough of them and into them to find this out; my mother was never without one in the house, and I looked into Warwick Deeping, A. S. M. Hutchinson, Fannie Hurst, Kathleen Norris, and the rest. This was not snobbery. I was in no position to enroll under the highbrow banner. I loved certain kinds of trash, detective stories, adventure, travel, and science fiction. A man who enjoys E. Phillips Oppenheim, H. W. Hornung, Mary Roberts Rinehart, S. S. Van Dine, Ellery Queen, Dashiell Hammett, Zane Grey, Jules Verne, Conrad Richter—the list is endless—can scarcely scorn readers of the best sellers. And my taste was oddly selective. For example, I disliked the Tarzan books. I don't know why, but I did. I have never been able to like Louis L'Amour, though I can see he's good. Emerson Hough, Owen Wister, Bret Harte, all leave me cold, while I like Jack Schaefer, Arthur C. Clarke, and especially A. B. Guthrie. I detested all the religious novels, Catholic or Protestant. I liked most dialect stuff, like *Nize Baby*, *The Letters of a Japanese Schoolboy*, and Mr. Dooley. But I hated *Abie's Irish Rose*. And so it goes. Reputation was no consideration. I can't explain why I loved Thackeray but found most Dickens heavy going. Or why I dislike the Bloomsbury gang, but find Compton Mackenzie and E. F. Benson charming. To this day I am no magazine reader. And to this day I do not collect books. My colleague, Joe Duffy, used to say he wouldn't read a book he didn't own, but my greatest debt to society is owed to the free public libraries of Davidson County, Tennessee, and South Bend, Indiana. Next to them come the university libraries, our own, Vanderbilt's, and Peabody's. I do honestly believe these have done more for democracy and the American Way of Life than any other comparable institution.

None of my contemporaries read as much as I did, and all of them read more than any student today can. Just as my camp permitted me to listen to those John McCormick records, so my schooling allowed me to read widely. And just as today's camps are organized to the hilt to keep the youngsters busy, so too is schooling designed to keep them from reading. We teach too much, assign too much, examine too much, and pay too little attention to what we do assign: the prose style of American academia is enough to ruin a taste for reading for life.

How about the other time wasters? I have, at different times of life, been a once-a-week bridge player and a passionate every-night poker player. I enjoyed both. I can't say that either did me any good, mentally or psychologically, though I may be wrong. I disliked the dumb card games of my childhood, hearts and euchre. I played little bridge in college, however; I didn't have time. And I never played enough ping-pong or bowled enough to generalize about either. Moreover, I think I am just not much suited to intellectual games. I never got into word puzzles or chess, which so many people seem to enjoy. I am just a reader. I wouldn't say obsessive. It's just that when I sit I reach for a book and try to have one handy.

We've never had a good bookstore. The first, in a corner of the main floor of the Main Building, was a shambles. It dealt in nothing but texts, and, considering the essential dependence of both faculty and students on them, was woefully inefficient. The next, in Badin, was little better. Here the new space was used, not for books, but for the bane of most college bookstores, souvenirs for the tourists. I wish this sort of store could be housed separately and a sizable building be given over to all sorts of books besides texts. This has been successfully done at Michigan, Chicago, and Boston Universities. But I have never been a worshipper of the physical book. I love readable type and have fooled around enough in book and other print design to find out a little about type. But rare books, first editions, and fine bindings leave me cold. This sort of bookstore, common in the halcyon days of A. E. W. Newton, has pretty well vanished from the shopping scene and is carried on largely by mail.

But a store full of all sorts of books arranged for browsing can be a useful help to education. I must confess I haven't the faintest notion of how to set up such a store, but I would enjoy dropping in it. The only time of my life when I could afford to buy books was in the heyday of paperbacks, and I did gather up a good number of them. I was not so stingy about phonograph records, although my once enormous collection was largely from two free sources: records for review, which I did for some years, and collections passed along to me by friends. However, I did buy some by and for myself: useful as they were, those collections passed on to me were not my own choices. When I began teaching I allowed myself to buy one record a month. Never, never did such care and research go into a small purchase. And never were records played more. I literally wore out some, like Glenn Gould's Goldberg Variations and Toscanini's account of the Brahms Variations on a Theme by Haydn.

What wore them out was the heavy steel needles we used. These eroded the deep grooves of the old 78 rpm's. I played my records on an old Victor Model 66E, manufactured for record-store testing and not ordinarily sold to the public. At about the same time, tutored by my Nashville friend and fellow record collector, Olin West, I began to experiment with thorn needles, plucked from bushes right under our windows. These did indeed preserve the records; some of Olin's are still usable. But collecting the thorns, or buying them, and incessantly sharpening them on circles of sandpaper, was a nuisance.

Reading and music have been a large part of my life. Writing, too, though I was not part of the campus writing scene, which was mostly fiction. I decided early on that I had no talent for that, but I did get involved with student publications. I got involved the way I get involved with everything, through friends.

Two of my closest friends were editors of student publications, Arthur Sandusky of the *Dome*, in our junior year, and Jim Kearns, of the *Scholastic* in our senior year. Sandusky talked me into doing the satire section of his *Dome*, and Kearns into doing a weekly column for his *Scholastic*. I greatly enjoyed doing the satire, not just because I liked that sort of writing, but more for the collaboration with my artist, Gerry Doyle. I still think my idea of doing parodies of texts with illustrations of collegians as three-year-olds was a good one, but I didn't quite bring the writing part off. Doyle did bring his part off. (In 1935 Doyle was left holding the bag when the *Juggler*, of which he had been named editor, was discontinued.) My *Scholastic* column suffered from inattention. I simply did not work hard enough at it, especially at gathering interesting material. If I had to capsule my shortcomings for all my life, it would be "Keep your eye on the ball." Even in tennis, my favorite game, I had a fatal tendency to the roving eye. I can forgive my youthful tendency to instruct my betters in my *Scholastic* pieces but not the filler to cover over my indolence.

Reading and writing, these have been my life. I think I taught them better than I did them, but my teaching was them. Music has been very important to me, but way behind these two. I can, and have, done without it for long periods of time, and I am an amateur who desires to be no more. I once studied piano with a well-known teacher but decided I did not want to get into music technically beyond what I could figure out for myself. In my youth I had a pretty good singing voice, along with my siblings, but I am also glad I never studied it. There are lots of things I like knowing a little something about, but no more. I love the trees and shrubs on the Notre Dame campus, but I don't want to go on from the pleasures of simple recognition to a knowledge of botany. Similarly with the stars. I know the zodiac and the major constellations, and love to see them marching through the night skies. But I dislike looking at them through a telescope, have little interest in the nebula and the black holes, and even less in the gaseous composition of the planets. I used to like the movies, but I care naught for the private lives of the stars. I used to like automobiles and their design, but bow out when I hear the words "overhead cam." I like to cook on a small scale, but don't want to know a carbohydrate from a protein. In short, I think the old adage "if a thing is worth knowing at all it's worth knowing well," is false and foolish. Give me a little learning every time. I don't think it a bit dangerous. I think it's fun.

6

I BEGIN TO TEACH

There was nothing in my college curriculum or in my own mind that pointed to a career as a teacher. Of course there should have been: my ancestry is filled with teachers and clergymen, and my dear Uncle Sam, who was paying for my education, was himself a thwarted teacher. But I did not, in my late teens, dwell upon such; indeed, I scarcely thought about the future at all. When I did, my first faint feelings of guilt were erased by one of helplessness. After all, what could be done in college?

I am now convinced that unconsciously I did the right thing. For me, and young people like me, a very large number indeed, college is a time of life when you don't have to think of the future. My dwelling in the glorious present of reading, grappling with the big ideas, finding one's self slowly rising from the self-conscious posturings of adolescence, was hampered by the lack of enough money to oil the process. But that didn't really bug me too much. Youth can handle poverty. It's only in old age that it's demeaning.

My laissez-faire attitude now seems very sensible. It's comforting to feel assured of one's vocation at an early age, as many clergymen and physicians do. But like so many students I have dealt with through the years, I knew I was fit for neither of these pursuits. Nor did I know what I was fit for. This was rather embarrassing, but nobody pressured me, thank the Lord. One of the hardest jobs I've had through my professorial years is to try to convince parents and students that vocational indecision is a natural stage in life and on the whole a useful one. The trouble with those self-assured physicians, clergymen, and others who seem to know their way through life is that they become narrow, interested only in their professions. The doubters become

99

more tolerant adults, more widely concerned with community, wiser. They have come to know that life is lived not out of rational decision making but out of the deep reaches in the self, some prompting of the blood, some urgency in the heart. Or, perhaps more frequently, something unexpected turns up and you gladly respond to its invitation, relieved of choice.

My personal experience was of this last pattern. I had been a good, not outstanding student; twenty-fifth in a class of 400, not first or even tenth. Nor had I been very active in extracurricular activity; my job as campus correspondent for the *South Bend Tribune* made that impossible. But I quit the *Tribune* in my senior year to do a weekly column for the *Scholastic*, our campus newsmagazine. This was Father John O'Hara's first year as president of the university. He did not as yet have the title; he was Father Charles O'Donnell's vice-president. But O'Donnell was, in 1933–34, mortally ill, and in various hospitals and clinics mostly away from Notre Dame. So O'Hara was in charge, already working vigorously away at the program which would eventually change the character of Notre Dame.

I became a tiny pawn in his game. He invited Shane Leslie, a well-known Irish leader of the cause of Irish nationalism, a convert to Catholicism, and a former editor of the *Dublin Review*, as well as a poet and litterateur, to spend a year teaching at Notre Dame. Wanting to assure Leslie of some graduate students, O'Hara invited me to return for a year of graduate study under Leslie, and also to work for him in the presidential office at correspondence and like chores. I happily accepted, and was getting ready to resume my old life and begin new work when, just before classes were to begin in the September of 1934, the then director of studies, Father Carrico, asked me to take over two freshmen English courses in writing. At O'Hara's suggestion I had talked to Father Carrico before I left Notre Dame for the summer. He told me that a teaching assignment was very unlikely, but one did turn up—I don't know why. I did not then know Father Carrico, and I feel sure he asked my former teachers of writing, Father Leo L. Ward and James Withey, about my credentials. And I know that the head of the English department, Father James McDonald, was my backer. But I also believe that Carrico and McDonald were favorable to me through that weekly column in the *Scholastic*. Talk about unforseen results! I undertook that column only because I was the best friend of the editor, Jim Kearns, and through endless discussions and planning had helped him formulate policies for his editorship.

I had never dreamed of teaching. I had dreamed of writing, and done quite a lot, for my age, of journalism, both paid and unpaid. (Kearns's job on the *Scholastic* was paid, mine not.) A natural career for me would have been journalism. But I didn't really like daily journalism that well. Moreover, my other best friend, Robert West, whom I met when we both worked for the *Nashville Banner*, had left his newspaper job to go to graduate school at Vanderbilt. This influenced me, for I knew we were of similar dispositions. Even so, I had never really thought of teaching, and I turned to it with many misgivings. After one week I thought I had done my all, but after six I was hooked for life and I knew it. I liked it so well, and did so well at it, that after a year I was hired for the regular faculty.

I had an excellent model. My own teacher of freshman English was the best I've observed in my sixty years at Notre Dame. This was the young James A. Withey. His method, which I adopted *in toto*, was simple, and suicidal. He assigned each of his hundred or so freshmen a piece of writing on a given topic, to be handed in at each of the three class meetings a week. These he corrected and criticized with incisive skill and brilliance, and returned, usually at the next meeting. This incredible load of work ruined him, of course. After ten years of it his always delicate health broke, and he spent the next ten in a tuberculosis sanitarium in his native Grand Rapids.

It just about ruined me when I used the same method. In teaching writing I am still faithful to it, though now a little more flexible and a little less demanding. Writing is learned by practice, and the good teacher is one who knows how to inspire the student to do it as well as he can, and to organize the work so that it grows into an organic unity. It's a superlative method for a few students. What made Withey's load ruinous was that one hundred, as I soon discovered. Yet in 1940, my old record book tells me, I was still handling around forty items of credit per student, in round figures four thousand a semester, three hundred a week. Some of these were brief quizzes, some simple exercises, but most were themes. And once the student took the bit, so to speak, he'd often run on to four or five pages. Even for upper-division students I think this long enough. The long paper, the standard at most universities, is one of the weakest teaching devices I know of to develop good writing. It encourages the worst faults of student writers, triteness, wordiness, and heaviness—"TWH," as Jim Withey called them, endlessly railing against them. And, relying as it does on one subject that often turns sour as the student gets into it, it often does not show him at his best. Three papers of ten pages each, even for seniors, are better than one of thirty, I believe. One good reason is that right criticism of the first and second may result in substantial improvement in the third.

This method assumes that professors are competent critics. They generally are, of the material being dealt with in class. It would make liberal education enormously more effective if they were also good critics of writing. Since they rarely are, the student's prose style is generally best left alone. But even so, I believe three papers better than one and five better than three. Not counting exams, of course. Most students are simply incapable, out of sheer funk, of organizing and phrasing a good answer to an exam essay question.

Withey was a superb critic. On my first paper he wrote, "Fine individual ideas that don't quite fuse to make a B effect." Like most students who get really sharp criticism, I realized instantly how true that was, of this paper and my writing generally. (It is still true, as I struggle with organizing this chapter). Most students ignore any criticism on their papers and exams. They look at the grade, no more. So the trick of teaching them is to set up a system which forces them to note the criticism. I had a paper due the very next day after I got the first one back. In it you may be sure I tried to fuse my ideas into something like unity.

I have tried, in my own teaching, to hit the nail on the head in my criticism. I think I have had fair success with my overall comments, but much less with my marginal ones, at which Withey was so stimulating. Often students would get papers back from him with more red ink on them than their typescript. (In those days we got as many handwritten papers as typed ones, and we were pathetically grateful for typing. Why don't educators make typing a required subject in middle school, the perfect time to learn it?)

So, I played the sedulous ape to Withey in method. Not otherwise, for in personality we were very different. Withey played down his classroom performances. He talked in such low tones that one had to strain to hear him sometimes and preferred not to talk at all. He enjoyed questioning the class, which he did with the same brilliance he gave to his criticisms, but his instruction was rather offhand. Only when he read good models did he brighten into something dramatic. He was a very effective reader, a good mimic, an adroit pacer. Like myself, he had done a good deal of acting in the University Theater as an undergraduate, the best possible training for a prospective teacher. If you can get through a bad play poorly directed before a student audience, you can get through anything short of a riot.

I had a better voice than Withey. His was rather nasal, and he himself rather disliked it. So, as a teacher, I found myself using my voice more and finding ways of using it better. As time went on, I became more and more far-ranging, talking, as the spirit took me, about music or art or reading or travel or whatever I thought might be interesting. I wanted my classes to be like good conversation. Withey, on the other hand, had beautifully designed classes, like a good play. I have no doubt that his were far superior, but his ingenious design and his creative inventiveness were beyond me.

Also beyond me was his performance in conference. He saw students outside class as often as possible, and in these conferences he was miraculously (it seemed to me) intuitive, sizing up the student's personality and ability with insight and accuracy. Like all such, he occasionally overreached himself, I thought, in moving into problems having nothing to do with class. Early on I decided I would have nothing to do with these, though they insistently turned up. I longed for a good counseling service. After much blundering I confined myself in conference to professional matters. But I did not have Withey's patience. He was an absorbed listener, the best I've ever known. And while we both thought of teaching as charity, as that one talent which is death to hide, his charity was richer and more bountiful than mine.

Actually we were very different. I am stocky, gregarious, open, vulnerable. Withey was faintly mysterious, rather remote. His startling attentiveness was focused entirely on the student.

He himself was utterly without vanity and gave full rein to that most self-centered of creatures, the adolescent male. His students never guessed that their interlocutor was a devoted and knowledgeable amateur astronomer, a pretty good pianist and a connoisseur of music literature, a keen bird-watcher and naturalist, and a fair linguist. In those formal days Withey was more formal than most, dressed like a dandy, and was rather jaunty in gait and appearance. He commanded the attention and respect of students like no other teacher I have known, and he did it, as he did everything, on purpose.

When I brought Jim Withey back from his sanitarium decade to teach in my journalism department after World War II, he taught with undiminished skill but with greatly diminished energy. Happily I was in a position to look after him. His friend and colleague in the old Freshman English Program, Frank O'Malley, was then well into his incredibly long run of nearly forty years. Frank and I had been undergraduates together. He was two years ahead of me in college and four years older— he had clerked in a drugstore for two years to help pay his college expenses. We were hired at about the same time and became fast friends, laughing at and teasing one another, incessantly discussing our teaching and its wayward course, sharing the same friends and dreaming similar dreams for Notre Dame and the Church.

After a year teaching American history, which he did extremely well, Frank shifted over to freshman English. Along with veterans Withey and Tom Madden, and Richard Sullivan, who joined us in 1936, we made, I think, a really good staff for that college curriculum standby, like-minded about aims and method but different in character, pace, and intensity. In teaching freshmen, Frank adopted the Withey method of frequent papers but handled his classes very differently. He was a little jealous of Jim Withey's success and eager to get his hands on some of Withey's best students. But Withey's illness, plus Frank's own rising star, settled all that, and Frank succeeded him as the great freshman teacher. For the rest of his teaching career he always had a class of freshmen. He loved that course above all he taught.

But his other courses were the ones that made him the most famous teacher of the humanities in Notre Dame history. In 1937

Father Leo L. Ward, by now chair of the English department, revamped the English major. He built the new curriculum around two central courses called The Philosophy of English Literature. He assigned the junior course, dealing with the earlier authors like Chaucer and the Elizabethans, to Professor Rufus Rauch. Frank took the senior course dealing with modern literature. In addition Frank taught to other than English majors a very popular course in Modern Catholic Writers. These courses are well described in John Meaney's excellent biography of Frank. They took hold of the Notre Dame student imagination like nothing before or since and made Frank the great Notre Dame professor in the humanities for the rest of his long teaching career, lasting almost to his death in 1974.

Frank was no model for me. He was a prophet-teacher, and I am not tempted to prophecy. I am fascinated by it, however. The most influential teachers I have known are of that kidney. Frank is the excellent specimen, the more so because his was a religious kind of prophecy. Perhaps all prophets are religious at bottom, but Frank was definitely so, and so rooted in Catholicism that I feel his case a special and a very Notre Dame one.

The times were ripe. The 1930s were dingy depression years socially. But they were years of religious revival in Catholic Europe. Frank's intellectual mentor and hero was a leader in it, Jacques Maritain. In the mid-1930s the Maritain message was taking root in the United States. He was highly esteemed at Notre Dame, as he was in all Catholic circles, nowhere more than among Frank's students. Maritain's teaching was a silent rebuke to the lifeless formulas of the Scholastic philosophy handbooks so widely used in Catholic institutions. His works sparked an electric sense of vitality in many other areas of intellectual life: European literature as well as the visual arts. Catholic literature in the United States was just beginning its slow rough passage through the muck of the standard U.S. Catholic press. Not until after World War II did it come with a rush.

But most of all the college students were eager for the new ideas. Some of these young people had touched on them slightly in high school, but most found little in the standard curricula of both high school and college to stimulate them. They were Catholic to the bone, they wanted to participate deeply in the life of a Church they could feel theirs, and prophet O'Malley caught their minds and hearts. Frank was an unusual teacher. He rarely looked at the class. But he spoke with the tongue of angels. He had a beautiful clear voice and a dramatic delivery. What he said was usually carefully organized and made excellent coherent internal sense. O'Malley had a keen sense of his mission to "redeem the times," his favorite quote from St. Paul. Above all he wanted to fill Notre Dame with real Catholicism rather than the sentimental slush of Irish devotionalism. He wanted the students to know the thinkers in the Church, he wanted to reclaim the deserted Church from the shallow Catholics who had drifted along into the soulless rationalism of secular thought.

O'Malley did not really care for anything but his "mission." How he came by it, or knew it to be his, I have no idea. He came from a lower middle class Irish-American New England family. He was devoted to his mother, but a certain type of Irish-American family is very like its analogue among the blacks, strong maternal, weak paternal. In such mother machree is the central shrine. But neither his mother, nor his numerous sisters—you wouldn't have any trouble guessing him to be the only male—had anything to do with his life's purpose. Neither did anyone else that I know of. Most prophets have a traumatic experience on the way to their assertiveness, but if Frank did I never heard of it.

He didn't look like a prophet. He was red of hair and face, thin-skinned, skinny, shapeless. He lacked the prophet's piercing eye; his were watery blue and, oddly like Jim Withey's, of almost no use without glasses. Nor did he dress negligently, as so many prophets do. He may have been the only prophet ever in tab collars, which he wore all his adult life. He was obsessively neat and clean. I often traveled with him, and his prolonged ablutions exasperated me. But he was notoriously selfish in personal relations. He broke engagements without a qualm, was always late for everything, especially class, was completely unpunctilious. He adored wit and cleverness but had little himself. And he had the most delighted, happy laughter I ever heard. He loved Notre Dame football—"It's the only thing we do really well," he once said to me.

He was a loner, a suspect outsider in the English faculty, though he had a few good friends besides myself. But he was very friendly with some of the visiting faculty from Europe, notably Charles DuBos, Desmond Fitzgerald, and above all Waldemar Gurian, to whom he gave deeply appreciated help in founding and developing the *Review of Politics*. I was a fellow worker in that vineyard, a minor hand at untangling the twisted English of some of the foreign contributors. But this sort of thing was tangential to both Frank and me. Our concern was our students.

I was never a disciple of Frank. I was a friend, no more. I loved and admired him, but I learned nothing from him about teaching. I knew I could never do what he did, any more than I could do what Einstein did. So I tended my little garden as best I could and by the time World War II took me away from teaching felt comfortable in my role. I never ceased entirely to do some journalism, though I certainly did not foresee a future in that field. I went through the war as I did through college, greatly enjoying the experience. I never thought of any branch of the service other than the Navy, which commissioned me for work in journalism. But I did that for only six months. I then wangled a transfer to the brand new amphibious forces and spent the next three years in the Mediterranean with them.

I learned nothing about teaching from the war, either. Indeed, one of my most resounding failures in the classroom was the required course in Naval Leadership I had to do as commanding officer of a naval training unit at the University of Richmond. I think that Frank O'Malley, who tried every avenue he could find to follow me into the Navy, could have done this well with no tour of duty at all. Frank always failed the eye test, but he could probably have given the course I found so trying the inspirational touch it needed.

But I had, during the Navy years and for long thereafter, ample opportunity to reflect on the contrasting styles of Withey and O'Malley. I incline to think the prophet style is the one students like best. Most of the famous teachers I heard of at other universities were along the prophet line—William Lyon Phelps at Yale, Edwin Mims at Vanderbilt, John Dewey at Columbia, Leo Strauss at Chicago. So also was the only teacher to rival O'Malley in student affections at post-World War II Notre Dame. This was Joseph William Evans of the philosophy department.

Evans came to Notre Dame as a graduate student in 1947, after sitting out the war in his native western Canada. His bad leg—he walked with a limp—kept him out of uniform, as Frank's bad eyes did him. He was successfully teaching before he got his doctorate, again like Frank, though Frank was working on his master's, not a doctorate. Joe kept on going through the 1950s, 60s, and early 70s, teaching with great success very much like Frank—that is, by his personality, sense of mission, and what used to be called loving-kindness. Frank proclaimed his prophecies; Joe's, though quieter, were no less firm.

But Joe's method was far less effective, and far less difficult, than Frank's. Joe's only requirements were three exams during each semester. These were not memory exams. They were based on assigned readings and Joe's lectures but were meant to provoke imaginative and meditative responses to the perennial problems. His classes were very large, as large as Frank's, and attracted the indolent as well as the serious—a passing grade was easy to obtain from either prophet. To his disciples, Joe's class meetings were like musical events. He had a beautiful clear low voice and never said a word he didn't mean, though he sometimes searched for long hoarse pauses to find the right one. He was fond of quoting from Gerard Hopkins and Antoine de Saint Euxpery, whose Little Prince was elevated in Joe's reliquary almost to sainthood. Somehow he made his classes love and remember these quotations, a surprising and rare achievement. He had little ways that students loved. He called the entire roll each class meeting, to hear, as he put it, "the music of the names." He learned nearly all of those names and put them unerringly to the right faces; students in large classes, which they generally dislike, love this trait. One of his favorite students told me that Joe never sounded prepared; his class talks seemed instead to come straight from the heart, full of wisdom and goodness. But after much experience with Joe and his courses, she decided that they were indeed carefully prepared. I wish I had heard some of them, as I did O'Malley's.

For Joe talked even in conversation with great charm. His big eyes beamed interest and affection. His laugh was from the depths of his considerable being—he was a big man—and he rarely laid an egg and never a cliche. Like O'Malley he was a devoted disciple of Jacques Maritain, but he was far more single-minded in his devotion. Joe was rarely seen without a volume of Maritain under his arm. Indeed, it sometimes seemed to me that Maritain was his entire intellectual equipment in philosophy. He sweated over his translations of his master's works and drove his collaborator, Father L. R. Ward, nearly to distraction by his doubts and hesitations. He was no scholar, nor was he much of an administrator of his beloved Maritain Center. But he was a great teacher.

Withey, O'Malley, and Evans were all bachelors. They were also devout Catholics. None had the usual ambitions of power and affluence—or, even in their chosen academic world, of renowned scholarship. None ever owned an automobile. Both Withey and O'Malley had to help out at home, but I doubt any one of them yearned for more than simple sufficiency—or, if they did, consciously renounced the dream for their work, or wryly settled for what they were going to get anyhow. They were indeed a part of the "living endowment," which we heard so much about in the old days of Notre Dame poverty. Not all their lives were lived in the old days. Withey died in 1967, O'Malley in 1974, Evans in 1979. Their memories live on, but their type is as dead as the dodo bird.

What's gone is the sense of mission, the dedication, the noblesse oblige. During the reign of the prophets at Notre Dame, as now, there were plenty of excellent teachers of the show-biz type. This is prophecy parodied, mock dramatics to catch the attention, clever ruses which sometimes make good newspaper features, and above all a classroom performance as in a play or from a platform, full of drama and enthusiasm. I see nothing whatever wrong with this. Students generally like the show and often profit from it. Most good teaching has an element of ham. Those who know how to turn this to the advantage of learning vivify their work. They avoid the dull and perfunctory performance which so often learned professors fall into in disdain of the show biz.

Yet the show-biz approach to university teaching is by nature ephemeral. It depends to a great extent on catching the tone of current student culture, itself a fleeting scene. Especially as time goes on it runs the risk of bathos. Nothing dates faster than fashions in social conventions; yesterday's rhetoric is today's corn. The show-biz professor has to move fast to keep his act effective.

I knew from the start the show-biz act would be as impossible for me as the prophet's. So I tried to settle for simple workmanship. By that I mean a constant stream of papers carefully criticized and promptly returned, combined with class meetings geared to the papers. This was for teaching courses in writing, which I have continued to do off and on. When, after World War II, I became chair of journalism I devised, like Father Leo L. Ward in English, a new curriculum in which I taught courses in modern culture. Here I had to lecture more but continued to use many writing assignments.

This approach goes against the grain of most professional thinking. For one thing, it has to be frankly elitist. The classes exposed to it must be homogeneous, or nearly so. I frequently hear professors in elitist schools like Notre Dame and Vanderbilt lamenting the homogeneity of their students. When I hear these complaints I know I am listening to a non-teacher. It is impossible to teach effectively a wide mixture of students, some with minimal English, some without motivation, some whose interior lives are entirely devoted to break-dancing or Calvin-and-Hobbes daydreaming. The plight of so many of our public high schools is owing very largely to this student mix and eloquent testimony to the impossibility of democratic education, no matter what the sentimental idealists say. I think a school composed entirely of disadvantaged students, most from broken homes and some even homeless, all desperately poor, can do more for its clientele, brothers in misfortune, than a mixed school. Especially foolish is the widely held notion that the bright students in a class will motivate the less bright. What happens is that the less bright get discouraged and the bright bored.

Even more destructive of decent education in colleges is the domination of the university by the graduate schools. I have long thought these ought to have separate faculties and if possible separate campuses. They are certainly separate endeavors. The professor who can do both at once, the norm at Notre Dame at present, is rare. The graduate approach is bound to creep into the undergraduate course, to its deterioration, I think. The methods of research are not the concern of most undergraduates and in my opinion should not be.

Since few professors agree with all this, I must think mine an old-fashioned approach to teaching, probably obsolete. However, it is what I tried to do, the whole thrust of my stupid sincere youth. For, like Withey, O'Malley, and Evans I never grew old in teaching and never tired of it. I have always been, quietly I hope, proud of my profession. Teacher is a beautiful word—I like to see it used of Christ. At its best it is Christlike, a raising of the human spirit to a higher level. Its effect on students ready for its message can be magical. Parental guidance is, of course, much more important, but the fact that it normally takes place in an atmosphere of easy familiarity leaves the way open for the good teacher.

In a democracy, the work of the good teacher is essential. It is the certainty of this that makes intelligent people uneasy at its present failures and eager to pour more money into the enterprise. But in my opinion we already spend too much. I think a good case could be made for the argument that higher education in the United States has been ruined by money, not least at my beloved Notre Dame. And as for primary and secondary education, the emphasis on plant, equipment, busing and other social purposes, and above all the non-teaching bureaucracy, have all but obscured its main purposes. Pay incentives, teacher-of-the-month (and year and no doubt eventually of the nice day), all such gimmickry is sheer folderol, the prize of the charlatans, the gleeful booty of the show-offs. Now that Mies van der Rohe's famous dictum about modern architecture is in eclipse, I'd like to see it applied to education. We need more of less–less at the periphery, more at the center. For the magic of the effect of a good teacher on a good student can still be there, the satisfaction of curiosity, the lift of the heart from art, the radiancy of what is humanly good.

7

THE BACHELOR DONS

When I began teaching I slipped without noticing into a tribe of long and useful history at Notre Dame. This was the bachelor dons, those youth-devoted teachers who never married, or postponed marriage till late in life. These dons usually lived in student dormitories, where their rooms were generally open to students. They often spent their evenings listening to them, gently advising them, being that disinterested older friend that adolescents need so badly and cherish so greatly. Since I never lived in a student dormitory after I began to teach, I am not really a fully accredited member of the tribe. I lived in the Lyons Hall Annex, that little wing of Lyons to the right of the arch reserved in those days for faculty.

Sorin was the favorite hall of the dons. When Paul Fenlon left it, after sixty years, in 1980, Sorin was for the first time since it opened in 1889 without a resident lay professor. That's almost a hundred years. For the briefer period of Notre Dame history before Sorin was built, the dons lived, along with most everybody else, in the Main Building. The earliest version of this cradle of Notre Dame, built in 1844, included rooms for lay professors.

But the archives are mute about who lived where for how long and in what degree of comfort; the only insight into the quality of professorial life there I know is the diary of Professor Charles Warren Stoddard, in the Notre Dame archives, for the winters of 1885 and 1886, which he spent there. Stoddard writes of his narrow white bunk and the clanking radiators, but his diary mainly records a steady stream of visitors, students and faculty, so his digs must have been cozy enough.

Similar rooms seemed to suffice for Professor James Edwards, the dandiacal Notre Dame librarian who lived near his collections in the Main Building for nearly forty years, as well as the redoubtable Professor Francis X. Ackerman, professor of mechanical drawing who lived there even longer, from 1902 to 1942. Ackerman, the third of his family to teach at Notre Dame, did not follow the fashion to Sorin. That was set by the famous Colonel William J. Hoynes, who was engaged to beef up the Law School in 1881. In 1889 he moved his Law School and himself to Sorin, where he lived for forty years more. The Hoynes legends are numerous; he provoked them, by his courtly and flamboyant manner, his 1880s rhetoric, his flashy wardrobe, and his classroom dramatics.

In his old age Hoynes became a figure of fun. The young, given half a chance, love to caricature their elders, especially teachers, hanging nicknames on them which sometimes stick but mostly don't, inventing stories, mostly mock-heroic, about them, and endlessly gossiping about their characters and habits. At Notre Dame — I can vouch for the last sixty years — there seems to have been very little ill-nature in this indoor sport, which naturally had for its favorite targets the bachelor dons living on the campus. From the evidence of Stoddard's diary, however, as well as what one would guess, the older Notre Dame, so much smaller and more restricted of movement, provoked rather more, the usual flaw of single-sex enclaves.

Hoynes, Edwards, and company were picturesque enough to make waves of remembrance breaking into Notre Dame history. Others are more muted. What about Arthur Joseph Stace, who taught mathematics and engineering and lived for years in the Main Building? His impressive monument in the cemetery at Notre Dame is a reminder of his former eminence, but despite scattered references in the *Scholastic* he remains shadowy today. Joseph A. Lyons, also memorialized by a cemetery obelisk, is omnipresent in the university archives; he wrote the silver jubilee history (1869), and he was dispatched to Montreal to bring Father Sorin back to the campus after the fire of 1879. The *Scholastic* is full of his activities. What a pity he didn't leave a diary — although, if I read his personality right, it might have been conventionally pious and quite unrevealing. For example, I can find, among his considerable documentary remains, no clear record of his Main Building residence, although I am fairly confident he did live there, as did, very quietly it would seem, Martin McCue, the prime mover of Notre Dame engineering education, for many years dean of that college. And think of all the others who came for a season and departed with scarcely a trace beyond their names in the university bulletins — professors of history, law, manual training, agriculture, and so much else that sounds quaint to us today. I am especially fond of Professor Thomas McKinnin, who was "Professor of Belles Lettres, Italian, Spanish, and Chemistry" in 1854, and his colleague Max Girac, "Professor of Greek, Latin, French and Vocal Music." McKinnin departed early, Girac stayed long, and I rather think both lived in the Main Building for periods of time, as did numerous of their colleagues. But I don't know for sure.

Perhaps the outstanding lay professor of those days was Timothy E. Howard. Howard attended Notre Dame as a student, went off to the Civil War, returned and taught a variety of subjects while living on the campus. Quite late in life he studied and taught law, married, and became a well-known figure in South Bend and the state, ending up as chief justice of the Indiana Supreme Court. He and Lyons are the only lay professors to have campus halls named for them. Less typical is Professor Edward Maurus, who lived in a Sorin tower room from 1893 till his marriage in 1926. Maurus was something of a scholar, to judge from the mathematical treatises he bequeathed to the Notre Dame Library, but I gather he did not participate much in the life of the hall.

These older lay professors are dim and shadowy figures. Of them I knew only Maurus by sight and the last Ackerman a little better. But even so, they seem closer to the dons I did know well than they do to today's unbuttoned faculty. My imagination pictures them as frock-coated and totally collared, even though the frock coats covered patches on their pants and the collars and cuffs were detachable and washable celluloid.

Although Professor Francis Wynne Kervick, who lived above me in the Lyons Hall Annex, dressed conventionally, he belonged in spirit to the faculty he joined in 1913. Kervick, like myself, was no proper don; he never lived in a student dormitory, and his fastidious sensitivity is unimaginable in its noise and confusion. The Lyons Annex was no Sorin. Rarely did a student penetrate its portals, and I am sure never a student of Kervick's. Indeed, his students found him difficult to find in his own bailiwick. As head of architecture he had two offices, one for business and one for his own work, in the spacious quarters of the former Law School he moved into in 1930 after seventeen years at the top of the Main Building. He disappeared into these after his daily mass and breakfast at seven, and reappeared for lunch at his regular dining hour of 11:30 in the cafeteria of the South Dining Hall — he was regular in all his doings. I knew him as well as a young person could, I think. I greatly enjoyed his company. He was charmingly old-fashioned; I remember how bowled over John Frederick was on hearing Kervick say his favorite painter was Frank Brangwyn. That was the kind of visual art he loved, simple, sweet, formal, good, but utterly conventional. This did not impair his able leadership of the architecture department. He created the excellent reputation it still enjoys, and despite his predilection for the Gothic style and his hatred of Rockefeller Center, just then going up, had the respect of his students whose tastes differed so markedly from his.

Joining Kervick and librarian Paul Byrne for many of their Cafeteria meals was Professor Thomas P. Madden. Madden came late to academia. After a stint in World War I he'd worked for the old Peerless Automobile Company in Cleveland and Boston but hankered after an education. He got it by working as a secretary to Notre Dame administrators while attending classes, and, blooming with Irish charm and style, after graduation slipped naturally into teaching freshman English. He also taught with great success the substitute course for religion for non-Catholics, World Literature. But his home base was freshman English, with which he became identified; the teaching award for freshmen is named for him. Although like so many of the dons he dressed like a boulevardier, the truth is that at bottom Tom was a domestic soul, devoted to his large Ashtabula, Ohio, family and their old home there. I believe he was the only don who prefected in student dormitories during the whole of his teaching career (1929–1958). He liked the domestic side of prefecting and the avuncular relationship it brought him with students, just as he enjoyed tea and kitchen snacks and small talk and jaunts and all that's familiar and tranquil and affectionate. He was very popular with the other faculty dons, not least the two youngest, Frank O'Malley and myself.

Of all the dons I think Joseph C. Ryan loved Notre Dame best. He loved the place with a passion I've never seen equalled, though heaven knows, unlike some Notre Dame lovers, he was far from uncritical. Profoundly simple and straightforward, he was also deeply sensitive and, under the cover of an amusing irony, warmly affectionate. Patient and persistent as a spider, Joe taught the freshmen English course between bouts of illness, till his last one, in 1976. I think of him, correcting freshman papers in his neat handwriting, in heaven, where he surely is. The only thing he cared for more than his Notre Dame freshmen was saving his soul.

Thomas Bowyer Campbell had been in the business, so to speak, of saving souls; a native Virginian, he was ordained a priest in the Episcopal Church and became a missionary to China in the early 1920s. The Lambeth Conference of 1930, however, which legitimized divorce, was the turning point in his road to Rome; within a year he was a Roman Catholic layman trying to earn his keep with a succession of not bad novels, which would, I believe, have had the modest success they deserved had they been published ten years earlier. As an Anglican he had come to know the brothers Staunton, Henry and John, themselves converted Anglican priests teaching at Notre Dame. Through them Bowyer joined our history faculty in 1931, teaching the freshman survey of European history almost exclusively. Campbell was no historian, but he was a lively and sharp lecturer in his hoarse and hybrid accent, part Virginia, part British, and part himself. He was by far the most donnish of the bachelor dons — indeed, it is likely the only one who ever met a real don — but this worked somewhat against his dealing with Notre Dame students; he was a little exotic for them. But he was a delightful host to many of the faculty, especially after he built a little house for himself near the campus. When he was building this, an ancient Virginia kinswoman wrote him, "So you are going to settle down in that far western land! How terrible!" It was never that, yet Bowyer was no child of the midwest soil, either. He flourished for a time at Notre Dame, but of all the dons he was the least a hard-core Notre Damer.

I never knew either of the Confrey brothers, Burton and Augustine, who made a considerable splash during their comparatively brief stay at Notre Dame in the 1920s. Burton came earliest and stayed longest, teaching English very effectively but with old-maidish methods. Gus taught education, which never caught on at Notre Dame during the regular school year. His lively and charming personality made him popular with his students, but they were few in number except for the summer sessions. After a few years of this lopsided career he departed for greener pastures. Burton followed in 1929, why I don't know. I heard much about them from their fellow Sorin Hall dons. And, of course, I knew the popular tune their youngest brother Zez had written, "Kitten on the Keys."

Perhaps the best-known of all the modern dons was Charles Phillips. His was a vibrant and picturesque personality, and some romantic youths were entranced by his enthusiasms. He was very active, especially in his early days. By the time I came to know him, in 1933, he had become so deaf that acquaintance with him was hard to improve. Phillips came to Notre Dame to teach English, from San Francisco journalism and freelance writing, not unlike Charles Warren Stoddard seventy-five years before him. Like Stoddard he was widely traveled and filled with enthusiasms; like him he was overemotional in classroom performance and overoptimistic about student response. But Charlie was a much more stable character than Stoddard and lived happily in his Sorin tower for ten years (1924–1933) till his death, greatly beloved by many students and greatly admired by practically everybody.

Phillips was a widower when he came to Sorin, reversing the usual procedure of the sometime bachelor dons who abjured donhood for marriage. Daniel Charles O'Grady was prominent among these. Until his happy marriage he flitted in and out of student halls, where he was a prefect of sporadic practice, and downtown apartments. In the halls, in the classroom, wherever, he was excellent company, witty, engaging, indolent, self-deprecatory, utterly tolerant. In one of the pleasantest speaking voices I ever heard he spoke pure Wodehouse, mock-elegance mixed with colloquialisms. His discipline was officially philosophy, but what he really taught was how to be cultivated without being priggish and how to be content without being envious.

But this last was the basic lesson of nearly all the bachelor dons, the built-in premise of their lives. It was true of the best-known of them, Frank O'Malley. It was true of John Towner

Frederick, who roomed next to me in Lyons Annex during his commuting days. It was true of George N. Shuster, a Sorin don for only a few years before he left to become perhaps the most prominent American Catholic layman of his time. And it was true of Clarence Manion, another Sorin don before his marriage.

Some of the dons who lived for enough years on the campus to have a place in this account of them I simply didn't know well enough to write about. Such a one was Herman Wenzke, who lived in Lyons while he taught chemistry. Another was John H. A. Whitman, the law librarian. And I am sure there are more. It is, of course, impossible to name all the birds of passage, those professors who lived on the campus for a year or so while they were getting oriented. I'll name some I knew, just to summon them up: Bill Leen, John Connolly, Ray Schubmehl, Devere Plunkett, Louis Hasley, Norbert Engels, Ray Snyder, Bill Coyne, Andy Boyle, Art Reyniers, Francis McMahon, John Fitzgerald, Eugene Guth, and the visitors from the British Isles, Shane Leslie, Arnold Lunn, Christopher Hollis, and Desmond Fitzgerald.

Of all the bachelor dons Paul Fenlon was the best-known, not merely because he lived his role longest and most fully. As Father Joyce said in his funeral eulogy of him, Fenlon had a gift for friendship, and on the campus he lived among his friends: priests, faculty, students. He acquired them easily and kept most of them firmly. His teaching was merely an extension of his Sorin life, the only life he wanted. He professed to hate the noise and misrule of the hall, and so he did when they disturbed his habits, the most adamantinely regular I ever observed, but he was desolate without its life and verve, reluctant to spend a single night in Sorin when it was empty of students.

Fenlon had style of his own making, as fresh as celery and as inviting as a sideshow at a circus. This is what he passed along to his students, a sense of style, a distaste for vulgarity, a love of elegance without show or snobbery. It ought to be the first aim of liberal education, and those who have it in ways that students can understand and respond to, as Paul Fenlon did, ought to be more cherished in the educational scheme than they are. Like the bachelor dons, it is going out of our culture, drowned in rock.

Fenlon dispensed his style in Sorin rooms almost perfectly described in a piece on the bachelor dons in the 1907 *Dome*, the university yearbook:

> His snug little chamber is crammed in all nooks,
> With worthless old knickknacks and silly old books,
> And foolish old odds and foolish old ends,
> Cracked bargains from brokers, cheap keepsakes
>   from friends.
> Old armor, prints, pictures, pipes, china
>   (all cracked),
> Old rickety tables and chairs broken-backed,
> A two-penny treasury, wondrous to see;
> What matter? 'Tis pleasant to you, friend, and me.

Drop the armor, and the pipes (but not the cracked ashtrays), and you have Fenlon's Sorin rooms in the third and first floor towers — they are interchangeable — set down nearly ten years before he came to Notre Dame. The tradition of the bachelor dons was there waiting for him; he wore it well and stayed content when his best friends, Shuster, Manion, and Frederick, shone in other worlds. The tradition has died with Fenlon, not, I think, to return soon. But for Fenlon it would have died sooner at Notre Dame.

8

WASHINGTON HALL

I suppose my friend Joe Carroll shepherded me into Washington Hall in the fall of my freshman year of 1930 for a series of lectures on the Victorian Age in English Literature. Green as I was, even I had heard of the lecturer, the best-known Catholic layman in the English-speaking world, G. K. Chesterton. But without some stimulus the accumulated wisdom of my seventeen years might not have spotted these lectures as something not to be missed. I doubt I had read anything more of Chesterton's than some verse. Carroll knew what seemed to me a good deal about Chesterton, and Belloc; the knowledge was, I think, a prop to his rather sketchy Catholicism. Looking back, I am happy that I went to the lectures. From almost every point of view they were indeed something not to be missed. But I am not sorry to have read so little of Chesterton's works. They are a taste of maturity, and only in my postgraduate days did I begin to see G.K.'s greatness of spirit and the brilliance of his works. Boys should keep away, except for the boyish verse.

In any case there I was, notebook in hand, in the balcony of Washington Hall on October 6, when, with his usual grace, Father Charles O'Donnell introduced the speaker. This must have been very gratifying to O'Donnell. Chesterton had been wooed by many American Catholic universities but had finally been signed by Notre Dame, only to have illness postpone the engagement — luckily for me. Seeing him safely in hand, healthy and in good spirits, adding greatly to the prestige of the university and its president, must have made O'Donnell happy. The auditorium was pleasantly filled with students. Some genius in the administration had figured out the way to build up the student audience and to emphasize the seriousness of the subject

121

matter, was to offer one academic credit for the successful passing of an examination after the six lectures. The student could take for credit only one of the two series, one on the literature, the other on the history of the Victorian period in England. I chose literature and faithfully attended the full course, though there was a noticeable diminution of attendance as we went along.

Chesterton, then fifty-six, was at the height of his fame. Although his energies were ebbing — he died six years later — his wit had not. I wish I had had the background to understand it all. I did enjoy his opening characteristic joke. He said, in that famous squeaky voice, "The first question is to ask whether there was a Victorian Age in English literature. If there is no such period, then to my considerable and your enormous relief, we may betake ourselves to lighter pleasures and let there be a vast and yawning chasm where I now stand." Chesterton was an enormous man, well over three hundred pounds, and getting him around the campus and back and forth from his rented South Bend residence, not to mention the parties he loved, was, I learned later, a taxing job for the faculty of the English department.

I understood the lectures only fitfully. Since I had read some Dickens, I could see the justice of some remarks about him, but of course I did not see what I came to realize only years later, that Chesterton is probably the best critic of Dickens ever. Again, my knowledge of Swinburne enabled me to appreciate only Chesterton's initial evaluation. "A burst of song," he called Swinburne's work. But of Meredith, Browning, and Hardy, I knew nothing; of Scott, only the school stuff; and of the poets, only "Lines for Remembering." I may have first heard of Thackeray here. In any case, I recall I was still reading him a year later, and no doubt I was stimulated to other reading. One could scarcely ask more of a freshman. Incidentally, even a freshman could see that the exam had to be little more than a formality. There were no grades. My transcript has written in longhand at its bottom, "English (Chesterton), I credit."

The commencement of 1930, which Chesterton had been scheduled to ornament, was re-invented for him alone at a special convocation on November 5, at which he received, with extravagant praise, an honorary L.H.D. But perhaps the most touching mark of the visit was a poem dedicated to Notre Dame which appeared the following March. This is a typical Chesterton performance, beginning with an imaginary chariot race in Nero's Rome (an allusion to the football team), then shifting to Notre Dame, Our Lady of Sorrows, but also "Causa nostrae laetitiae," surveying from atop the Dome her "Youth untroubled, youth untortured, hateless war (football again) and harmless mirth." The Nero gladiators turned into football players, those about to live saluting the Queen of Heaven. I think Chesterton was deeply touched by his Notre Dame experience. His celebratory poem is not very successful, though. The gladiator-football player comparison is forced and rather bathetic, and the rhetoric, like the initial metaphor, too fanciful. But it seems to me in spite of this an affectionate gesture to a visit he enjoyed. Perhaps it made him recall the visit of his brother Cecil a generation earlier. Cecil, to whom he was devoted, died during World War I: tragically, of a disease he contracted in the dismal trenches of that ghastly war.

I believe that the Chesterton lectures are a historical watershed in the history of Notre Dame and especially the history of Washington Hall. From the year of its erection, 1879, until roughly 1930, Washington Hall was the home of the lecture. College campuses have always been a target of the lecture business. Most of the time some attendance was guaranteed, forced by faculty or administration. Since the target audience was concentrated in one place, publicity was minimal. And finally, a lecture at a university looked good on a resume.

This is, of course, still true, but mostly for specialized audiences. The pre-Chesterton lecturers were meant more for entertainment than knowledge. At Notre Dame the visits of the lecturers began in the administration of Father Thomas Walsh in 1883, when Washington Hall was only four years old. Walsh thought the lectures would widen the horizons of the student listeners. The rain of lecturers continued to increase till it reached a climax during the administration of Father John W. Cavanaugh. The list of speakers in Cavanaugh's second year as president is typical: Vice-President Charles Fairbanks, Hon. Adam Bede (sic), Hon. Edward McDermott, humorist Opie Read, Irish writer Seumas McManus, among the known. The unknown are more numerous: Frank N. Robertson, Willis N.

Moore, Col. H. A. J. Ham, Thomas E. Green, and a trio of physicians, Doctors Hall, Monaghan, and Stafford. Try that gang on your trivia club.

This list would lead one to suspect that the run-of-the-mill lecturers were no great shakes. And it seems to be true that faculty and students more and more disliked being turned out of their classrooms and into Washington Hall for an address not worth the effort. The best were different. Even if they were not the best talkers in the world — famous men of letters are especially noted for their platform deficiencies — still, it was something to write home about. I'd like to have heard Thomas Henry Huxley, the Abbé Felix Klein, Dom Aidan Gasquet, Eamon De-Valera, Guglielmo Marconi, Wilfrid Ward, Joyce Kilmer, William Howard Taft, Samuel Gompers, Al Smith, Will Rogers, and Henry James, all of whom spoke in Washington Hall. I wish I could have heard "Honey Fitz," the grandfather who bestowed his name on John Fitzgerald Kennedy. And many more. Stars will always fetch a crowd. Bill Buckley, Art Buchwald, and Tom Wolfe pack the house even today, and in their cases it was still Washington Hall. For really big occasions, like commencements and the visit of President Franklin D. Roosevelt, the old gym was converted into an auditorium. I still remember the feel and smell of the dirt floor as I sat at the press table for Roosevelt's visit to assist the visiting newspapermen. More than any other speaker I recall the grating voice of Cardinal Mundelein of Chicago.

But the days of oratory are over, and it was Roosevelt's intimate radio "Fireside Chats" that helped kill them. Because of the informality of radio and television, we tend to forget what a hold old-fashioned ranting had on our ancestors. As I read the day-to-day history of Notre Dame in the *Scholastic*, I often get the impression that college was mostly for training in public address. In literature Twain, Lardner, and the other vernacular writers had set a new style, but in public life high falutin' oratory still held the stage. Woodrow Wilson was perhaps the last great exemplar of it, with Senator Everett Dirksen of Illinois a kind of amusing and faintly parodistic echo.

Washington Hall fairly shook with it. At the Notre Dame commencement exercises in the early years of this century, three student orations were standard. To be chosen for one of them was the highest honor a student could aspire to. Oratorical contests were still common in my youth, and in my college days the Breen Medal for Oratory was still perhaps the most popular of intellectual prizes. Almost as popular was debate, both intercollegiate and interhall, which got more space than football in the early yearbooks — the first *Dome* was published in 1906.

It is not too much to say that Washington Hall was also built for it. The great event of the school year in high school and college in the second half of the nineteenth century was the "exhibition," and the most important of these was the final one of the year, later called "commencement." An exhibition meant just what the word implies: the exhibit of what the students have learned during the year. Obviously, this could take many shapes. In girls' academies needlework might have a prominent place. Music recitals were common. So were elocution pieces; if memory serves, the famous "Spartacus to the Gladiators" was written for just such exhibitions. At the exhibition, the proud parents were the principal guests, but as time went on it became customary to invite a speaker as well, the governor or mayor or some other public official being the usual choice. The original building especially for exhibitions at Notre Dame was a simple wooden structure, pictured on page 101 of Schlereth's history. It was called "Exhibition Hall," and so was Washington Hall when it was first opened in 1881. "Washington Hall" was thus to be taken literally, as a "hall," a big room, one of several in the structure. Since the north wing was reserved for music, and was for nearly seventy years the home of the music department, the building was also called the Music Hall, or the Academy of Music. Not until 1900 does "Washington Hall" appear below the engravings of the building in the yearly university catalogs.

The first commencement held in the new building was something special. It featured the usual student oratory, a band concert, and a performance of Sophocles' *Oedipus Tyrannus* in Greek. Creon was the younger Zahm, Albert, then an undergraduate. This odd mix characterized the early years of the old hall. There were concerts by the Swiss bell ringers, who played simple tunes on bells of different pitches strung out on a table before them. There were steropticon shows of all sorts, frequently by Father John Zahm, whose science shows had been a weekly event in old Phelan Hall behind the Main Building and transferred well to the new house. There were impersonations, skits, vaudeville and minstrel shows, all sorts. Some of these were simply terrible, "Unbelievably bad," says Father Arthur Hope, the university historian. "And the conduct of the students sometimes created terror in the hearts of the performers." No doubt of that, considering that they were mostly preppers.

Students themselves got up all sorts of shows. The big holidays, Founder's Day (October 13), St. Patrick's Day, and Easter Monday were traditional targets for shows which must have been of immensely varying quality. But the biggest splash was for Washington's birthday, February 22. George Washington was one of Sorin's heroes, and his birthday was a major Notre Dame holiday, the biggest secular one. The programs through the years varied somewhat, but it was a dead serious occasion. There were speeches, of course, often by the president of the senior class and sometimes by a visitor of distinction. The crowning event was the presentation of the official university flag by the senior class to the administration and its acceptance and blessing. The flag was flown for the first time at Commencement. This ceremony went on for years and years, down, I think, to the 1960s, and a remnant still survives. I suspect it originated to demonstrate that Catholic patriotism was as staunch as any, a proposition that needed emphasizing in the early days.

By my time the holiday was gratefully enough received, but the "exhibition," with its unabashed display of patriotism, was as out of date as a shivaree. The lectures for general audiences also went out of fashion, not without some latent show of persistence. I recall, for example, during my student days attending one by that hardy perennial of Catholic chauvinism, James J. Walsh, delivering what must have been the ten thousandth rendition of his "The Thirteenth, Greatest of Centuries." In my senior year I heard two famous men talk in Washington Hall, William Butler Yeats and Jacques Maritain. But it is significant that the next lecture by Maritain was held in the smaller Law Auditorium. There were more lectures than ever, but they were more specialized, held in smaller rooms and halls. The excellent series sponsored by the Committee on International Relations in the 1950s and 60s, for example, were held in the lounge of the Rockne Building, whose furniture as well as size was more conducive to discussion.

Washington Hall's exterior has changed little through the years. It was designed by Willoughby J. Edbrooke, who also designed the Main Building, and it is, in baroque-ish fancy, twin to it. Edbrooke also designed the present LaFortune Student Center, but here he reverted to a rather severe — unusual for him — classicism, perhaps for the sake of economy. Whatever, it is a rather pleasant change from the extravagances of Washington Hall, whose huge side windows were no doubt designed to illuminate the auditorium. The big windows are pleasantly echoed in ones of similar shape in the tower, but it is the tower, itself pleasantly repeated in the side entrances, that gives the building its character. The whole entrance wing, with its staircases and foyers, make a little, separate, attached building. The north music wing is plain, its severity lightened by limestone touches at the tops of the upper windows.

The date 1881 appears in big block stone figures on the base of the tower; the tower itself was not finished until 1887. Since the ground floor was for many years recreation rooms, mainly for the dormitory students in the Main Building, the auditorium and the music rooms were both reached by long flights of stairs, as in the Main Building. The north stairs still stand, handsome in their wrought-iron elegance, the railings ending in small horse heads. The front steps went in 1933 when they were thought unsafe.

The interior remained the same from its completion in 1884 till Father Arthur S. Harvey's tasteful and intelligent remodeling in 1956. The original decoration was the work of one Signor Rusca, the *Scholastic* for 1884 tells us, though most of the figures were done by Gregori, still working on his frescoes. These were portraits in the corners of the ceiling: Shakespeare for tragedy, Molière for comedy, Mozart for music, and Dante for poetry. Over the proscenium was a circular portrait of George Washington, flanked by fancy curlicues. Many other curlicues and stencil vine-leaves and fruit motifes took up the rest of the ceiling and proscenium, intertwined with the names of Rossini, Verdi, Gounod, Beethoven, and other musical greats. As a student I was puzzled by two of these names, Girac and Lilly, and was pleased later on to discover they were two Notre Dame professors of music. As if to emphasize the role of oratory, the two largest figures, one on each side of the proscenium, were life-size paintings of Cicero and Demosthenes, made to look like recessed statues. In my time the colors were attenuated beige and gold; perhaps they were brighter when new.

The history of theater in Washington Hall reflects pretty faithfully its course in the United States. This was from the beginning a sketchy affair and a very mixed one indeed. Recall that the agent and producer of the tours of Jenny Lind, the great "Swedish nightingale," were the work of P. T. Barnum, whose other theatrical ventures included shows of freaks and oddities, county-fair stuff raised to a high pitch of salesmanship. Theater was like that. Shakespeare was followed by plays like "The Corscian Cousin" and "High Life Below Stairs." Actors were poorly paid; the dissolution of a road company in the middle of nowhere is a legend in American theatrical history. Stability was unknown. Practically every town big enough for a horse trough in nineteenth-century United States boasted an "opera house" for plays (and, very occasionally, even opera), but the management of these was as ephemeral as the dew. Big stars like Joseph Jefferson could fill the house with their favorite vehicle; he starred in a sorry play called *Rip van Winkle* for forty years. James O'Neill was almost as well known the country over for his *The Count of Monte Cristo*. On one tour he stowed his boys, Eugene and Jim, at Notre Dame Prep while he played the Middle West. He even, when old and fat, made a film of it.

What Americans loved was melodrama. They got it in full measure on the numerous showboats, but the more elaborate stages of the opera houses provided a field day for the ingenious stage designers. They loved to show on stage the battle of Gettysburg, or a fire at sea, or, most enduring of all, Eliza crossing the ice in touring companies of *Uncle Tom's Cabin* so numerous that "Tomshow" was a backstage name for any down-at-heel touring company. Viewers of old films know how the directors loved to show melodramatic scenes of war and disaster, but they learned their trade from the stage, not the other way around.

What went on in Washington Hall is a muted version of most of this. Shakespeare was a perennial favorite, as he was everywhere, partially at least because of his melodrama. At Notre Dame he tended to be done in costume but without scenery,

or at least without very much of it. Also, well-known professional actors and actresses appeared in programs of recitations
from Shakespeare. These were, I guess, good introductions to
the poetry of the bard, although, as I can testify, learning the
parts was a wonderful experience for the actors. Of course you
learned not only your part but the others as well; there was a
time when I could quote yards from the plays I acted in, *The
Taming of the Shrew, The Merchant of Venice*, and, in prep school,
Julius Caesar. Strange how these Shakespearean lines stick with
one while other parts, from *Richelieu, Abraham Lincoln*, and other
such pretentious dramas are mercifully forgotten.

The level of playwriting was so low that anyone thought
he could do it and at Notre Dame frequently did. A tradition
developed of an original play presented on St. Patrick's Day.
Fueled in part by the Mitchell Award for Playwriting, this lasted
into my own time. I acted in one such, based, as so many were,
on some subject of classical literature. The play I was in was
set in the Trojan War, but it was a comedy about how the great
Achilles couldn't cope with a woman. More common, and I
suspect more popular, were skits developed by students about
eccentric faculty, kittenish athletes, and, I regret to say, girlish
boys. Women's parts had, of course, to be taken by men; K. K.
Rockne actually did a transvestite part for a play in his student
days. It was a dumb situation, especially at Notre Dame, with
St. Mary's across the road. I think transvestism a worse evil than
any possible with both sexes, but it was a time when theater,
and especially actresses, were morally suspect.

This suspicion may have helped put theater in the basement
of Notre Dame art. Everything else, from 1865 on down to 1940,
was better. The band was better and far more stable. Public
address and debate were far better. Writing, both in poetry and
prose, was better. But the theater was their poor relation.

Here, I believe, it reflected both a Jansenist suspicion of the
stage and a tradition of bad plays in parish halls. While the
legitimate theater was slowly evolving better standards in the
1920s, as shown in the work and influence of the Provincetown
group and the writers and players associated with the Princess
lyric theater in New York, the still active and popular Catholic
school and parish theater was mired in *Seven Keys to Baldpate*
and *The Octoroon*. Not until Father Gilbert Hartke and Walter

Kerr at the Catholic University virtually remade Catholic theater in the 1930s did things change. The influence of the Catholic
University theater and its touring companies was immense because it re-formed teachers and directors, who imbibed the good
taste and good sense of both Kerr and Hartke, and because the
imprimatur of the Catholic University re-assured pastors and
principals.

The theater of and at Notre Dame did not participate much
in the CU renaissance until it got Father Harvey as its head, a
CU product. There was some good theater sporadically. Young
people love theater, and Notre Dame had its share. There were
Allen Dwan, who went on to be one of the great pioneering film directors, Charles Butterworth, who followed a distinguished stage career with a film one, and Walter O'Keefe,
who flowered eventually into a radio personality. The great
star of the women's parts in the theater just before World War
I, Cecil Birder, returned as director of a memorable series of
Gilbert and Sullivan productions beginning in 1940. There was
a much-praised production of *Journey's End*, a World War I
play which had no women in its cast, by Frank Kelly. Father
Leo L. Ward directed a number of plays at Moreau Seminary
of excellent quality and style. There were at least an equal
number of failures, some downright bad, some just silly and
unworthy of university patronage. But there was no stability,
no planning, no academic structure until Father Harvey took
over in 1952.

Harvey did for Notre Dame what Hartke and Kerr had done
for Catholic University. He made the University Theater. He
saw what had to be done and did it, bucking as he went the
inherited indifference of the administration. He wanted Washington Hall, which he rightly saw as an excellent theater with
great acoustics, for theater and theater only and almost brought
this off, shunting most other attractions elsewhere. He engaged
an excellent staff. He planned and organized. He himself directed a series of musicals that would bear comparison with
any but star productions. But above all he brought the theater
status. Gradually administration supported him, including even
the renovation of the old hall and some badly needed technical
improvements. All this he did with unswerving persistence and
determination. He left the University Theater on a par with the

other arts, with the Glee Club and the Band and the new Snite Museum.

But the great student memories of Washington Hall are the Saturday movies. Films were shown there as early as 1916, when *The Birth of a Nation, Quo Vadis, The Man from Home,* and *The Warrens of Virginia* drew big houses, and John Barrymore was voted Notre Dame's favorite light comedian. After World War I, however, free films were shown every Saturday. At first there were two evening shows and later a matinee also. These attracted a cult following that lasted till 1965, when Father Harvey finally managed to get them out of Washington Hall and into the Navy Drill Hall. There the cavernous gloom dispelled the chummy atmosphere of the old house, and the growth of serious film interest shamed the juvenility of the old Saturday programs, which were originally designed in any case to keep the students on the campus.

The Saturday films might be good or they might be bad. The audience didn't care. The worse they were, the better the occasion for the roars of applause, yells, mimicry, chants, hall-shaking laughter, anything the herd could think of. The frequent breakdowns of the projectors were received with joy, as were the deliberate stoppages of the film till the noise subsided somewhat, and the hapless brother in charge tried to stop the riot short of carnage. Many students attended both showings, especially if they had seen the film previously, and so could chant the telling lines of the dialogue along with the actors. The printed dialogue of the old silent films was naturally delivered by the entire house. The only Notre Dame institution to compare with the Saturday films are the football pep meetings, but they are much more serious. What went on in Washington Hall on Saturday nights was mock rites of passage. Adolescents need this sort of blowing off steam, of course; the rock shows at the JACC serve the same purpose. What interested me most about the Saturday films, however, was the tolerance of an otherwise rather strict University disciplinary attitude toward them. Behavior which would have met with stern measures in the dormitories was not seriously reproved in Washington Hall.

Thus in the end, at least as late as 1965, the old function of Washington Hall was reestablished. It was meant to be a fun house as well as the house of art and serious endeavor.

Perhaps its most wholesome use comes when the Muses depart. The post-Harvey theater has seen a reversion to the early days of Washington Hall, although the locales are elsewhere. The Keenan Hall Follies, now in its tenth year, is a wild student frolic, and other halls have followed suit with productions *de haut en bas*. This is, I think, as it should be. There is no reason why a group of college students shouldn't do *Hamlet* in the lounge of a student hall, or, following the pattern of a lively group just before and just after World War II, do original musicals. The only difficulty is to get them to stop short of pornography, that perennial bugbear of college administrators.

At the same time the University Theater itself has shown signs of vitality. Professor Fred Syburg's production of *Amadeus* in 1989 was a brilliant success, easily taking its place with the Harvey musicals of the 1950s. Professor Reginald Bain has introduced audience participation in his innovative productions, and prospects are bright for a new center for the performing arts. Film series abound.

The new center is planned for a site southwest of the stadium, part of the new campus being built on the big parking lot south of Dorr Road and east of Notre Dame Avenue. It will be interesting to see what sort of character this new complex of buildings develops. The Notre Dame I came to still revolved mostly around the church, the Main Building and Washington Hall, plus a little assist from what was then Science Hall. This was pretty primitive. Especially skimpy were the recreation rooms in the basement of Washington Hall. There were none in the Main Building and none in Sorin. Yet somehow we made out. Since so many rooms were singles, roommates were carefully chosen for compatibility, and no one had to spend half his energy escaping from an undesirable one. We spent much more time in our dorms than students do today. But, however much I muse over our differences — in my junior year our tuition leaped up to $250 a year — I can't decide which was better.

TJS as a student, 1933.

John Zahm
Holy Cross Provincial, 1898–1906

John W. Cavanaugh
President, 1905–1919

James A. Burns
President, 1919–1922

Matthew Walsh
President, 1922–1928

Charles O'Donnell
President, 1928–1934

Hugh O'Donnell
President, 1940–1946

John J. Cavanaugh
President, 1946–1952

Howard Kenna
Holy Cross Provincial, 1962–1973

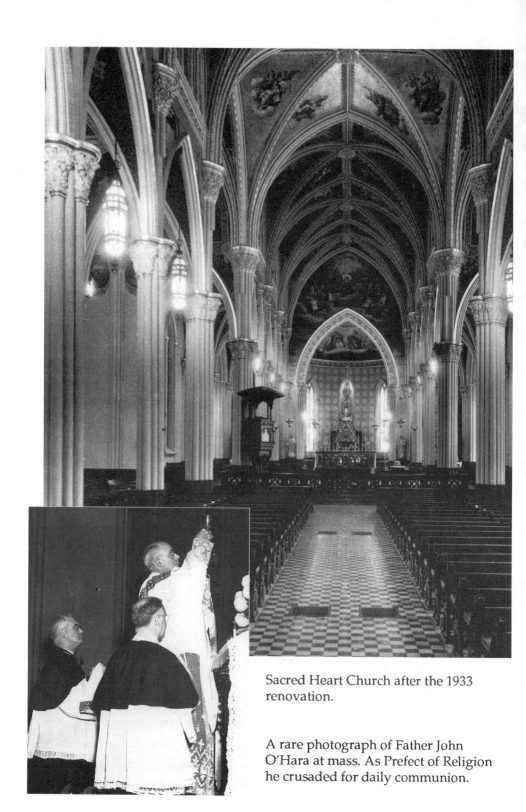

Sacred Heart Church after the 1933
renovation.

A rare photograph of Father John
O'Hara at mass. As Prefect of Religion
he crusaded for daily communion.

Left: Father Charles C. Miltner, first dean of Arts and Letters; right: John J. Becker, professor of music from 1919 to 1929.

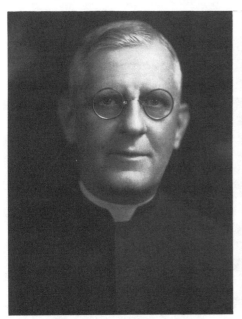

Left: Father J. Leonard Carrico, head of the English department and later Director of Studies; right: Father Leo L. "Literature" Ward, teacher of writing and later English department head.

The dime matinee at the Orpheum plus a nickle ride on this vehicle spelled a fun afternoon in the 1920s.

Professor Vincent Fagan's charming sculpture for Howard Hall has the owl of wisdom cocking a wary eye at the student weeping over his test paper.

Morrissey Hall was the first to boast a lounge, 1925.

Notre Dame Agrarians
John T. Frederick and Leo R. Ward

This group of Nashville Agrarians includes (l. to r.) Allen Tate,
Merrill Moore, Robert Penn Warren, John Crowe Ransom
and Donald Davidson.

Some members of the
O'Hara Foreign Legion.

Waldemar Gurian

Christopher Hollis

Desmond Fitzgerald

Karl Menger

Sir Shane Leslie

Yves Simon

F. A. Hermens

Track coach John Nicholson, as much a character as Rockne.

Knute Rockne, circa 1912.

George Keogan coached, by turns, freshman football and baseball, but longest, basketball.

When it opened in 1930 the stadium was not always filled.

Frank O'Malley

Joe Evans

TJS at the South Bend Press Club Gridiron Dinner of 1952 with host
Walt Sweitzer and a very young Father Hesburgh.

TJS as head of
Communication Arts, 1950s

James A. Withey

Edward Fischer

Ronald Weber

Ed Fischer and TJS with students filming Fischer's documentary, *Life Without Germs*, 1954–55.

My uncle and my brother, Samuel Cardinal Stritch and Father Morris Stritch.

The Review of Politics gang circa 1980, M.A. Fitzsimons, Phil Gleason, Fred Crosson, and TJS surrounding Father Leo R. Ward.

Father Sorin

Father Hesburgh

With Father Charles O'Donnell, "So well I love these woods . . ."

9

SPORT

I hate Notre Dame football.

Not the team. I fell in love with it on January 2, 1925, when I read a newspaper account of its Rose Bowl win over Stanford. It was a long story, almost certainly an Associated Press one, and I savored every word of it. I even remember a subhead, "Hunsinger's Great Play." If I was reacting like every other twelve-year-old Catholic boy in the USA, I came late to the party, because I don't remember the earlier story of the win over Army, which occasioned the famous Four Horsemen christening. The Army story was by Grantland Rice, a Nashville boy, and I ordinarily read every Rice word, with pride and pleasure.

However, football was not prominent in my boyhood. For us, baseball was *the* game. We knew baseball. We knew how to play it from attendance at Sulphur Dell, the home of the Nashville Volunteers in the Southern Association. In my last year of grade school I became a box usher at the ballpark, wondrous boyhood bliss. On ordinary days you had the best seat in the park when business was done, around the third inning, and even when the boxes were filled you sat in the aisle on upturned soft-drink cases. From here, in that memorable year, I saw many major league stars, stopping in Nashville for exhibition games on their slow way north for the season. Memory serves up Harry Heilman, Tris Speaker, Earl Combs, George Sisler, Burleigh Grimes, and even, in uniform but not playing, Ty Cobb on his last legs. But my favorites were Babe Ruth and his fellow Yankees, largely because Ruth came to church the Sunday of his game to the delight of the local Catholics and the local press. I missed the sight, but not the photos in the papers.

I have never lost my love for baseball. When I began to write sports for the *Nashville Banner*, I didn't cover professional baseball. That was the perk of the sports editor, Fred Russell, who did the best job of covering it I've ever seen. But Fred did get me into the World Series of 1932 at Wrigley Field in Chicago, after I had come to Notre Dame, as *Banner* correspondent. From the temporary press quarters for outlanders like myself atop the third base line, I saw Ruth hit his famous homer, the one many fans thought he had predicted by gesturing toward right field. Maybe he did. I saw the gestures, but thought he was merely keeping up his hassling the Cub bench for their failure to give Mark Koenig, a former Yankee who joined Chicago late in the season, a full share of the series swag—a big item in those days. Anyhow, I was happy to see once again the great Ruth. He was a long ways from the figure he had in his Nashville appearance. He was paunchy, swathed in rubber from head to toe to hold his bulk together, but he still projected the old charisma. Never mind who was the greatest player. Ruth was the most dramatic, and drama is the soul of all sport.

It was during Ruth's great Yankee years that football began to rival baseball as the nation's favorite game. Although some rivalries, like those of Harvard and Yale, and some teams, like those of Michigan, go back to the nineteenth century, actually the football of that early time was an odd sort. Many teams, especially prep-school ones, played only one game a year, against some archrival. What happened at Notre Dame, I think, is that the growing fame of nearby Michigan roused the Irish fighting spirit to field a team to play them. Of course they lost, but the die was cast, and football began to fire the imaginations of Notre Dame students. Nevertheless, student journalism tells me that baseball remained more important till Dorais and Rockne shocked the Knights of West Point out of their moleskins in 1913.

From that day on Notre Dame and football became inseparable. It was a long time, however, before the Holy Cross Fathers faced up to that clear fact. The 1930 stadium should have been built years before; football revenue was a big help in the building program of the 1920s and 30s. But most of that revenue came from playing elsewhere. In the fall of 1923, notes historian Father Hope, over 188 thousand saw Notre Dame play.

Of these only 53 thousand saw the home games, in rickety old Cartier Field, which seated only 35 thousand even with the two expansions in the 1920s. By this time the old joke about Rockne going about with a shoe box full of tickets and receipts was obsolete. Football was becoming a big business, and homegrown J. Arthur Haley and Herbert Jones were engaged to run it. They have not been given sufficient credit for setting up the most efficient athletic business I've ever seen.

There is something endearing about the modesty of the Holy Cross Fathers, who seemed suspicious of the golden spheroid. And there is something attractive about the man who turned the pigskin into gold, Knute Kenneth Rockne. In all the golden years, he never seemed to take his Notre Dame post for granted. The pre-golden Rockne was a deep-dyed Notre Damer, active in theatricals, journalism and music—he played the flute—as well as sports. He and his wife were frequent chaperones at student dances. He lived near the campus, on St. Vincent Street, and students streamed in and out of the place all the time. As his fame, and the demands on his time, increased, Rockne gradually drifted away from all this campus-centered activity. But he still was part of the place.

This is the Rockne I like, the right man for Notre Dame, shrewd yet simple, confident yet unpretentious. There was still something of this quality left in my only encounter with him in the fall of my freshman year. One morning I went to the president's office, and there, cooling his heels in the reception room, was K.K.R. I was too flustered to say anything, but he said something like "Hi, kid." President O'Donnell then appeared and got rid of me with a kindly but firm word, and took Rockne into his office with him.

It's the Rockne legend that I don't like. The St. Kenneth of the gridiron, the master of psychology, the oracle as well as the orator of the locker room, the father figure of American football (Rockne looked venerable even as a young man), the master showman, all the legendary stories and superstitions that fans of all ages love to repeat and revel in. Many, I think, are fictitious. Professor Paul Fenlon, who knew Rockne in his man-about-the-campus days, once told me he asked him about one of his famous between halves speeches. "All I said," Rockne told him, "was watch Cagle." Chris Cagle was a famous Army star. Rockne called him Caggle. I often wondered where he got his odd accent. It reminded me a little of Al Smith.

That little story encapsulates the Rockne I like. I also liked the way football developed at Notre Dame, and I feel sure he did most to make it the way I like. I liked seeing the coaches on the campus. I came to know many of them. As a student I liked living with the players. I am uneasy when I encounter places where the athletes are virtually segregated. Even the bums, and we had our share, were bums in reality, not legend. I don't want to project the holier-than-thou image we've brought on ourselves lately. I suppose that now I'm being the romantic, but I like, liked, *college* football. It's basically a college game.

But I am of two minds about it. I liked the collegiate feel of the game, young men doing battle with their bodies, a remnant of chivalry and knighthood, a romantic echo of the past. But now that the sportsmanship is gone, swept away in the competitive fury of getting psyched up, my affections have gone, too. I just plain don't like the orgy of self-congratulation, the meanness, the almost-hatreds stamping out the fun and combat joy. Yet there is something left of what I do like.

I am afraid my feeling is too much that of the person who never left the shadow of the Dome. I have usually resented the football crowds. I know I ought to smile on the tailgate parties, the welling up of alumni emotion, the old boys reaching back for their youth, bringing with them their anxious kids. But I don't. I resent them and their litter. I feel that they are intruding on my turf, my country, my own. Somewhat irrational, I concede; I have the same feeling about the townspeople who hang around Notre Dame, eating in the dining halls, using the library, walking their dogs, as if the campus were a public park. This is an especial spasm of selfishness, since I have done exactly those things on the Vanderbilt and Peabody campuses in Nashville since I was fourteen. Why can't I be as generous as my Nashville hosts? I'm not. I can't altogether stifle my irritation when I see a gang of preteens racing their bikes along the Notre Dame walks or hanging around the student center selling something, or just messing around.

I am all the more impious in view of my indebtedness to Notre Dame football. What little spending money I had as a student came in good part from writing about football and its coaches and players. Moreover, I liked a great many of them, Ed Krause, Hughie Devore, Jack Robinson, Ray Brancheau, Elmer Layden, Frank Leahy, Terry Brennan, George Kunz, Dan Shannon, many more, and I greatly enjoyed the company of ever so many football writers and staffers. I have contributed to the legend. But on the whole I dislike it. I loved the game but am turned off by the worshipful acolytes it spawned.

I dislike the foofaraw, the hype, the sports talk, the stats, the hoopla. Most of all I dislike being the ticket agent everybody at Notre Dame is supposed to be. Through the years I have expended much energy, and even some of my own money, getting tickets for people I like. I am often besieged by those I scarcely know, and I don't mind shaking them off. But when a third cousin of my mother's calls to see if I can get tickets for her son-in-law, I feel weary. I have been there so often. And, of course, it's always for Southern California. They'll accept Michigan, but Air Force or Purdue, nah, nah.

It is incredible what people will do in their ruthless drive to get tickets for a Notre Dame home football game. Most try more sources than one, so you often have the experience of turning up something for a friend of a friend, only to hear that he's been taken care of, thank you. As recently as last week I had once again the unbelievable experience of dealing with a woman who has some claim on my attention, wanting tickets. "Mind you," she said, "I'll pay for them." The assumption underlying that remark is mind-boggling. Did she think I wouldn't have to pay? Does she think faculty get tickets merely by asking for them? Does she believe they abound, like a fall of walnuts?

Since I came to Notre Dame the football mystique has grown and grown, like Jack's beanstalk. Along with many Notre Dame people, I used to think it wouldn't. I thought that the memory of Rockne would fade away, like that of matinee idols of the theater. But since World War II and Frank Leahy, I have come to believe that college football is one of the hardiest vessels of our civilization. And there is no doubt that Notre Dame is its flagship. I have seen the ship dead in the water in season after season of inept coaching, but each time new leadership has brought it back to lead the fleet.

The genius of Rockne, of course, began it all. He was the great innovator, the man who changed the game from one of brute strength into one of speed and timing, the man who brought the grace and style, almost, of ballet into the game. Rockne was once asked who he thought the best football coach in the country. "Modesty forbids," chuckled the old boy, "but if I had to pick the two best, one of them would be Clark Shaughnessy." Here, again, is the Rockne I like: he recognized the maker of post-Rockne American football.

Frank Leahy was not of this stamp. He was not an innovator. But he was an organizer. He foresaw the development of the game. He wanted what is now standard, a coach for every position—some said, every player. Of course he didn't get even half that, but he tried to make up for it by doing the work of half a dozen. What a contrast between the Leahy organization, itself ahead of the times, and today's Holtz tribe of eleven full-time coaches, five graduate assistants, and a support staff of fifty.

Leahy was a fierce competitor. When Admiral Nimitz visited the campus shortly after World War II the word came that he enjoyed pitching horseshoes. Someone arranged a match, surely for publicity photos mainly, between him and Leahy. Faced with this challenge, Frank practiced for hours on end. Of course he won. Something he said to me in the press box about halfway through the first quarter of a football game we were watching after he stopped coaching is a good clue to his character. "You know, Tom," he said, "that offensive line of ours has a good charge." Then he breathed heavily and clenched his fist and added, "But they don't do it every time!"

Still, speaking as one who loves Notre Dame better than Notre Dame football, Leahy is not my beau ideal of a coach. That would be Ara Parseghian, whom I did not know. He won enough to soothe the partisan hearts, but more than that, he represented the university to near-perfection. He was exactly what Hesburgh's Notre Dame needed. Hesburgh turned Notre Dame's image from athletics to academics, a magnificent achievement, and Parseghian's style, good sense, and charm helped the process enormously. The only similar case is that of Elmer Layden in the late 1930s, during the O'Hara administration. It was Layden who patched up some of the fences Rockne's success had smashed. He got us back on the Michigan, Ohio State, and Illinois schedules. But Parseghian knew best how to steer the flagship of college football. He understood that the flagship has to keep a little better order than the ships down the line.

Of course the whole picture has changed so much in the wild scramble for television money that the early days I knew now seem mastodonic. When the Notre Dame Stadium opened, in 1930, you could walk up to the ticket window ten minutes before the game and buy, for two dollars, what is to me, with my farsightedness, the best seat in the house, high up in the end zone. Occasionally the place sold out, as for the Southern California game of 1932, but if all you wanted was to see the Irish in action at a lesser attraction, all you needed was two bucks. This was on a par with other sports admissions. I happily recall the time when I could take the State Street trolley from downtown Chicago either north to Wrigley Field or south to Comiskey Park, and there, for under two dollars, get a grandstand seat—and ordinarily, again, on the spur of the moment. No planning, no ticketron, no waiting in long lines, and no bank loan.

But, for one of my peculiar temperament, perhaps the nicest inducement was the quiet. Like most Americans brought up on sports, I watch them on television. But I rarely have the patience to sit out a whole game, and I nearly always snap on the blab-off after a few minutes of the constant chatter of the commentators. To me, part of the pleasure of watching baseball or tennis in the stands is its quiet. Or should I say *was*? Even in tennis, goaded by its new vulgarity, the crowd begins to intrude, and the baseball parks I attend are usually so crowded that noise is inevitable, even without the spur of the organ or the jabber of the public address system. The days when I used to sit alone, and watch, as I once did, the great star of the Athletics, Robert Moses Grove, outpitch the White Sox's Ted Lyons 2–1 (time of game 1:32) in peaceful content are gone forever. I like best going with a friend or two, but ones who know the game and talk sparingly. I will never, never, never understand why people talk at a movie, a concert, a play or in church.

I was almost never a spectator at Notre Dame football. I sat in the press box. My position there was, at first, professional. For some years I dictated a play by play for the Western Union, who sold the service to small radio stations and newspapers especially near the hometown of the visiting team. When radio network killed off this service, I was free for other chores. I ghosted Jock Sutherland, the former Pittsburgh coach, for some games he covered at Notre Dame, and I wrote for any medium the directors of sports information asked me to. But increasingly, especially in the 1950s and 60s, under the kindly eye of my former student, Charley Callahan, the sports information director, I simply attended.

Heaven knows the press box was no haven of quiet. It was filled with the noise of typewriters, teletypes, a public address system of its own, and the dim echoes of stadium noises. But there was no show biz about the P.A. I suppose I am in a small minority thinking there ought never be. The attempt of so many P.A. announcers to tart up a simple listing of the lineups with phony drama is nauseating to me.

This is the key to the negative side of my attitude to Notre Dame football. I know that it is the great bond among alumni. They love it. But it might surprise most of them to know how little football impinges on the daily life of the Notre Dame community. I hear more baseball than football talk among the faculty. Most of us go to the home football games. Until I got too old to move easily I went as a matter of course. I would no more think of missing a home game than I would miss Sunday mass, and frequently went to nearby away games. But these were simply pleasant excursions, as one might go to Niagara Falls. They meant more than going to a game at Princeton, to be sure, but not much more. Come Monday, the whole thing was forgotten.

I often did not discover that a student in my class was on an athletic scholarship until I got a list of them from their academic mentor asking about their work. I think most of the athletes liked it that way; they wished to merge with the student body, which has always been Notre Dame's policy. I don't mean to suggest that college athletics present no problems to faculty and administrators. They do. But I don't know what to do about the problems except live with them. One's children also often present family problems to which there seems no solution, but it's no use pretending that there are none. It will come as no surprise, then, that some of my favorite sports-watching at Notre Dame and elsewhere are the sports which used to be rewarded with a small monogram. I have been a tennis player and fan

since high school, a player of more style than success but a
spectator of the usual vanity. One of my favorite Rockne stories is of tennis. I tell it with the blessing of Tom Fallon, our
long-time superb tennis coach who established tennis as a major sport at Notre Dame and brought us the most unlikely sports
honor we ever won, the NCAA tennis championship in 1959.
That even surpassed Paul Harrington's NCAA champion indoor pole vault (12 feet, 11 inches, 1927). Both Tom and I are
a mite unsure about the authenticity of this story, but it rings
true to both of us.

In 1923, the story goes, some tennis enthusiasts in the Notre
Dame student body thought it was time we had a varsity team.
They elected one of their number to call on Rockne in his capacity as athletic director, asking him to sponsor the team. Could
be, said Rockne. "But," he wanted to know, "are you any good?
If we are going to field a team it will have to be up to our normal collegiate opposition." "I think we're good enough," said
the suitor. "Well, I'm pretty good myself," said Rockne. "How
about a match? If you can beat me, we'll talk about a team."
Accordingly, the match was arranged.

But the tennis representative was perplexed. He thought that
if he beat him, Rockne, a fierce competitor, would be so angry
he'd never get his team. So at first, in the match, he deliberately
lost. But after a while he hated the dishonesty and the trick,
pulled his game together, and swept Rockne off the court. Prop-
erly impressed, Rockne, anything but sore, agreed to a team.
"But," he added, "there's no budget for it and no chance for
one. So I'll have to add you to the football squad for your away
matches." Which he did.

All I find in the official annals is that we did indeed have
our first tennis team in 1923 and that then, and in the following
year, it did pretty well in intercollegiate competition. But I hope
this story is true. Again, it's the Rockne I like.

Even keepers of the Rockne flame often forget that he was
interested in more sports than football. He had been a star of
the track team and coached it till he engaged John Nicholson
for that post in 1927. I was a track fan. Some of my pleasantest watching in college was of the indoor track meets in the
old fieldhouse. For one thing, the indoor track itself was, to me,
something very special. I had never seen one before and thought

it very big league indeed. I used to try to get the top row of the temporary bleachers, from where you could see most of the dirt track—as well as trickle a little water down on the runners. The outdoor meets were fun, too. There was something casually festive about them, something like a racetrack atmosphere, something you might see pictures of in fancy magazines, like *Country Life* or *Yachting*.

I kept on being a track fan after college. I recall with special pleasure traveling to Chicago for the big *Chicago Daily News* indoor invitational meet, with Coach Nicholson and our great two-miler, Greg Rice. On that occasion Greg set his long-standing indoor two-mile record on dirt, 8:58 if I recall correctly. A group of us track fans often went to Chicago, or Bloomington, or Ann Arbor to see a Big Ten meet, and I twice made the NCAA meet, once in Minneapolis and once in Chicago, though this last may have been an AAU meet. My memory is fuzzy about this.

Coach Nicholson was, in his way, as much of a character as Rockne, though only in track circles. He had been a champion high hurdler in college, and was the favorite to win this event in the 1912 Olympics at Oslo. The tradition is that after winning two heats in easy fashion, he was leading the field in the finals when, amid ruffles and flourishes, the king and queen of Norway entered the stadium. Flustered, John turned to look, fell at the last hurdle, and did not finish the race. His winning the heats and the melancholy "DNF," did not finish, are in the record books. I don't know about the rest, nor do I remember where I first heard it. Maybe from John himself.

Steeped in track, Nicholson coached it at various colleges until Rockne tapped him for Notre Dame in 1927. He found a home here and stayed on till he died suddenly, in 1940. He was, when I knew him in the 1930s, a craggy faced big man with a rasping voice. But he knew his business. He was smart and innovative. He said he'd invented starting blocks. I believe that was in some controversy, but he certainly did invent his own type. He knew, however, that there was more to it than things like starting blocks. He once said to me something like—I've forgotten the phrasing, but not the sentiment—track is a branch of abnormal psychology. He was right and wrong. Track, like tennis, depends on good form. You can't do the high hurdles at all without form, and the same applies, though in less measure, to the field events. But, also like tennis, form must be backed by a fierce competitive spirit. John Nicholson laid the groundwork for a splendid Notre Dame track tradition, one that continues to this day.

Rockne is seldom thought of as an athletic director as well as a football coach, but as a spotter of talent he was brilliant. Well before he hired John Nicholson he spotted George Keogan, who was at nearby Valparaiso. Keogan was a real find. Coming to Notre Dame in 1923, he coached freshman football, baseball twice, and basketball longest and most memorably. He was the last but by no means least of the great triumvirate of coaches I found at Notre Dame.

Like his two colleagues, Keogan was very visible on the campus. He was a brilliant recruiter and a good game strategist. He was also loud, tough, an umpire baiter and a voluble quote-maker. It seems to go with the game—Keogan was very like his great rival at Purdue, Piggy Lambert, and not unlike Indiana's present coach, Bobby Knight.

I scarcely knew Keogan personally, for the excellent reason that I dislike college and pro basketball. I went to all the home games of my college days but rarely thereafter. I am not so anti- as my friend Red Smith, who once said that if they were playing the NBA finals in his backyard he wouldn't raise the window curtain to watch. Unlike Smith, I see the merits of the game. It is without a doubt the best kid game ever, great exercise, highly competitive, and exhaustive of even teen energy. You can play it alone, one on one, two on two, and on up to five. And the closest the average American boy comes to an esthetic experience, even including dancing, is handling a basketball and practicing the moves. The truest symbol of American sport is not the great stadium but the basket suspended from the garage entrance.

It is a modest symbol. I think it basically a modest game. Although I gave up the deafening spectacles of the college game, I continued to go to the high-school games as long as they remained somewhat modest. Here were neighborhood kids and their parents and schoolmates enjoying what still seems to me a neighborhood game, more like marbles and hopscotch than football. A full half, perhaps more, of the kids got on the team from talent and practice, not carefully tutored freakish height and reach. But I am clearly out of step with the American people who have made basketball at all levels perhaps the centerpiece of American sport, like soccer abroad. I forget which sage said it, but I agree with the proposition: basketball has exceeded the natural limits of the game. The players are better than the game's structure, unlike baseball or football.

Baseball has had an odd history at Notre Dame. Until 1913 it was the premier campus sport. Then, as football rose, baseball declined. In some sense it was an old-fashioned sport. Jake Kline, its long-time coach, was the last major coach to teach an academic subject. He had some good years and some good players, but in my college days and for some years thereafter it generated little enthusiasm. I used to feel that the climate was against it. But it was popular before, in the early part of the century, and is now popular again, as success has come under Coach Pat Murphy. On fine days I like to drop in on the games, but there are few fine baseball days in the Indiana spring, and the fall season seems somehow, to me, out of place.

When I came to Notre Dame the minor sports were golf, fencing, tennis, and swimming. Of these we excelled at golf, in some good part, no doubt, because we had a course in our front yard. I don't understand why we have always excelled at fencing, but we have, spectacularly so in the recent years under the excellent coaching of Mike DeCicco. Tennis had some good years under the excellent professor-coach Walter Langford, but the real father of Notre Dame tennis is coach Tom Fallon. Swimming had to wait on the construction of a pool in 1938 when the Rockne building went up. It has flourished under the intelligent and devoted ministrations of Dennis Stark.

I rejoice at the recent expansion of these nonrevenue sports, giving more and more students a chance to be part of a team. Rugby, lacrosse, volleyball, rowing, sailing, all claim their adherents. Boxing continues at the sensible pace Dominic Napolitano set for it, a strictly in-house big tournament, and wrestling stays a small-time intercollegiate competition. Hockey has had an up and down career since we got an indoor rink. We tried it for a while as a major sport, but in recent years have played it in a lower key. Soccer may be reversing that trend, rising gradually to major status as more and more American boys and girls are playing it. The most spectacular example of sports populism at Notre Dame is, of course, Bookstore Basketball, whose annual tournaments attract hundreds of players and stand-up crowds. It is still the delight of all sorts of less than top players, but succumbing, too much I think, to semiprofessionalism. And of course the big story is women's sports, gaining enormously in popularity and interest since the first women graduated in 1976.

And now, the perennial question. Are college athletics good for the college and for the public? Is Notre Dame football helpful to the legitimate aims of the university, or have we now, or at times in the past, been a rogue university? Is this inevitable? Do sports, however clean, intensify the natural human tendency to violence? I spoke of Babe Ruth as a boyhood hero, but is he really a demonic figure? "Bam busts Two," yelled the old *New York Daily News* headline, with a photo of the Babe finishing his famous swing. Was this really a part of the seamy underside of American culture of the 1920s, in which Al Capone was busting a few as well? Is football a sport or mayhem? Has sportsmanship dissolved in the orgiastic dance of the scorer in the end zone, the frantic self-congratulation of the play maker, the vanity of the star outfielder, and the greed of the promoter?

These are the eternal questions raised wherever "sport" becomes popular. It was as true of the Greek Olympics of antiquity as it is of much sport today. There was in them as much infighting, as much finagling to lure the best to switch teams, and as much bribery and hypocrisy as Joe Jackson, Pete Rose, or the sorriest tanker in a boxing stable ever displayed. In his posthumous book *Take Time for Paradise* Bart Giametti says that the heart of sport is "serendipity." That's nonsense. It is as far from the heart of the average player as it is from that of the avid fan. The heart is *win*, and that's no heart at all. The truest prophet of American sport is Leo Durocher.

These questions apply to more than the United States. They pop up wherever sport is a popular spectator event. The Super Bowl hoopla in this country is minor compared to what the bicycle Tour de France generates. A capacity crowd in Notre Dame stadium would fit into a corner of the soccer stadium in Rio de Janeiro. No American college team for any sport was ever so completely detached from intellectual endeavor as an Oxford crew training for the big race with Cambridge. And for general all-round violence, gambling, cheating, quarrelling, and politicking reaching into the highest levels of government, nothing modern even comes close to the chariot races of Constantinople in the days of its Byzantine splendor.

For the *New Yorker* for September 10, 1990, George Steiner notes that with the wonderful feeling of liberation in a Central Europe freed from the domination of the Soviet empire there also is the onrush of what is "shoddiest in modernity, in the media, in down-market entertainment." Kept partly at bay by force until now, with the coming of freedom "the drug pusher, the salesman of kitsch, the hoodlums have moved into the East European and Russian vacuum." This is the price of freedom. In the United States we know it all too sadly as we contemplate the commercial success of Andrew Dice Clay and the 2 Live Crew, amid so much more. And we don't know how to check it short of tyranny.

A minor example of Steiner's lament is the scene in sports. The successes of Kenesaw Mountain Landis in baseball and Avery Brundage in the Amateur Athletic Union misled some sports fans into thinking that strong leadership could keep the games clean. But the fact is, it now seems, that both of them throttled the individual player and unconsciously bolstered the owners and promoters. It's like tax loopholes: the wise guys will always find them. I remember my disbelief that bingo, as my mother used to play it in the church hall, could do a community any harm. But I found, looking deeper into the matter, that the crooks and the con men were operating in that seemingly innocent pastime, too. I would not now be surprised to learn that tiddely-winks has some racketeers.

The deep puzzle, one that has intrigued academics for long, is this: why the public passion, the big crowds, the publicity, the industry, the commercialism—and the gambling, the fixers, and the crooks? Everyone knows that young people need to exercise their bodies. Why can't they, and the public, be satisfied with intramural play, no pay-contests between classes, dorms, and fraternities? Notre Dame has always seethed with this sort of sport. I remember that, when I turned out for the Howard Hall football team in the fall of 1930, I found twelve high-school captains on a squad that looked to me to contain half the hall's occupants. All my teaching career I've been running into unlikely bespectacled students playing evening basketball in the Rock, noon handball in the old Fieldhouse and baseball everywhere. They'll organize into teams and leagues between dribbles. I know this is true to some extent of all youth, but I believe it's more true of Notre Dame than anywhere else. And I note with interest that since we began admitting women nearly twenty years ago, they have caught the fever, too, as bad almost as the men.

For me, the intriguing question is, would these students play as much and as intently if there were no varsity sports? But it is a purely hypothetical question. Cockfighting, outlawed in forty-eight of the fifty states, still has enough adherents to support a trade magazine. That sport, like golf, flourishes on small-scale gambling. There is no way that betting on golf holes can be out-lawed. Nothing wrong with that, you'd think. Nothing wrong, either, with betting on a basketball game, except that it invites the fixers. There *is* something wrong with them. But it's like problem children again. You just have to live with it. The ideals of fair play and sportsmanship, the constant themes of school-boy fiction, were even in it always being challenged by the bad guys who wanted to fix the games. The true story of sport lies in the sad remark of the kid to Shoeless Joe Jackson, "Say it ain't so, Joe."

10

THE ARTS AT NOTRE DAME

One of the charms of the Notre Dame campus is the wide variety of outdoor sculpture. At first you simply don't see it. You see the buildings, the big trees, the paths, the vistas. You see the lakes, "sleeping with open eye," as Notre Dame poet Charles Warren Stoddard put it. The sculpture comes to you only later, as you stroll and stop to look around. Then you feel that only you have spotted the student crying over his quiz paper above the Howard Hall arch, the Romanesque athletes holding up the decoration over the west entrances to Dillon, the niches filled with the likenesses of saints and scholars. As you go deeper into the campus you see Ernest Thompson's beautiful outdoor stations of the cross, the glorious Anthony Lauck stained-glass window of the Moreau chapel, set in exquisite exterior relief panels, and the sharp contrast of Ivan Mestrovic's neobaroque large figures with the attenuated expressionist ones of Waldemar Otto.

But what impresses most is the sheer volume of it. The old cast-iron figures, the Sacred Heart on the Main Quad, the charming St. Edward (Sorin's patron) holding Sacred Heart Church in front of the hall, Our Lady in the Brownson garden, the modern constructs in front of the Library and the Snite Museum, all these and many more. The impulse to adorn public places with pious and monumental sculpture is as old as Western civilization, yet still its profusion at Notre Dame amazes me. Emphasizing its attraction to Holy Cross is the interesting presence on the campus of three Holy Cross priests who are sculptors and good ones, Anthony Lauck, James Flanigan, and Austin Collins.

Instruction in drawing and painting is almost as old as the university. A Notre Dame president, Father August Lemonnier,

149

Sorin's nephew, taught drawing before he assumed his high office in 1872. His obituary says he was an "amateur" of oil painting, whatever that may mean — perhaps simply that he liked it, as I do. Well before President Lemonnier the first of the three professors Ackerman, Jacob, is listed in the catalog for 1854 as "Professor of Academic and Linear Drawing and Painting." The last of the Ackermans, Francis Xavier, was still teaching mechanical drawing when I came to Notre Dame and living in the Main Building, as he had all his adult life. He lived on till 1948 but not in the Main Building; his last days were eked out in a nursing home.

Mechanical drawing is a hardy perennial of the Notre Dame catalog, tied, as it has been historically, to the physical sciences. Artistic drawing has had a spotty history, though nearly always mentioned in the old catalogs. But it, too, has usually been tied to something else, the handmaid of painting. The catalogs and bits of history about the arts give an impression of itinerant artists dropping in at Notre Dame for a season or so and doing some work that rarely survived. We undergraduates who took most of our classes in the Main Building will recall the wall painting in so many of those ancient old rooms. Some survived in the basement, relics of the dining hall decorations. On the second floor of the Main Building there was a room known privately as the Chamber of Horrors, filled with scenes of European churches and monuments. This tradition of the itinerant artist lived on into my time; the murals in the Oak Room of the South Dining Hall are the work of such a one, Augustin Pall, and Eugene Kormendi, a protégé of Bishop John F. Noll of Fort Wayne, did a good deal of outdoor sculpture.

It is against this background that the work of Luigi Gregori, hired from Rome by Sorin to decorate the interior of his new church, should be understood. Wall decoration was thought a necessity for churches and public buildings — recall the fuss about decorating the Capitol in Washington, as well as numerous state capitol buildings. Sorin wanted the best of this kind of thing and went to a good deal of trouble to get it.

Gregori came in 1874 and seems to have turned the entire Main Building into his studio. All, priests and students alike, were delighted to pose for him. Muralists need help, and Gregori absorbed any student with talent into working for him.

He himself was a dynamo of energy. He did his murals, he did sets and costumes for plays, he did portraits, he even did a commemorative medal for the Columbian Exposition in Chicago celebrating the four hundredth anniversary of the voyages.

Sorin was the most enthusiastic of new Americans. He was fascinated by the whole idea of the New World, and upon rebuilding the Main Building after the great fire of 1879, he suggested to Gregori, by now nearly done with the church, Main Building murals of scenes from the life of Columbus. Gregori responded with twelve large murals, pleased to commemorate his fellow Italian. He returned to Italy, however, before the "White City" was opened in Chicago.

As Father Hope noted in his official Notre Dame history, the Columbus murals are no great shakes as art. Neither are the church murals, so carefully restored in the renovation of 1990. They have, however, some historical interest. It's interesting to spot the various faculty members, including the Gregori family, who posed for the scenes. In one of these, a rejected suitor of his wife's, is shown breaking a wand over his knee, reminiscent of the great Raphael of 1505. But Gregori was no Raphael, and his brand of Roman art not much worse than what Pius IX was decorating the Vatican with. It wasn't a good time for religious art. Sorin was on firmer ground when he designed the church in the style of his home parish in LeMans and landscaped his grounds at Notre Dame in the French mode.

However, there is no question that Gregori made a sizable splash in the history of Notre Dame. Whatever the art quality of his work, the publicity value was considerable. It still is. Tourists came to see the murals as soon as they were done, and they still do. The Catholic press reviewed them in detail. The religious themes in the church and those of patriotism in the Columbus paintings, combined with the new theme of American native Catholicism, were highly attractive to the turn-of-the-century Catholics, and boosted Notre Dame into prominence. Long before Rockne and football came Father Hudson's *Ave Maria* and Gregori's art, along with much else, to give Notre Dame a major role in American Catholic life.

After Gregori the studio atmosphere seems to have declined at Notre Dame. It went into a phase of misfortune. Paul Wood, Gregori's favorite student, was clearly meant to be his successor, but his career was cut short by his death in a Chicago hotel fire the very next year after Gregori went back to Italy, 1892. Misfortune also hit T. Dart Walker, a Goshen boy who had studied and taught at Notre Dame before he began winning prizes, at home and in Paris, where he studied. The great favorite of the Notre Dame galleries in the 1910s and 20s was his *Salute to the Rising Sun*, very much in the romantic Maxfield Parrish style of his time. Walker, too, died young, in 1914, only seven years after he graduated from Notre Dame. The mainstay of studio painting till World War I was John Worden, a pupil of the celebrated French academic painter Gérôme.

It was during this time that Father Matthew Schumacher was cooking up his plan for revising the Notre Dame curriculum, which Father Burns put into effect in 1921. By then Schumacher had departed to become the president of St. Edward's in Texas, but his reforms filled the Notre Dame academic stage. Among them was a School of Fine Arts, involving painting, music, drama, and speech-debate.

Father Schumacher's first move was the establishment of the Notre Dame Summer Schools. This brought to Notre Dame swarms of religious, mostly women, fulfilling the teaching requirements being established in every state of the union just about then. This marks the real beginning of graduate work at Notre Dame. And graduate work from this beginning involved women, so this is also the start of coeducation.

The team Schumacher picked to run his fine arts program were Ernest Thorne Thompson and his wife Florence. I don't know how Schumacher got wind of them. They had just graduated from the Massachusetts School of Art, where they had met. Schumacher must have been a good judge of talent, at least of artistic talent, for the Thompsons proved a good choice. They were very versatile, adept between them not only at oils and watercolors, but also lithography, etching, and sculpture, although I believe Ernest's sculpture was mostly designs for it, not the craft. The only Thompson legacy at Notre Dame are his beautiful bronze-relief outdoor stations of the cross, which show an expert sense of the medium although they were cast by others.

Thompson ran the fine arts school for the decade of his Notre Dame tenure with apparent success. I find no record of his trials and not very much of his successes. There is some correspondence with Father Walsh in the archives which indicates that Thompson had Walsh's steady cooperation, but I find no minutes of faculty meetings, no records of disagreements and disappointments, though these must have abounded.

The Thompsons left Notre Dame in 1928 to start an art program at the College of New Rochelle, New York, where they worked till his retirement in 1967. The archives there tell of his success as a teacher and artist, but I don't know what prompted him to leave Notre Dame — perhaps just a desire to return to his native East.

Excellent as the Thompsons were, the really big success of the School of Fine Arts came from music. The star of this department was John Becker. Becker is little known in Notre Dame history, but he is one of the few assured of a place in the annals of his discipline, like Julius Nieuwland in chemistry, and Emil Artin, who taught mathematics briefly. Becker earned his spot in the history of American classical music only after he left Notre Dame, in the 1930s and 40s. He then became associated with an outstanding group of American composers, Charles Ives, Henry Cowell, Carl Ruggles, and Wallingford Riegger. These regarded Becker as their peer and in some ways their leader, for Becker wrote well and promoted this regional school of music by word as well as musical notation.

Becker came from a devout and cultivated family in Evansville, Indiana. He was brought up in an atmosphere of music and had a good musical education. He went as a very young pianist to teach at Kidd-Key, a well-known college for women in Sherman, Texas. From Sherman, Becker went every summer for further study to Chicago with Alexander von Fielitz, and to Kansas City with Carl Busch. Becker became lifelong friends with these two able teachers — Becker's entire life is filled with the warm and devoted friendships of some of the most distinguished musicians of his time. Stimulated by these he began to compose and by 1913 or so had a sizable list of original compositions to his credit. By then he had made a happy marriage and decided to return to Evansville. He participated in the musical life of the state, where he came to Schumacher's notice. A mutual and lifelong admiration and friendship developed between the two men. Becker came to Notre Dame's faculty in 1917.

Schumacher had his eye on Becker as a prospective star in his summer program. He was not disappointed. By bringing to the campus mostly in the summers the musicians whose friendship he had cultivated, he made the Notre Dame music department widely respected in the Midwest and eventually the entire country. These include, besides Busch, the well-known Chicago organist and composer William Middleschulte and the popular composers Charles Wakefield Cadman ("At Dawning," and "Land of the Skyblue Waters") and J. Lewis Browne. One of the best-known music educators of Chicago, Glenn Dillard Gunn, was a popular feature of many summers with his lecture-recitals of the Beethoven piano sonatas. Otto Luening, along with Becker a composer likely to have a permanent place in the history of American music, heard his compositions performed for the first time in the Notre Dame summer sessions.

During the regular school year Becker was no less productive. He took over the recently formed Glee Club and made it known throughout the Midwest for its professional excellence and high musical standards. Its continuing importance in the musical life of Notre Dame undergraduates owes much to John Becker. He warmly supported the liturgical music program and the Moreau Seminary Choir. He beefed up the music faculty and its instruments until by 1925 he was able to offer a master's degree in music.

Becker also became involved in the musical life of South Bend and northern Indiana. South Bend loved the Glee Club concerts Becker arranged especially for the city audience, as well as other concerts by star soloists. Becker also blossomed forth as a music critic for a local newspaper. I have read quite a few of his articles and found them remarkable for their good sense and understanding of the audience, as well as musical insight.

The loss of Father Schumacher from the Notre Dame scene must have been keenly felt by Becker. Unlike Thompson, Becker seems to have clashed with the administration. Father Burns replaced him in the Glee Club with J. Lewis Browne, for reasons not clear thus far; Becker's high standards may have left the Irish Americans out in the cold, although their own hero, John McCormack, a one-time Becker soloist, managed to mix the classics with his Irish balladry. In any case, Becker lost favor with the Notre Dame administration. He left in 1927, after ten years of accomplishment, for St. Mary of the Spring, in Columbus, Ohio. This small and progressive Dominican college had set up an "American Composers' Foundation," which Becker headed and worked with for two years. But financial support slipped away, and he then followed once more the beckoning of Father Schumacher, who had taken over the presidency of St. Thomas College in St. Paul, Minnesota, a new fief of his Holy Cross Community.

It was here that Becker really flowered into an important figure in American music. Composing straight along, at Notre Dame and in Minnesota, Becker gradually became a strong proponent of the "new" American music. The leader of this growing band of composers was the great Charles Ives, whose firm friend and steady correspondent Becker soon became. But even more important was friendship with Henry Cowell, the founder of the quarterly magazine New Music and a tireless promoter of the new. Becker soon became a contributor to the magazine and a prominent member of the ring of composers associated with Cowell, Carl Ruggles, Dane Rudhyar, Ruth Crawford Seeger, Adolf Weiss, and Wallingford Riegger. Once established in St. Paul, Becker became a strong advocate of these composers and developed his own style. He composed in all seven symphonies, six concerti, many songs, much chamber music and music for the solo piano, along with several stage works and some church music.

Despite a permanent small place in the history of American music, such as the one in Howard and Bellow's Music in America, Becker never has achieved the reputation he deserves. In 1958 Leonard Bernstein conducted his third symphony in a concert in New York, and the Louisville Symphony has recorded his Abongo. But these are rarities. The reasons for his neglect are easy to speculate on; an important one, I think, is the overwhelming emphasis in the media on the studio of Nadia Boulanger, the Paris idol, and the performance time Serge Koussevitsky gave its members with his Boston Symphony. But still more important is the reason which lies in the simple word Becker so rejoiced in: Midwest. In time and in inspiration, Becker's music was drawn from the same regional roots as the painting of Grant Wood, Thomas Hart Benton, and the other regionalist artists, whose reputation has also so markedly declined. The same has happened to the writers, and to Notre Dame Professor John Frederick's *The Midland* magazine. A few greats survive, of course: Ives, Willa Cather, Jackson Pollock. Becker does not belong in that august company. Still, he is the only artist nurtured by Notre Dame and on its faculty for a considerable time who has attained a national reputation.

Becker was succeeded at Notre Dame by his Glee Club accompanist, Joseph J. Casasanta, whose versatility and steadiness helped the music organizations through the depression years. Casasanta handled both the band and the Glee Club, no mean achievement. The excellent Willard Groom took over piano and organ, and in 1936 the beloved Daniel Pedtke began his long tenure with the Glee Club. At about the same time Father Carl Hager took the Moreau Seminary Choir to new heights of musical excellence and spiritual fervor. Like Becker, he was also a composer, but directing the choir and administering the music department left him too little time to develop his own charming and original talent.

Becker was not even a memory when I came to Notre Dame. Although several faculty members, both in and out of the music department, must have known him well, I never heard him talked about. But I heard no talk of Father Schumacher, either. His pet "School of the Fine Arts" foundered and split into the several departments it had merged. Father Hesburgh tried, in 1956, to inaugurate a new such division with myself as chair. After six years of experiment with theater and speech, and some informal work with the art department, I concluded that St. Cecilia herself couldn't run such a venture. Administratively, as Hesburgh saw, it's inviting; the arts are indeed connected, and, especially in performance, constantly call on one another for assistance. But artists are anarchists by nature and spoiled children by nurture. They need to be constantly cosseted, flattered, soothed, and sweet-talked. At the same time they also need to be checked from their extravagant enterprises, made to see that the university has concerns other than theirs, and to understand that wounded vanity is not really a dread disease. To manage a stable of them, as in a repertory theater, is tough enough, but to ride herd on a passel of different sorts of artists is a job for Superman. This, to me at least, makes the achievements of the 1920s School of Fine Arts all the more remarkable.

The longest, steadiest, and most remarkable musical tradition at Notre Dame is that of the marching band. The fact that ours is the oldest continuous marching band among all United States universities may be the direct result of the interest of our founder, Father Sorin. One of his first acts was to organize a band — not an orchestra, not a choir, but a band. This may have been a reflection of his youth in France; the French of the nineteenth century were very big on bands.

The bandmasters of Notre Dame have had a rougher job than many of their opposite numbers, especially in the land-grant schools of the Midwest. These have the resources of large graduate music schools training musicians for bandwork, especially in high schools. Seeded throughout a large band like Michigan's, such graduate-school musicians provide a nucleus lacking in the strictly undergraduate amateur bands of Notre Dame, Yale, Vanderbilt, Southern Methodist, and other such universities. It speaks well for the Notre Dame band leadership that our band has resisted the temptation to go cute, as have so many, to play any old way in or out of tune, to get themselves up in all sorts of non-uniforms, and to play parodies of all sorts of pop music from ragtime to rocktime. But, even if it is often much smaller than the other band on the field, the Notre Dame band proudly displays its stuff between the halves of football games and at all sorts of other university functions. The loyalty of its members, who turn out for practice with devoted regularity in all weathers, is truly admirable. And the members are all sorts, from the girl whose admission to the charmed group is like getting to heaven early, to the blase intellectual whose love for bang-bong-bang may be happy release from mental chores. But they are all highly conscious of their importance on the Notre Dame scene and buoyed up by it.

The Glee Club, too, continues the proud tradition established by Becker and continued by Brown, Casasanta, and Dan Pedtke. Indeed, Becker, I believe, would be proud of our present music faculty, a remarkable group of composers and performers.

However, the outstanding developments in the arts at Notre Dame since World War II are the two museums of art, the first as part of O'Shaughnessy Hall (1954) and the second the new Snite Museum of Art (1980). I played a small part in both. I even played a tiny part in the Wightman Galleries, tucked away at the top of the old library, out of sight, out of mind, and out of range to most Notre Damers. My tiny part was simply to be one of the few students who ever was seen in the galleries. I used to poke around in them every now and then. I hung around the library, of course, as I have all my life, and naturally explored the attic as well as every other floor.

Yet when I think of the Wightman Galleries the first picture that comes into my perverse imagination is not exactly of a work of art. It is of my classmate Arthur Sandusky, the galleries' custodian, asleep in the Medici bed. This bed, a canopied and highly decorated article, said to be from the Medici Palace at Fiesole — there is a picture of it in the university bulletin for 1934 — was part of the bequest of Mrs. Frederick Wickett, the widow of an Oklahoma oil millionaire. It was, according to its sleeping beauty, rather uncomfortable — and that is the final irony in this unshakable image of my imagination. Sandusky was the very embodiment of the handsome and charming college boy, his happy countenance incongruous in this medallioned and flossy objet d'art.

Both the Wightman and Wickett collections were brought to Notre Dame by one of the most colorful figures at the university in the 1920s. This was Maurice Goldblatt, a member of the well-known and wealthy Chicago department store owners. Merchandising did not interest Maurice. The arts did. He began as a musician, good enough to be engaged for the violin section of the Chicago Symphony Orchestra. But the quiet life of a second fiddle wasn't nearly enough for Maurice. He turned to art connoisseurship and aspired to be the Bernard Berenson of the Midwest, an advisor and agent to collectors. As such he came into the orbit of Dom Gregory Gerrer, a Benedictine priest who first came to Notre Dame as part of the Schumacher summer sessions. Dom Gregory taught in these, but he also became the curator of the art collections. He was an expert at restoration and repair. So he spent some time during the school years in the galleries. I often encountered him there, working away in the shadows, like the industrious copyists one sees in that favorite subject of nineteenth-century art, the gallery itself. In his painter's smock he looked the artist, stooped, with a mane of white hair. At the same time he was working for Notre Dame he also founded in 1915 a museum at his home base, the College of

St. Gregory in Shawnee, Oklahoma. Its handsome new building is now called the Mabee-Gerrer Museum.

Goldblatt seemed to me just the opposite of Dom Gregory. But I never met him and so never experienced his charm, which certainly captivated many. He loved the dramatic and was constantly attracting press notice by discovering masterpieces hidden away in attics, or denouncing some well-regarded work as a fraud. Many thought him a charlatan; certainly, he had a touch of that style. But Dom Gregory and other artists at Notre Dame seemed to have thought well of him. In 1932 he was named the gallery director and two years later awarded an honorary degree.

In addition to the Wightman and Wickett collections, plus some paintings that had been around for years, Dom Gregory presided over the Braschi collection, purchased in 1917 by Father John W. Cavanaugh. This large group of paintings, around 125 in number, was picked up by Cavanaugh, so far as I can ascertain, simply as a bargain. Actually, it wasn't. Little of it remains in the Snite Museum, perhaps seven paintings. The Wightman fared even less well, with only two paintings remaining. And there are only a few small objects from the Wickett. In the early 1950s, as part of the move to the new O'Shaughnessy Building, the university hired the well-known experts Hans and Erica Tietze to evaluate all the paintings. Thus began the movement to weed out the poor, restore the damaged, and cherish the best. Meanwhile, more bequests came in, notably from Mrs. Fred Fisher of Detroit and Peter C. Reilly of Indianapolis.

Besides prowling around the Notre Dame collection I began, around 1933, to frequent the splendid collection of modern painting in the Chicago Art Institute. In that year I lived across the Alumni Hall corridor from George Rocheleau, a Chicagoan, who had been practically brought up in the Art Institute. He became my guide there and my lifelong intimate and deeply cherished friend. After graduation Rocheleau went on to a career in art, becoming an outstanding teacher and painter. He introduced me to other Chicago artists and I began to make friends with some of them, Francis Chapin, Max Kahn, George Buehr and his wife Margo, among others.

Rocheleau also introduced me to Mr. and Mrs. Joseph Randall Shapiro, the well-known Chicago collectors. Joe had a superb collection of modern art, which he loved to show and I loved to see. From it he provided us with two excellent exhibitions to open up our new O'Shaughnessy Galleries in 1953, and from it he gave us some of our best modern paintings. Through the generous and delightful Shapiros I came to know other Chicago collectors, and Notre Dame soon became known to them.

It opened up a new era in art at Notre Dame. What the O'Shaughnessys did in effect was to move art out of the library attic and onto the ground floor of their big building. Its great hall was adorned by a beautiful crucifix by Ivan Mestrovic, the gift of my good Chicago friend John Muldoon. Mestrovic himself was soon to occupy a studio adjoining the galleries, today a museum of his works. But to me the great change was exposure. Hundreds of students perforce went through the great hall every school day. The art galleries were right off it, *there*. Good art, all kinds, became part of the normal student experience.

My old friend from undergraduate days, Father Charles Sheedy, was the new dean of the college. He knew of my interest in art and asked me to help him with the management of the new galleries. Paul Byrne, who, as director of the library had, willy-nilly, some direction of the galleries no matter who was officially in charge, had retired as head librarian to become curator of the new art galleries. Byrne, a good friend, also lived over the gallery, in O'Shaughnessy. But Byrne had small knowledge and less interest in modern art and was glad to have me lend a hand.

I also lent a hand to Father Sheedy's fine idea of an annual "Festival of the Arts." These brought students into the galleries as nothing else could. They also introduced music performance into the galleries, a pleasant innovation which the Snite has continued.

As we all grew in experience, we came to recognize that the man to run the galleries was Father Anthony Lauck. Father Lauck, who was comparatively new to the faculty, needed to get used to the idea. Himself a sculptor of skill and taste, his knowledge and interest extended to all the fields — painting, textiles, graphics, as well as sculpture. But most importantly he had the style and charm that appealed to prospective donors. His development of an arts council was a natural next step. This brought to our help such distinguished advisers as John Walker, the director of our great National Gallery in Washington; Wilbur Peat, the director of the Indianapolis Herron Gallery, and many more. It is to Lauck more than any other person that the Snite collections owe the most. He and I came to emeritus status at about the same time, and we have both watched the development of the museum and its new administration with pride and pleasure.

The Snite was dedicated with festivity. I rejoiced at the honorary degree awarded my old friend Agnes Mongan of Harvard. I presided over the banquet speeches. This was my last act in the Notre Dame art world. I end up as I started, prowling the galleries of the museum, like the bums at the zoo. I prefer my tigers out of Henri Rousseau rather than nature. And as I prowl I recall, when I see how the collection has grown in quality, the happiest hours of my academic life, those spent on Saturday mornings when Father Lauck, John Howett, our first art historian and also curator, and I met to decide which of the many items Lauck had sent in from his shopping trips to buy. I learned a lot about art, but I learned even more the pleasures of the companionship of my colleagues over something worthwhile. I thank the Good Lord this took place in the 1960s before the wild inflation of fine art prices.

In between all this I tried to teach a little art appreciation to my journalism students. I found the best way is the way of the Snite Museum: put the good in front of their eyes. You can say the same things about a bad painting as well as a good one. You can point more morals from Greuze than Matisse. You can hang a symbol on a beer can as well as a hero. But in the long run quality will out, even though the teacher can only stand before it and gawk. It is increasingly worth doing in a world where art and commercialism are becoming practically synonymous. They actually are at opposite poles. The difference is that between honesty and dishonesty.

In the literary arts Notre Dame has a curious history. There is little fiction. Until recently, the only really serious good fiction done at Notre Dame was that of Richard Sullivan, working from roughly 1936 to 1970. Sullivan was a Notre Dame undergraduate and began to write then under the tutelage of Father Leo L. Ward and, later, John T. Frederick. But if you except Frederick's own fiction, none of which was written at Notre Dame, all that's left is Leo L. Ward himself and the little group that he inspired. Fiction has never been congenial to the Holy Cross community. Only Father Patrick Carroll kept at it all his life, and his was mostly for young readers. He made no attempt at art.

Ward himself had some talent. I helped put together a posthumous book of his stories, *Men in the Field*, and it was something of a struggle to get enough to fill the covers. His energy went into teaching and administration. It was what was needed. He knew it and wasted none on regrets. From 1927 to 1940 there was much Ward-led student fiction, often quite respectable. But little flowered into serious adult work. Harry Sylvester, Hemingway's pen pal, did a little, but he seemed unable to reach into other than undergraduate life at Notre Dame. Only Richard Sullivan managed that.

Sullivan's best work, in his own view and that of his Notre Dame friends, hewed firmly to Frederick's regional standards. *The World of Idella May* and *First Citizen* are excellent examples of the genre. I myself thought Sullivan's fantasy, mined only in *The Dark Continent*, was more his natural vein; in private life he excelled at theatricals and fanciful tales, and he enjoyed the fantasies of Karel Capek and James Branch Cabell in his reading. Financial stress kept his nose to the grindstone. His depression-born books never sold as well as they might have ten years earlier, and he was forced to do a great deal of book reviewing to keep afloat. It's a wonder he could do as much as he did, with an invalid wife, two young daughters, and a full program of teaching. His character of genuine sweetness and decency made him much loved by both students and colleagues, myself not the least.

If fiction is oddly missing from the Notre Dame artistic life, poetry certainly isn't. One would scarcely think, from its macho football image, that the Muse of Poetry also dwelt in the halls of Notre Dame, but if profusion is any index, it seems to show she settled here. "Poetry," says the foreword to *Notre Dame Verse* (1917) "is in the tradition of Notre Dame."

It is indeed. The bound copies of the *Scholastic*, Notre Dame's all-purpose student weekly magazine during her first hundred or so years, is full of it. The 1883 volume contains more than a hundred poems, that of 1917, when the anthology was published, more than two hundred. The production of poetry fell off sharply after 1920. The *Juggler*, Notre Dame's excellent humor magazine, siphoned off the lighter verse. A humor magazine was as much a part of the college scene as the new football mania in the 1920's. The *Scholastic* itself, diminished as a mass publication by the more recent Notre Dame daily newspaper, slipped into the news magazine format popularized by *Time*.

Most of all, I think, the writing of poetry ceased to be a requirement in English classes. Clearly this was the source for most of those early *Scholastic* poems. They smell of the labor under the night lights — laborious is the word for most of them, laborious and pious. They are highly imitative.

Most of these seem to me Tennysonian in approach, if lacking that noble lord's elegant ear. Listen to this:

> I ask'd an aged man, a man of cares,
> Wrinkl'd and curved, and white with hoary hair,
> "Time is the warp of life," he said, "Oh tell
> The young, the fair, the gay, to weave it well."

It is signed XYZ — many of the poems are signed with initials or pen-names, no doubt to avoid the jeers of the writer's friends.

But Alfred Lord Tennyson was not the only model for Notre Dame poets. Publius Vergilius Maro is also prominent, as witness these limping hexameters:

> Anni per spatium semper labor acriter instat,
> Fructus erit dulcis: solatia digna dabuntur.

This charming pep talk for exams was one of thousands of class exercises in writing Latin verse in the schools of England in the United States — and for all I know elsewhere, too.

This reminds me of the rash of translations from Horace and Catullus that lasted to my own time. I am guilty of several that I can't get out of my memory:

> Ye tender maidens sing Diana,
> And you, fair youths, Apollo hail.
> Then all in swelling chorus hallow
> Beloved Latona's high travail.

I can't remember when I impugned the great name of Horace with this laborious fakery, but I am sure it was for some class —

maybe one of Father Hebert's. My verses are at about the level of many in the old *Scholastic*. Some things are slow to change.

The stilted foreword to *Notre Dame Verse* recalls the faculty influence. "One does not speak," it went on, "of poets, though such former professors as Eliot Ryder, Arthur Stace, Charles Warren Stoddard, Maurice Francis Egan, and Austin O'Malley wrote better poetry than much that is nowadays 'boomed'. Rather, one thinks of the influence these men had to plant this interest among us. One remembers that the writing of verse has always been a part of the local method of teaching English. Consequently our book represents something more permanent than a mood of popular taste: it would exhibit something historically characteristic of Notre Dame. And, fittingly, it makes its appearance in an historic year, the seventy-fifth of the University's life." In this sesquicentennial year it is good to look back again.

The poet-teachers named were indeed prolific in the old genteel tradition. American poetry was dominated around the turn of the century by such writers as Thomas Bailey Aldrich, Adelaide Anne Proctor, Fitz Greene Halleck, Joaquin Miller, Edwin Markham, and many more of the same ilk, plus the lighter verse of Eugene Field and James Whitcomb Riley, so dear to the Midwest. Easily up to this standard is the work of the Notre Damers. Charles Warren Stoddard was perhaps the best of them. Although this poem about his newly adopted state is rather forced and precious, its fanciful play on the name, the Indians, and the seasons is both clever and honestly felt.

Indiana

> "What's in a name?" the poet cried:
> Sometimes less than is implied;
> Sometimes all — and more beside.
> Tell me, Indiana, why
> Thy name, so like a lullaby,
> Droned in wigwam to papoose
> Seemeth unto me a truce?
> Is it that the soothing word—
> Musical as song of bird—
> Seeks to make in melody
> What we should not know or see?

Here are only the first few lines of a long poem. It must have been written in 1885 or 86, making it the oldest poem in the anthology. More modest, and much more youthful, is this poem by Charles Flynn, of the class of 1914.

In March

A wild wind and a flying moon
And clouds that drift and lower;
A heart that leaps at the thought, how soon,
The earth will be in flower,
Behind the gust and the ragged cloud
And the sound of loosening floods
I see young May, with her fair head bowed,
In a waking world of buds.

Another anthology of student writing was published in 1927. This covered only the one year, and includes stories, plays, and essays as well as verse. It shows an enormous increase in student sophistication. I thought the plays perhaps the best section, the one most even in quality. But the poems are very good, too, though very uneven.

From a College Window

I see the days
Twang by
Like curving arrows
Feathered
With old memories
And tipped
With new hopes.
        — Henry James Stukart

The Marsh Hawk

Flap—flap—flap,
Lazy sweep,
Dynamic motion,
Stroke—stroke—stroke,
Climbing spiral stairs to heaven and the vaulting
    arch of cirrus,
Up the wall of bowl cerulean, crawling speck on

glaze, opaque,
Up the shaft of dew ascending, where the
    mountain molds the raindrops,
Up the archway of the rainbow, up the scar by
    lightning torn,
To the empyrean firmament.

— C. Everett Michael

There's much more of this shower of imagery. Both these efforts show a new sophistication, a far cry from the genteel tradition. They reflect the growing maturity of Notre Dame, which in poetry reached a professional stage after World War II. It is ably described in James Walton's new anthology of Notre Dame verse of the last fifty years, *The Space Between*. Walton's perceptive choices and critiques make Notre Damers aware that "poetry is in the tradition of Notre Dame" perhaps more forcefully in recent years than ever before.

11

REACHING OUT

Since the age of fourteen I have been consciously attracted to journalism. I wrote then most of the *Buzzer*, a sort-of yearbook for the lower division of my prep school. This is a mimeographed and stapled set of sheets containing the usual yearbook features of class history, prophecy, fortunes in sports, and so on. I still have a copy, and the perusal of what I wrote leaves me affectionately amused at my pretensions. But what I remember best about its production was my betaking myself to the mezzanine of the downtown Gibbons Hotel to write.

I think I remember why I did this: to get an afternoon or two free from interruptions. But it now seems to me a tiny little symbolic act, the unconscious turn of the real writer, the reaction to the stimulus of a deadline, an embryonic gesture of dedication. Anyhow, to come back to terra firma, I got the damn book out eventually.

At about the same time I was sending in accounts of our school sports to the *Dayton Herald*, a local afternoon paper. In an early one of these I wrote of the bad play of one of our linemen. One of his teammates told me of the grave hurt I had inflicted on him. This was my first inkling of the power of the press. It was a good lesson, for it told me the nature of that power. I had already observed that the power was not what it seemed: that papers did not always elect the political candidates they supported so diligently, and that the causes the press backed got nowhere without wide support from the public. The real power lay in the ability to hurt Mike Corrigen. Its reverse was also true: that the paper could elevate Mike, and others, to heights of public esteem beyond any merit of theirs.

I have pondered this all my life. Why do people seek mention, however ephemeral, in the newspaper — or today, on television? It is as if public mention increased their own stature, magnified their identity, gave them a power almost magical that they did not possess before. I don't, of course, mean people who, perforce or by choice, live their lives in public performance, politicians, entertainers, and athletes mostly. I mean ordinary people, like the ones whose heirs splurge on a big paid-for obituary. But the ways and means of public relations are mysterious and chancey. I early learned to be wary of those who thought they could command the public.

My thoughtless swipe at the hapless tackle did not deter me from continuing to write sports. It did make me more careful and woke me up to the difference between Mike Corrigen, playing for his school, and professional performers. My journalism gradually took me away from trying to play football, which I wildly wanted to do, to writing about it. I sadly accommodated to this. I realized, at about age fifteen, that I was still the same height and heft (five feet four, 126 pounds) that I had two years before, when I weighed in for football. By age thirteen I was big for my age, well advanced in puberty, had already a voice that rumbled like a bassoon, and was strong enough to bully smaller boys. Many of my mates in the junior division were four feet five eighty-pounders. But they grew around me like Jack's beanstalk while I stayed still.

I got my first tutelage in journalism from Jake Frong, the sports editor of the *Herald*. He was the first of the many kind seniors who helped me over the threshold of the profession. What a fine lot they were to me! I found out as I went along that many of them were anything but, drinkers of prohibition whiskey, frequenters of brothels, connoisseurs of lowlife. But to me they were as stalwart in virtue as bishops and as protective as police. I often chafed under this vigilance. It was not till I was out of college and, especially, into the U.S. Navy that I got any education in the streets. But even in the Navy my crews went out of their way to look after me. I have often felt that this treatment has kept me from being no better than I am at fixing things, the do-it-yourself syndrome I am so poor at. But still, I was born awkward and ill-made. I remember well what a good older athlete said to me when I was in my early teens: "You'll never make a boxer. Your arms are short and your weight is in your rear end. But you are pretty quick. Stay out of range till you can get close enough to hurt the other guy." A mechanic might have slipped me similar advice. I never learned to tie the Navy knots. I can't draw. I have always been a sloppy typist. I fall downstairs, off ladders, and on the ice. It has been for many years my unrealized ambition to wrap a present neatly.

All through my high-school years my mother nagged me into summer employment, as a magazine seller, a Fuller Brush man (boy), and a factory pieceworker. I hated all these, and finally took things into my own hand. With good clips and a good recommendation from Frong, I wrote the *Nashville Banner* for 1930 summer employment writing sports. I caught the department at the right time, adjustment after the departure of popular Ralph McGill for Atlanta, and reshaping under a youthful new editor, Fred Russell. I came to know McGill only much later, when, as a shining star of southern liberalism, Notre Dame gave him an honorary degree. Russell became, almost at once, a dear and lifelong friend, as loyal and generous to his friends as a man can be, and a journalism success far beyond the boundaries of Nashville.

Thus began a new chapter in my education, not for academic credit but more important to my intellectual development than any course. For also on the sports staff was the man who was to become my closest friend for the rest of his life, Robert West. We soon found we shared similar tastes in literature and much else; a college generation older, he quickened my pace into maturity. He also opened the door to the second university of my education, Vanderbilt. I took no courses at Vanderbilt, but I belong to it in love and loyalty almost as much as I do to my own beloved Alma Mater.

West was a Vanderbilt man of deepest dye. His father had studied medicine there, taught it, and took an almost proprietary interest in the progress of its School of Medicine. Doctor Olin West went early into civic medicine. He was a pioneer in fighting the dietary diseases which so plagued southerners of the early twentieth century, notably rickets. This brought him into prominence in medical politics, and he was chosen to be the general manager of the American Medical Association, with headquarters in Chicago. Both Bob and his younger brother Olin Jr. attended old Hyde Park High School there. But their hearts, like their father's, were tuned to Vanderbilt. Neither retained a single friend from high-school days and both flourished at Vanderbilt. Bob was a natural for a newspaper sports department. He had played on the Vanderbilt football squad and was a star high hurdler on the track team. His long and lean physique was ideal for the high hurdles and good for most anything; he was an excellent handball player and wrestler. Olin, more gregarious, ran their common fraternity, the Vandy chapter of Phi Delta Theta, and made Phi Beta Kappa in his junior year.

However, Bob was the more scholarly. In college he was miserable at math and science, which kept him off the Phi Beta Kappa turf, but a whiz in the humanities. I did not need him to take my mind off sports reporting and divert it to more intellectual matters. Although like most boys we both loved sports, I fear we both were something less than devoted to our work. I was especially derelict. I was faithful enough to the in-house duties and presided contentedly over the late afternoon sports pink-sheet edition, which did not go to bed till about 4:30 or 4:45 and kept me in the city room till then. But I did not do much legwork or dig up the local stories we so badly needed. Instead of the sandlot baseball diamonds, I headed to the Carnegie Library on my way home. West was better than I in the fields of his interest, football, tennis, and track, and the fourth member of our staff, Tom Anderson, was a minor genius at the bright ironic feature. But he, too, wayward and fitful, was no model staffer. I don't know how Russell, the only steady one of us, put up with the rest. Perhaps he knew we would drift elsewhere, West and I to academics, Anderson to do a daily column in Knoxville.

The West brothers introduced me to a friend of theirs, Francis Robinson, who followed me to the *Banner*. But not to the sports department — anything but. Robinson's sport was music. He guided me into a reaching out that has lasted all my life into that marvelous art.

Robinson covered music and theater for the *Banner*. He'd had some training in music, especially for his pleasant baritone singing voice. But he realized early on that he was no Tibbett (Lawrence Tibbett was the great American baritone of our youth), and settled for music journalism, like many another before and since. His little apartment on the Vanderbilt campus was crammed with phonograph records and theatrical memorabilia. Because of my late afternoon chore at the paper I was free at noon, and Francis let me play his records while he was at work. In the evenings we often gathered on his little front porch for music. How I learned! In that first summer at the *Banner* I absorbed musical taste and music literature as if through the pores of my skin.

The glory of the old phonograph repertory was the human voice, which, as the 1990 re-creations show, recorded almost as well in 1910 as it did in 1960. Robinson was an opera fan and had a choice collection of arias. He finally collected all the Caruso records there were, save one, and wrote a book about this great singer whom he never heard in the flesh. Olin West finally collected all the John McCormack records save one or two, and so I had wide access to the two greatest tenors of the early twentieth century. Gradually I began to form my own taste and began my own collection of vocals, to which both West and Robinson contributed handsomely. I recall especially that, many years later, Robinson found in Toronto a rare Frieda Hempel recording I'd been looking for. He sent it to me with a note reading, "Tosca, finalmente!"

Robinson took me to my first opera during the Christmas season following my first *Banner* summer. This was *Carmen*, at the old Ryman Auditorium in Nashville. It was the door to a lifetime's pleasure, my favorite comic book, my never-failing indoor sport. Here was one I could pursue from Notre Dame. The Chicago Opera of the late 1930s was, except for some star singers, scarcely any better than the San Carlo company I heard in Nashville. But you could get a gallery seat in the big almost new Wacker Drive house for very little money, and from there I could see the stage clearly and hear a whisper from a well-focused voice. The overall performances in the tattered and dusty sets of the great old Chicago company of the 1920s, the band a gaggle of pickups and the conducting often of beer garden quality, could be sad, but singers like Frida Leider, Friedrich Schorr, Lauritz Melchior, and Lotte Lehmann could make up for everything. Not until the great early days of the present company in the 1950s, with Callas, Gobbi, Vickers, Ludwig, Nilsson, Tebaldi, Schwartzkopf, and Seefried, plus the greatest conductor of Italian opera I ever heard, Tulio Serafin, did I hear their match.

Before long Robinson himself reached out, to New York, where he was clearly destined to go. One of the ablest press agents and managers of the day, William Fields, lured him to work for his firm, and in a very short time Francis was more partner than employee, as he was with all his employers. One of Fields's premier clients was Katharine Cornell, the first lady of the American stage in the 1930s. Robinson took over for a tour with her, and before long became indispensable to her. She paid him the year round whether she had a show going or not. Opera came for Robinson just after World War II when Sol Hurok hired him to help with the Metropolitan Opera's annual tours, which Hurok managed for some years. Soon Robinson joined the Met full time as an assistant manager.

Robinson's new career was wonderful for me. From 1948 to 1978 I missed very few new productions at the Met and even fewer at the Chicago Lyric. Francis introduced me to his good friend the Chicago critic Claudia Cassidy, and we became firm and lasting friends, a delightful connection which has lasted till this day. I frequently sat with her at performances and often had her tickets for repeats she didn't want to attend. We went together to the summer performances at Ravinia and to theatrical performances as well, many of which had as their press representative our good friend Gertrude Bromberg. Later on I became the good friend of another music journalist, Mary Jane Philips-Matz. Thus, for me, journalism and music became fused, to a considerable extent, since I gradually introduced Robinson to my Notre Dame music circle, Fathers Carl Hager and Howard Kenna, and Professors Fred Pike and Richard Kilmer, our "Mozart & Gin" Society. Robinson's kindness and generosity extended to them as well as to me.

All who shared in that generosity rejoiced when Francis became, at the end of his career, a celebrity himself as the host of the live Met performances on television. He also became a frequent performer on radio, a nonsinging actor in opera, and a trustee of Vanderbilt University, where his music and theater memorabilia are now housed.

Earlier I wrote of my introduction to the Chicago theater. Since I also acted in the Notre Dame University Theater and from time to time wrote lyrics and libretti for small-bore stage production elsewhere, it was natural for me to get to know critics and journalists of the arts. For years I hovered on the fringes of theater and especially music, as well as dance. Perhaps the most thrilling single evening I ever had in the theater was at my first performance of the old deBasil Ballet Russe de Monte Carlo, probably in 1933. I became a fan from that evening on, and my pleasure in the productions and their dancers rivaled that I derived from my favorite Italian operas. When, after World War II, Georges Balanchine revivified the art, I went when I could, often again with Claudia Cassidy, who loved the dance above all the arts.

But the fringes were close enough for me. I was when young tempted to a career in the arts; managing artists is close akin to journalism, and I knew several managers through Robinson. But the closer I came to backstage, the more I backed away. I am in daily living, an orderly person; I have to be, because my mind is so disorderly and my awkwardness so omnipresent. So far as my daily routine goes I like to be conventional, up at seven, lunch at one, dinner at the other seven, bed at eleven. A life in the theater is the most disorderly of lives — not, be it noted, in the film and TV studios, with which I have only a very slight acquaintance. But the lack of rhythm in the theatrical world, the furious activity of launching a play or new production, the ennui of a long run, the eternal bickering of temperamental stars and their ambitious underlings, the endless rehearsals, appalled me as I got to see them. The undeniable satisfactions of a successful opening did not, for me, as it did for the professionals, make up for the trials. I keep gratefully returning to teaching, where there's a new production every class meeting, a new cast twice a year, and where the risks are more calculable.

The second aspect of my reaching out in Nashville was my getting to know many of the circle of poets, critics, and fiction writers centered on Vanderbilt. This had begun about the time of World War I and flourished in the 1920s. The group, known as the Agrarians, included John Crowe Ransom, Donald Davidson, Allen Tate, and Robert Penn Warren and later on added Andrew Lytle and John Donald Wade. I came to know all these except Warren fairly well, even eventually including a visit with its founder, Sidney Mttron Hirsch. The creative energy of this group extended to many younger writers. It continues to this day. It was very important to me. Its manifesto, *I'll Take My Stand*, appeared in my college freshman year. I devoured it.

I wrote in an earlier chapter of agrarianism as my youthful radicalism, rather than communism or New Dealism. As such, it is immensely more important to my intellectual development than music, of course, and though I call it radicalism, it might better be labeled a substitute for radicalism. If taken literally, agrarianism in the twentieth century is indeed radical, that is, "rooting" up industrial civilization and living subsistence-style on the farm. My friend Conn West, Robert's wife, used to maintain that true agrarianism would advocate ploughing up the roads, and she's right. But nobody took the Nashville agrarianism to be that. Some Notre Dame people, and many others in the East and Midwest, became literal agrarians, acquired land and worked it. But the Nashville thinkers attacked, not so much the actual machinery of industrialism, but the kind of materialistic thinking machinery induced and faith in unlimited progress and reason as the ultimate solver of all the ills of the world.

I was not aware till decades later how much the Scopes trial in Dayton, Tennessee, over the teaching of evolution in the state schools, inspired the agrarians. The gibes at the South and its mind by H. L. Mencken and the smart easterners set southern teeth on edge, and in some sense the southern literary renaissance is an answer to Mencken's charge that the South had no literature. What Mencken and his crowd failed to see was that the trial, whatever its outcome, set the teaching, and to some extent the research, of evolution back at least a generation in parts of the United States. School administration and textbook makers simply avoided the subject for fear of the courts.

Notre Dame's Father Zahm had long before this found evolution compatible with Catholic theology, so I had no trouble with this controversy. But my Catholicism added a new dimension to my sympathy with agrarian ideals. I began to think, as I still do, that a combination of southern style and sensibility, with Catholic doctrine and discipline, was the best way of life possible to us.

Other agrarians began to think the same. Allen and Caroline Tate were received into the Church, along with their and my good friends Brainard and Frances Cheney, a little later. Donald

Davidson, like his good and my great friend John Frederick never became formal Catholics but were deeply sympathetic to Catholic ideals. John Ransom, whom I never knew well, seemed to me to edge away from the religion of his forefathers as he grew older. However, I think he did retain a respect for religion, as did most of the other members of the Nashville group, John Donald Wade, Andrew Lytle, Clarence Nixon, John Gould Fletcher, Stark Young, Robert Penn Warren, perhaps others.

So, reaching out for me became at this point a reaching back, back to my roots in the Catholic religion, back to southern agrarianism and its profound troubles, back to what endures beyond and above modern technology. This came to a climax for me in my friendship with Flannery O'Connor. Reactionary radicalism, maybe.

I first met some of my Nashville agrarians in the North. It was my good friend and colleague John Frederick Nims and his wife Bonnie who introduced me to Allen and Caroline Tate. And it was my good friend and colleague Robert Fitzgerald who introduced me to Flannery O'Connor. I incline now to think Tate the best of the Nashville group, in both verse and criticism. Fitzgerald was no southerner. He had left *Time* magazine to devote himself to writing poetry and translating Homer and later on Vergil. He and his family were living in Italy when Allen Tate backed out of an agreement to come to Notre Dame as a visiting professor in 1957 — typical Tate. We hired Robert instead. He and I became good friends. It was he who brought Flannery to Notre Dame for a lecture, and she and I became close friends almost at once. She visited me in South Bend a couple of times, and I visited her at her mother's family's historic old farmhouse, "Andalusia," near Milledgeville. My close friends the Robert Wests had settled in Athens, Georgia, at the state university there. Milledgeville was close by, so I combined visits to both places for the several years of my friendship with Flannery. The Wests also became friends and admirers of Flannery, and Marion and Dot Montgomery, also of the Georgia English faculty, rounded off our little circle.

I had grown up in a very religious home, very conscious of my two uncle bishops and other relations who were priests and nuns. I am more Catholic than anything else, though I am also a southerner. Flannery and I were both cradle Catholics, rare in the South. She knew some of the Agrarians, notably Caroline Gordon, whose literary advice she cherished, and Andrew Lytle, who taught her at Iowa and later published some of her works in the *Sewanee Review*, which he edited for several years.

As I came to know Flannery I began to see Catholicism a little as she did, as all or nothing. I never pretended to the depth of her spirituality. But I caught on a little. In Flannery my southern-ness, my agrarian connections, and my Catholicism all merged. I was as easy with her as a biddable child. I cherish the collection of her letters, to which I contributed a few of mine. Well edited by Sally Fitzgerald, they bring out Flannery's personality clearly.

Early on in our acquaintance Flannery told me about her inherited lupus, and I realized she was almost certainly doomed to an early death. When I went to her funeral in Milledgeville in 1964, her mother told me it had been a wish of her last illness that I be her literary executor in case Robert and Sally Fitzgerald, because of their residence abroad, did not wish to serve. Thank God they did wish to. Greatly to my astonishment it has turned out to be nearly a full-time job, one I am wholly unsuited for. Shortly after Flannery's funeral I presided over my mother's. The main influence of my childhood thus came to merge with a major one of my maturity.

I have often wondered at the enduring southern-ness of my character. And for that matter, the enduring southern culture itself. For, in my opinion, there is still a distinctly southern strain left in the South. Many observers have denied it, maintaining that television and other modern technologies have leached the vitality out of the old breed and made the South indistinguishable from the Midwest. I don't think so. I rather think that the new southerners, who have moved south since World War II (always excepting Florida, of course) are more likely to be converted to the old southern manners and attitudes than the other way around. It's true that the great homes which so fill southern literature are gone—although my experience was enriched by "Glen Leven," Conn West's ancestral home, Flannery's old farmhouse, and the Cheneys' "Idler's Retreat." But in spite of the monotonous subdivisions on the farmlands of the old mansions, something of their spirit survives. The work of the southern writers is full of it, from Faulkner and the Tates on down to Walker Percy and William Styron.

The Agrarians didn't have and mostly didn't want a coherent political program. Like the English distributists, whom they resembled, they wished to influence the conduct of public life without rearranging it. Some were deep into politics — Brainard Cheney notably, active enough to be cited as a sage in V. O. Key's seminal study of southern politics. So, I can't trace my own interest in practical politics to them. Perhaps some to Don K. Price.

Price, like myself, started in journalism in Nashville and ended up in academe. A Vanderbilt undergraduate and a Rhodes scholar, Price came back from England determined on a career in public service. Politics was a passion with Price, as it had been with his mentor, Louis Brownlow. It's the title of Brownie's autobiography. This remarkable man served his apprenticeship on Nashville newspapers, where he also used to pay some court to one of my aunts. He then went on to a highly useful and somewhat self-effacing career in public administration. Price joined him in the Public Administration Clearing House, then went to the Ford Foundation, and finally to the deanship of the Harvard Graduate School of Public Administration.

I saw much of Price while he was at the Clearing House, whose headquarters were in Chicago. I don't know that his influence had anything to do with my own interest in practical politics, but they are too coincidental to pass over. When, just after World War II, I returned to Notre Dame as chair of the journalism department, I returned to two close South Bend friendships. One was with W. R. Walton, Bob to his enormous circle of friends, who had hired me to do part-time reporting for the *South Bend Tribune* in my student days and was now managing editor of the paper. Another was with John A. Scott, the first and best of my student secretaries, who had returned to South Bend after a distinguished wartime career with the Marines and was working in the city school administration. Walton half-jokingly said one day to Scott, "Why don't you run for Mayor? Your war record will be a big asset in the race." Scott did and was elected by a narrow margin in 1951.

I became a member of Scott's kitchen cabinet and our association became close once again, after the long hiatus of the war years. I tried to run him for governor — he would have made a good one — but failed dismally. Scott was a Republican in a normally Democratic district, so his support was slender even in his homeland. It has long been almost impossible to get support for a candidate from northern Indiana in the traditional Republican strongholds further south in the state. So am I Republican in local politics; the two best mayors we've had since World War II have been Republicans, Scott and Lloyd Allen. However, temperamentally I incline to be independent, supporting those who seem to me the best candidates whatever the party affiliation. That attitude will get you nowhere in American politics unless you are Dwight D. Eisenhower.

This knowledge did not quench my fascination with politics. It is without doubt the greatest game in the world; no sport comes close. In possible permutations and possibilities, chess is way behind, and only automobile racing (which I used to be addicted to) comes close in risk. My journalism connections made me a sometimes privileged spectator after Scott became himself a newspaper executive, going on to a distinguished career in the Gannett chain. In fact my next venture into politics was in the newspaper world of the American Society of Newspaper Editors, in which we journalism deans were honorary members. I tried to get Bob Walton's successor at the *South Bend Tribune*, Paul Neville, then the managing editor of the *Buffalo Evening News*, elected to the board of the association but once again met with failure, though this time by a very narrow margin.

I was very close to Neville and even closer to his successor in South Bend, my former student John J. Powers, as befits a journalism teacher in his home city. But I was lucky in having Franklin D. Schurz as owner of my local paper. However, I found my friends in the ASNE uniformly high-minded, or very nearly so. Newspaper people at the local level, the editors and their staffs, are in my experience admirable people, genuinely desirous of the public good, intelligent, sensible, clever, and amusing. Not so the publicized stars: they are like all other stars, arrogant and egotistical, taken as a lot.

My interest in politics in the 1950s and my professional interest in journalism led me to become a citizen of South Bend as

well as a Notre Damer of pure faith. I'd always liked the city.
It's the right size for a university of Notre Dame's dimension,
big enough to get lost in yet small enough to find your way
in. I used to think it too far removed from the life of the mind,
but association with some other university towns whose citizens take a proprietary view of the academic enterprise in their
midst has led me to think we're lucky. But I like to know where I
am. When Ivo Thomas, the interesting English Dominican who
taught math at Notre Dame in the 1960s, first came here, he
early sought me out. "I understand," he said, "that you know
the route LaSalle took on his pioneering trip through this area in
the late seventeenth century." I did know the route, or as much
of it as can be worked out since the draining of the marshes
through which LaSalle made his way to the St. Joseph River,
and happily took Ivo over as much of it as we could manage in
a pleasant afternoon. Most English know their local history; few
Americans do. Southerners do, but theirs is a family interest —
the history is incidental. Until World War II there was very little
immigration into the South, and most everybody was ticketed
by family. As the Virginia lady said about Whistler's mother,
"I don't understand what all the fuss is about. She was only a
MacNeill from South Carolina." Or, as my own mother used to
say of recent arrivals, with an air of dismissal, "Oh, they came
from away from here."

It was family that led me reach back into my tribal history
after my formal retirement from the Notre Dame faculty — formal, because I have since taught now and then, when asked.
I had for some time been feeling that I ought to write some
family history, history that I probably knew better than anyone
else. After all, having two uncles who were bishops, especially
on both sides of my family, was a mite unusual, to say the
least, and they and their mentors were very interesting people. So, in my first year of retirement, 1977, I stayed long in
my native Nashville researching there, and in Memphis and
Arkansas, the lives and works of the Stritch, Morris, and Farrelly families. That's three bishops. Farrelly was no kin but
might as well have been. He, too, was a bishop, but it was
as a priest that he took my uncle John, later the bishop of
Little Rock, under his wing, and later on, as bishop of Cleveland, Ohio, became the great friend and older adviser to my

Uncle Sam, the bishop of Toledo, Ohio, consecrated the year Farrelly died.

I wrote all this up in a long article entitled "Three Catholic Bishops from Tennessee," which was featured with a cover photograph of the old Nashville Catholic cathedral in the spring 1978 issue of the *Tennessee Historical Review*. This done, I returned to South Bend and occasional teaching. But it was that article which led the present bishop of Nashville to commission me to write the history of the Catholic Church in Tennessee for the 1987 sesquicentennial of the Diocese of Nashville. So, beginning in 1983, I spent at first about half my time, then in 1985 all of it, in Tennessee, writing and publishing the book. It is more journalism than history, but the historical parts are sound without being as deep as they might.

Reaching back indeed. I made a shoal of new friends among the staff of the Nashville diocesan offices and also among the historians of the state of Tennessee. But mainly the book deepened my love and respect for my ancestors in and out of religion and my admiration for the Catholics of Tennessee. These, mostly of Irish and German extraction, with some Italians coming along later swiftly adopted southern points of view along with the accent.

I have always been fond of history; journalism is history writ small. Notre Dame has long been conscious of its academic mission to preserve and encourage the history of American Catholicism. Two of my closest present faculty friends, Father Marvin O'Connell and Philip Gleason, have contributed with style and scholarship to this enterprise. Our American historians were stimulated by the addition to our faculty of the great historian of English Catholicism, Monsignor Philip Hughes, who became a close friend. Another dear friend, Fred Pike, has recently written of the history of the Latin American Church, amid a glittering array of other publications on Latin America; he and I collaborated on one such book during my editorship of the *Review of Politics*.

Editing the *Review* brought me unexpected rewards. In some ways it was like getting to know the guest lecturers I brought to my modern culture classes. I came to know many Notre Dame professors who reviewed books for me and even more usefully read and criticized the manuscripts submitted for publication.

Correspondence with the authors of these from other universities brought new interests. I especially enjoyed meeting these authors and prospective authors on the trips I took for that purpose. Everywhere I was welcomed with the courtesy toward their fellow workers which is the hallmark of American academia. I became convinced that the *Review* was the best service to the outside academic world in the humanities Notre Dame had.

Travel is reaching out in its most literal sense. I am very grateful I was able to go when the going was good. My first visit to Europe was a long one, over two years in Mediterranean ports with the U.S. Navy. Twice in my life I have been so fed up with what I was doing I would have happily taken a job as a mailman — anything. The second of these I describe in my next chapter. The first came in 1941.

It wasn't that I was tired of teaching, or South Bend, or had any difficulty in daily life. It was, I now think, simply a youthful desire to reach out, go away, do something different for a while. Thus when a former student of mine, Leo Buchignani, tore down the steps to my Lyons Hall Annex room to tell me about Pearl Harbor, I knew my deliverance was at hand. At once I began to look into how and where. Once again journalism came to my rescue. I never thought of any branch other than the Navy and was given an officer's commission to do naval public relations work by the time 1941 turned into 1942.

World War II was for me a time of excitement, interest, change, growth. I began with a happy summer at the Great Lakes Naval Training Station just north of Chicago, where I made a raft of new friends who lasted till I firmly wrote finis to my Chicago life when my uncle died in 1958. The summer of 1942 was golden. The war was popular; if I went to a Chicago restaurant in uniform I rarely had to pay the check. The way of life the uniform bespoke was no wrenching experience for me; I had been living barracks-style for nearly twenty years of boarding school and teaching. I had no idea of staying at Great Lakes beyond what I thought a decent duty to my reason for being commissioned, and by fall I had wangled my way into active service. This was in the new amphibious forces, which I chose because they were new.

I was firmly resolved not to do anything in the Navy that echoed what I had previously done. Throughout my time in training and overseas I stayed rigorously away from teaching and journalism. I was so fearful I would be tapped for teaching at Princeton, where I trained for the amphibious force, that I deliberately did poorly in the courses. When, toward the end of my time there, I went to see the commanding officer to intercede for a stateside post for my friend Bernard Muller-Thyme, a professor of philosophy who had blundered into the Navy as he did into everything else, the skipper, a very decent fellow, after telling me he'd do what he could for Muller-Thyme added that his staff had regretfully given up on me. I have rarely felt so relieved. The thought of spending the war at Princeton, which I loved, revolted me utterly. I wanted to get into the fighting. Incidentally, Muller-Thyme was spared for his wife and babies.

I trained in Chesapeake Bay the bitter winter of 1942–43 and by spring was languishing in the Brooklyn Navy Yard with my crew for our LCT (Landing Craft Tanks, to you), waiting for transportation to the Mediterranean, where the European war then was. This happened so swiftly I had no time to prepare. We were confined to quarters in the Navy Yard, but I was able to telephone my good friend Tom Walsh at Scribner's to bring me some books. He chose them wisely, classics that lasted me throughout the war. I especially recall finishing *War and Peace* one day, and immediately starting it again from the beginning.

I was right about the Amphibious Force. The regular Navy people knew little of use about it and so left it to us reservists to work out our salvation. This was at first great fun for me; one of my British friends in landing craft once said that handling a landing craft was like working a hunting dog. But after a year or so of participation in the invasions of Sicily and southern Italy I wearied of the long winter of inactivity and transferred to the shore and staff duty where I had really belonged in the first place. Bossing a landing craft is very like being a farmer. In both cases the land and sea, as objects of love or hatred, are unimportant. The main talent required is that of a mechanic, and that was distinctly not my line. I was in any case acquiring more rank than my job called for. Commanding an LCT is a young ensign's job. My two stripes were more suited to LSTs, Landing Ships Tanks, but I'd had no experience of them.

I learned nothing in the Navy of use to my academic career. I hadn't the slightest trouble handling the crew; my college teaching helped me with that. I still think of them with affection. The man best suited to command the ship was my cook, Henry Bosworth, the closest approach to Robinson Crusoe I ever knew. Henry could make, or make do with, most anything. Once, when we were out of soap, he made some of that. But like all good cooks Henry was rather temperamental, and I wonder whether he could handle the crew. He certainly could handle the ship. But the entire war experience was for me simply the big change I yearned for, the great adventure of my life tinged with a touch of romance. Had I stayed at Princeton, or wangled some stateside job where my talents could be better employed, I would have contributed far more to our war effort. But I could not have borne it. Like Stendahl's Julian Sorel, I just had to go to the war.

My war experience certainly changed me for the better. I became more confident, more sophisticated, better educated. Travel, even wartime travel, does indeed broaden those ready for it. College students love to travel, but they aren't ready for it. Most of them enjoy meeting new people, but they meet them as they meet their classmates at college. They learn new names for old things, as they do learning the foreign language most young people now master — a resounding change from a generation ago, when most collegians dutifully studied a foreign tongue but came out of it with only a few phrases. But the young aren't ready for the museums, the architecture, the monuments of antiquity, and the literature that spells out the true cultural differences. War travel started me on a quarter century of travel, both here and abroad. I think I was ready for it and only wish I had done more; I missed Japan and the Middle East.

My traveling days are done, I fear. I have no desire to go to any place which may be strenuous or uncomfortable, little hardships I once enjoyed. Little, be it noted. I am speaking of a snowstorm overtaking my companion, dear Elizabeth Starr, and myself in our Volkswagen and our trepidation making our solitary way through the mountains north of Sparta. And then, presto! The sun upon a snowless Olympia. I am thinking of being the outside rider going over the Grand Corniche road outside Monte Carlo, and my acrophobia rising like an ugly passion. Strange, that this acrophobia doesn't trouble me in aircraft, thank goodness, but it has atop the Empire State, Sears, and most of all the huge big bridges, like the one my friend Joe Herrington finally sweated driving me over the Firth of Forth. And I hate to think of the inevitable digestive difficulties which always accompany me on strenuous travel; they were a steady minor curse during my sea time in the war.

But there are kinder things that sweeten my memories. Automobile trips (before I had a car) with Tom Madden and Bowyer Campbell, fellow dons at Notre Dame, genial traveling companions. A long trip to the West Coast with my sister Kate, and my happy summer stay at the University of Portland. The return trip to Notre Dame with Fathers Kenna and Hager, and many, many short trips with them, and alternately with Fred Pike, Dick Kilmer, and Sal Asselta, to the Chicago opera or symphony, with dinner at the two best restaurants of my life, the old Henrici's on Randolph and the old Corona on Grand, both in Chicago. I took many trips by car with the Robert Wests. He was the best chauffeur of my long experience, since I prefer to ride rather than drive — very reasonably, say my friends. My first civilian trip abroad, and my most recent one in this country, were with that best of traveling companions, Gene Sullivan. He and his charming wife, Marilyn, have been my comfort and my joy from the days when Gene roomed next to me in Howard Hall, 1930.

I don't regard my shuttling back and forth to Nashville as travel, exactly. These days I like to get Nashville students to drive my car there while I take to the air. Nor do I think of my early and frequent visits to the delightful home of Elizabeth and Robert McGaw there as visits, any more than a ten-year-old thinks popping in and out of his best friend's neighboring home as visits. These are the stuff of life, life at its best, savoring of community, rootedness, good habits, and reassuring traditions. Nashville is filled with all these for me.

But the most meaningful, as well as the most satisfactory, of all my friendships were with my colleagues in the Department of Journalism, and my friends in the other departments who supported my work. To these I now turn.

12

HEAD, DEPARTMENT
OF JOURNALISM

That's what I was, for nearly twenty-five years, from 1946 to 1970. That's a big chunk of a person's maturity. If you think of your life as one you'd like to be useful to society and satisfactory to your own ideals, a quarter of a century should provide a fair sample. A look at my tenure as chair of journalism interests me especially because it came out of nothing, flourished its little time, and has now sunk back into nothing. That is, there is little or nothing in the history of journalism education that suggested it and now there is little trace of it in the Notre Dame curriculum. In addition, it provides a look into a teacher's life in the 1950s and 60s. That, too, has changed beyond recognition. I am like the iguana and the ginkgo tree, a relict of a time which has disappeared into the moving scenes of evolution.

Toward the end of World War II, while I was still in the Navy, I began to feel disinclined to go back to teaching freshman English at Notre Dame. I wanted to do something different. When therefore I got word in Richmond, Virginia, where I was in charge of a Navy V–12 training unit, that the longtime head of Notre Dame's journalism department, John Michael Cooney, had died, I saw an opportunity to do something new. This was in 1945. I was thirty-two years old. I applied for Doctor Cooney's former position and got back the answer I expected from Notre Dame: until the war is over we're in limbo. When it's over and the university returns to normal, we'll decide.

When Father Howard Kenna, then the director of studies, told me the job was mine, in the spring of 1946, I had long since decided what I would do. The first thing was easy: engage Jim

Withey to teach writing. The second was harder: find someone to teach journalism skills the way I wanted. The third was revolutionary.

I had avoided journalism courses in my student days because I thought I had learned from experience on the job what they taught. I further thought they dispensed an overdose of journalism skills. I wanted enough of these to get the student through the front door, so to speak. And I wanted them tied to their roots in liberal education: writing to the good writing of our time, design, photography, and layout to their roots in the visual arts. Above all, I wanted to avoid teaching the tricks of the trade.

Even in my limited experience I had learned the truth of H. L. Mencken's criticism of American journalism of the 1920s: "The majority of newspapermen in almost every American city are ignoramuses, and proud of it. All the knowledge they pack into their brains is, in every reasonable cultural sense, useless; it is the sort of knowledge that belongs, not to a professional man, but to a police captain, a railway mail clerk or a board boy in a brokerage house."

I had seen enough of this. It was what was taught in many schools and departments of journalism: how to steal a photograph, how to shock a bereaved woman into an interview, how to deal with a blustering politician, the voting records of every precinct in the city, a speaking acquaintance with every minor grifter and madam in town. Good schools of journalism looked upon this with the same contempt that I did, but particularly in Catholic places there was still lots of it. When a school felt it needed some work in journalism, it tended to choose a well-known local reporter, who usually had no more idea of education than a newsboy.

It was this sort of thing that gave journalism education a bad name. Yet, as with college courses in education, which had the same sort of bad name, I thought both enterprises worthwhile. Both need, far more than the traditional disciplines, intelligent teaching. No matter how poor a teacher of Greek is, something of the language's splendor may seep into the course. But a journalism teacher who teaches nothing but the tricks of sensationalism or the simple facts of typography scarcely scratches the surface of his students' intelligence.

But—dismiss the entire venture, as desired by most traditional academicians? Ignore the importance of the media in contemporary life? Banish training in communication just when democracy most needs it? Turn the operation over to the trash merchants? These I thought more contemptible than the many failures of journalism education. And I thought part of the remedy might be to add a dimension of intellectual life to journalism education. The trouble with skills courses is that they are not intellectual by nature. I thought to curtail the number of those courses and add the revolutionary part, courses in modern culture, the life around us, which ought, it seemed to me, to be the intellectual side of education for journalism.

So, I set out to try to give budding journalists some sense of their own American culture, just then beginning to inundate the rest of the world, plus some feeling for the visual arts, and finally some idea of what was going on in postwar Europe and the restive colonial world. In the prewar university I had left for the Navy, there was very little that was contemporary, and even less confrontation of the central issues of our times. I noted earlier that in my own college days I never heard any serious discussion of Marx. But I don't recall hearing, in the classroom, of Proust either, or of Cezanne, or Stravinsky, or Waugh. Or, in humanities courses, of the new atomic scientists, Max Planck, Werner Heisenberg, or Niels Bohr. We had all heard of Einstein and Madame Curie, of course, because they were the subjects of newspaper features which made little attempt to explain their importance. But even in journalism there seldom was heard any discussion of the seminal American thinkers in other than political fields, such as Willard Gibbs, William Graham Sumner, John Dewey, C. S. Peirce.

What did we study? Texts, mostly. These are by nature coolly academic, inviting neither agreement nor disagreement. Nor, above all, involvement. The classroom text must not offend, must not take sides, must not arouse. Some of our texts were better than others, and these were usually rather controversial also. But most were prim, dull, and unimpressive. I can name a dozen books that influenced my emotional life or changed my thinking, but not a single text.

My idea for educating the journalist's intellect had something in common with the Great Books Programs just then getting up a full head of steam. But the differences were marked. I've always thought it a flaw in the Great Books approach that it does not emphasize writing. Nor does it have the contemporaneity I wanted for journalism. Still, we both worked at texts we thought important, and that's kinship. And I certainly admired and liked Otto Bird, who inaugurated the Notre Dame program, and his staff.

The anthologies we used in class were very good. In prep school as well as college I thumbed through mine a great deal, learning especially lyric poems and reading the short stories and excerpts. But they seldom had anything substantial. I genuinely missed *Paradise Lost* (all of it!), *Don Quixote* (all of it!), and *The Divine Comedy* (well, not quite all of it). Going through such heft is, I think, one of the best things about the Great Books Programs. We were all helped very much by the cheap editions of the classics published by Modern Library. But the main enemy of the study of real books rather than texts was simply the stodgy old tradition of American schooling. It took a long time to break away from it.

I began my break with a careful study of *The Revolt of the Masses*, by Ortega y Gasset, the Spanish philosopher. It was a good choice; the book holds up well after more than fifty years. Dated by the discovery and use of nuclear energy is *Technics and Civilization* by Lewis Mumford, but it was excellent for the 1950s, as was Ken Galbraith's *American Capitalism*. *The Communist Manifesto* was a great success with students, *The Education of Henry Adams* a flop with them. Not my fault: I still read the book with pleasure. We read some fiction, saw some films, went to see the art and architecture of Chicago, and heard a good many guest lecturers. I wrote and distributed copious notes about everything from feudalism to federalism. And the students wrote and wrote and wrote.

This sampling doesn't sound revolutionary, does it? On the contrary, it sounds, in 1990, old-fashioned, "the canon" so despised by today's radical professors. All the goals of my little "revolution" have long since been absorbed into the college curricula and pushed way beyond anything I ever envisioned. Much too far beyond, in my opinion. I wanted to explore with my students good books, not the cryptic illiteracies of France's new Dada-ism. I wanted to study the cultures of the North

American Indians, not their little shards of literature. Am I wrong to prefer Faulkner to Toni Morrison? Matthew Arnold to Harold Bloom? The wheel has come full circle. A sizable portion of university faculties in the humanities have abandoned the books that have survived critical estimate and the judgment of intelligent and cultivated people. The critics who deplore the ignorance of our students have the wrong targets. It's the faculties who have abandoned the good and the true to the whims of the fashionable illiterate.

The Notre Dame faculty that helped me with my courses in modern culture was of a happier breed. They knew what the students needed. Bill Shanahan made ideas like *liberalism* and *Junkerism* intelligible to them. Ernie Sandeen did the same for *romanticism*. Aaron Abell made clear the virtues of American pluralism and federalism. Willis Nutting dealt with Lord Acton and his circle, Frank O'Malley with some modern literature. Al Hermens was eloquent on his favorite subject of the dangers to democracy. John Frederick broke new ground for me and the students on the influence of the American land and climate on our history. But it was the generous unselfishness of these dear friends that led me gradually to call on them less and less. There was no way I could pay them, and I was embarrassed to add to their burdens. They taught me as well as the students, and I gradually took over the courses myself. Further, as foreign affairs in the 1960s became more and more muddled and I myself less and less in sympathy with our government's policies, I concentrated increasingly on American Studies and so brought this rather new concept to Notre Dame.

The idea of a concentration in American Studies had some pre–World War II history; it was a graduate program at Harvard as early as the mid-1930s. I became greatly taken with the idea largely through my friend John Frederick, who pioneered in studies in American social thought as seen through literature. His Northwestern colleague Baker Brownell was doing the same sort of thing, writing about native American architecture and art. An early book then called *Made in America* by Columbia's Professor John Kouwenhoven (it is still in print as *The Arts in American Civilization*) just about clinched the matter for me. And, of course, my interest in the southern agrarians and the problems of the South generally whetted my study of the larger picture of American civilization.

However, the most basic reason for the general interest in American Studies was the war. During it, and just after, scholars and thinkers and politicians and journalists all began thinking and writing about our war aims, the goals of peace, the meaning of *American*, and above all the national character. There were still many followers of him *Fortune* called "The Lord High Keeper of leftist illusions, Harold Laski" and his ilk, but more took the turn toward studying the country and its institutions. A spate of books of excellent quality on the presidency, the political campaigns, democracy, capitalism, and especially various aspects of American social history became almost the center of intellectual interest. Even the Marxists moved away from economics and historical determinism to cultural criticism; Herbert Marcuse replaced Harold Laski as guru. The universities followed suit, and programs in American Studies began to spring up all over the place, especially in the Northeast and Midwest.

I was lucky to have so many veterans as my first students in these courses. Their eager intelligence, pent up for so long in barracks and cockpits, loved the material, and their maturity glossed over my deficiencies. From 1946 to 1960 was a wonderful time for me, a time in which I seemed to have enough energy to develop new courses, administer the department, work with art and music programs, and spend most weekends in Chicago. This was the change I yearned for in my Navy days. Jim Withey was teaching writing with his old skill, and I could keep an eye on his shaky health. My own courses in modern culture seemed what the students wanted, and their enthusiasm gave me extra strength. They absorbed all the new paths I tried to open to them. Even though I had only prints to use—our slides were few and dim—they fell with eager interest on my introduction to the study of modern painting and architecture. With equal zest they worked on contemporary problems: Robert Dahl on democracy, R. M. Carew-Hunt on Marxism, Pendleton Herring on the way our government works, deTocqueville on the fascinating fact that it has always worked that way, even John Stuart Mill and Lord Acton on that eternal problem of humankind: freedom. We skipped merrily from history to political science to art to literature to

technics and back: I believe mine was one of the first interdisci-
plinary programs at Notre Dame. I stayed away from theology
and philosophy because I thought our curriculum already over-
loaded with them. But we tried much else, from cosmology
to comics.

No one could be more aware than I of the dangers of such
freewheeling. The curse of American Studies is that they fall
so easily into the trivial, the commonplace, the vulgar, and
the special interests. I wanted to steer carefully among these
shoals, always working at student papers to drive home ideas:
why does Ortega call ours a "self-satisfied age"? What does
Langer mean by "virtual"? In no more than two carefully win-
nowed pages try to summarize Herring's idea of government
as a pressure-chamber. And so on.

I was lucky to find in Edward Fischer the ideal teacher of the
skills courses. Fischer saw my goals more clearly than I did. He
taught the students how to relate makeup to fine art and how to
put the techniques of journalism at the service of good writing
of any kind. He had a great classroom presence, modest and low
key, yet still authoritative. I rejoiced in his taste, his cooperation, his penetrating intelligence and delightful companionship.
With Jim Withey the three of us made a good journalism troika.
Neither Withey nor Fischer showed the slightest interest in or
aptitude for administration, so that was left to me.

I did not find administration onerous. In the halcyon days
right after the war, there was scarcely any bureaucracy at Notre
Dame. We department heads were left pretty much to ourselves
to devise curricula, set up requirements, and even, within narrow limits, to hire and fire. My own teaching methods had
always included much personal contact with students and until we were overwhelmed with numbers I knew them all. With
them my new program was a resounding success. In fact, success did us, me especially, a lot of harm. I did not know how to
check the rising tide of students in a department I had devised
for twenty-five juniors and twenty-five seniors. I was at a loss as
to how to scare off the indolent and the vulgar from a program
with so much appeal to them. For a time mine was the second
largest major subject in the college, which was way out of line.
The problems of success, I found, though more gratifying, are
just as bad as those of failure.

But for the first years, between 1946 and 1960, I rejoiced in what we were doing—although I didn't think about it much. I had decided twice, once after I'd been teaching for a couple of years and again after returning to it for a couple after the war, that teaching was the life for me and teaching at Notre Dame its best setting. And when I started, in 1935, making fifty dollars a week was good pay, if one could supplement it a bit in the unpaid summer months. After the war American prosperity made the supplement almost necessary, though once again I didn't do as much fee work as I should have.

Jim Withey used to say that unless you saw teaching as a form of charity you shouldn't do it. I heartily agreed with this and understood that the charity also extended to the institution. Unless you loved Notre Dame, I felt, you shouldn't teach here. I was always taken aback by the teachers who lived on their resentments, eternally griping about administration and pay and such like. In the 1950s you could get a job, teaching or otherwise, quite easily, and I used to think, love it or leave it. I loved it and left it not.

I think this attitude applies best to our summer work. From 1946 on, as the summer school began to re-form after the year-round wartime operation, our department offered summer courses to be taken as a minor—we did not offer a degree program. But, in the mid 1950s, the *Wall Street Journal* gave scholarships which paid for journalism teachers chosen by the paper, mostly from high schools, to take summer college courses. The remarkable group of men and women who came to Notre Dame on these scholarships practically forced me to offer a degree program so that they could return in later summers and finally receive an M.A.. And this, like our program in the school year, grew and grew and grew.

But what a difference, especially as the 1960s rolled round. Teaching in the summer sessions was even better than teaching the veterans. Here were adult, highly motivated men and women, nearly all religious at the outset, who had given their lives of self-sacrifice to Catholic education, eager to learn, eager to work with and learn from one another, delighted to feel free from the restraints of pastors and superiors, seeking something useful to take back to their classrooms. Moreover, they were the best public relations we could have, for they brought back good word about Notre Dame to their students. Withey, Fischer, and Ron Weber gave them full measure of the good word. I saw the good of these programs, and administered them cheerfully, but I was not enthusiastic about teaching the year round. And administration, so simple in the school year, was a real pain in the summers, full of problems not only of Notre Dame requirements but those of the various state boards of education.

I had learned the pleasures of adult education in a series of Workshops in Writing in the early 1950s. I joined with Professor Louis Hasley in administering these, and worked with John Nims, their vigorous promoter. We augmented our home faculty of John himself, John Frederick, Richard Sullivan, and Ed Fischer with visiting writers and editors like Caroline Gordon, Jessamyn West, Anne Freemantle, J. F. Powers, Robert Giroux, and others. I don't know why these workshops petered out. But I do know that I forsook them for different summer pursuits elsewhere.

But I still was tied to our academic summer programs, and I think back on them now with the emphasis time gives to features scarcely noticed then. In an earlier chapter I wrote of their inauguration in 1917 by Father Matthew Schumacher, and their success in the 1920s. This was very important, I now see, in two principal ways. One was their usefulness in accustoming our faculty and administration to keep graduate studies in mind when planning, for many of the summer students wanted to keep a-going in the regular school year as well. But the most important is the bringing of women to Notre Dame. The first women to attend Notre Dame were summer school students, the first to live on the campus were summer school students, and laywomen began to appear among the dominant religious.

In the 1940s the Department of Journalism graduated the first black person to earn a degree at Notre Dame. Almost from that time I was also pressing for the admission of women where possible. As the nominal head of theater in the late 1950s and early 1960s I worked hardest at merging the Notre Dame and St. Mary's theaters. After many a stutter this finally came to pass. Our journalism courses were among the first to admit St. Mary's women in our exchange program. It isn't that I believe coeducation ideal under all circumstances. It's just that I see no other way in our society.

I found that I personally liked teaching women. I found them more intelligent, more mature, and more responsive than men of the same age. They were mostly women, the men mostly boys. But I quail before the task of saying why I have, all my adult life, gladly taught. Some aspects are easy to note: the freedom, the life of the mind as opposed to routine, the feeling that much of it is what you do you'd want to be doing anyhow. What's troublesome is the responsibility, the tacit commitment to do the right thing by your students.

But how do you know the right thing? I think the answer to that ends in mystery. You don't know, any more than I know that what I am now writing is useful or interesting or even honest. You just have to feel right about it. Student opinion is worthless. They admire an interesting rascal, dislike a plainly superior intelligence, and are gullible bait for a pious though honest fraud. There is no way they can tell the good from the not. I have always disliked teaching that gets down on all fours with the students. Good teaching is sort of like naval gunfire: you need a little distance for your shots to take effect.

Moreover, students are unable to tell what it is they like about teaching. Frank O'Malley was the most admired, beloved, and effective teacher of the humanities in the modern history of Notre Dame. Yet I have never heard a student able even to hint at why. The same is true of Joe Evans. Their disciples just glow. They are much more able to say why they dislike certain disorganized professors. Students like good organization above all. They want to know what is required of them and where they stand in meeting the requirements. But they are wonderfully generous and good-hearted. If the teacher who knows his work is ineffective can somehow manage to appeal to student generosity, he'll get undeserved approbation.

The 1960s movement to bring students into administration decision making and teacher appointment is absurd, I think. Students can't judge anything much except the one thing they are good at, athletics. I rejoice to see the teenage champions in tennis, swimming, and other sports. The youthful body, full of dash and energy, is beautiful in spending its strength and determination in the disciplined ways of games. But the youth are incapable of choosing their very coaches, let alone their teachers and governors. They haven't lived long enough to make wise and prudent decisions. And they are by definition irresponsible.

They cannot be responsible while they are dependent on their parents. That very dependency shields them from the demands and duties of adult life. Only when they set up on their own can they begin to live autonomous lives. The person who, for some reason, however good, stays home with mother usually becomes dependent on her, emotionally if not financially, and most mothers dislike surrendering the controls. Practically everybody over the age of twenty-five knows this. Why, then, all the indulgence to the petulant outbursts of the immature?

Anyone who has survived student journalism will testify to the invincible immaturity of college students. My experience with it at Notre Dame was deliberately peripheral; I wanted both administration and my students to understand that I did not propose either to supervise or to police student publications. Nevertheless, I inevitably had something to do with them, if only because many of my students wrote for them. During the 1950s all the editors of the venerable *Scholastic*, the student weekly newsmagazine, were in my department. Because nearly all of them were veterans, mature men who knew how to deal with administration, it was a happy time. One mark of their maturity was that they never dreamed of asking for academic credit for their journalism and never missed a beat of their regular classes. The teenagers will usually expect special treatment and sulk if they don't get it.

As enrollment in the university increased in the 1960s, plans for a daily paper were inevitable. I supported these plans as I could, within my self-determined limits. The founder of the modern daily newspaper at Notre Dame was not Robert Sam Anson, as usually claimed. It was Barry Johanson, a brilliant student in my department. I tried to make it clear to him that I would not turn the department over to his paper, the *Voice*, but that I would urge students to work with him. We needed a daily paper, no doubt of that in my mind, but its proper administrative connection was with the Office of Student Affairs, not the Department of Journalism.

The *Voice* floundered, mainly, I believe because neither the students involved nor the overconcerned administration had enough experience to know what difficulties lay in their path.

When Robert Sam Anson tried again with the *Observer*, things went better. In the youth-conscious atmosphere of the late 1960s the students responded warmly, especially as the paper took on their tone. When this became strident, as often happened, the paper was a nuisance. *Sic semper* student journalism.

To my way of thinking the arrogance of youth is the sad legacy of the 1960s. As Pat Moynihan sagely noted, the real trouble lay with the demographics of the baby boom: there were just many more youths than was normal, and they in their majority called some of the shots. But this isn't all. How account for the support of the faculty—the "Greening of America" nonsense?

These reflections are not born of any personal experience. I was oddly untouched, in the classroom or out of it, by the student activism of the 1960s, and I was in Europe on a sabbatical for the worst of it, the Kent State horrors and the testing of President Hesburgh in 1969. All during the 1960s my classes grew larger and larger, including the summer classes, which reached their peak in 1964. But I knew I had been in the saddle too long. I felt control of my life slipping away from me and I longed for deliverance.

Jim Withey retired in 1962, succeeded by the excellent Ronald Weber. Fischer, at my urging, followed up his remarkable feeling for the visual by pioneering in film studies. It will be hard for the young to believe that film study was suspect in academia thirty years ago, just as media studies are now. By his books and the films he made Fischer helped to bring respectability to the serious study of film as art and documentary. Fischer became an international figure in these studies, a juror at Venice and elsewhere, and greatly in demand as a lecturer. I am very proud of this.

Ronald Weber had been an undergraduate student of ours before becoming a highly respected newspaper reporter and the editor for the two years of his graduate study there of the *Iowa Daily Student*. But he had the urge to try the teacher's life and got his Ph.D. in American Studies at Minnesota. Almost from the time of his appointment at Notre Dame I saw in him my ideal successor. But he did not want the job, thinking it my baby that could acknowledge no other parent. When at last he did take over he remade the department into American Studies.

I still think it should have been Communications and American Studies. But I would have made terms with Beelzebub himself to get out. The work which has interested me most since then has been with the *Review of Politics*, our only learned journal in the humanities, with which I had long been associated and which I edited off and on during the 1970s.

By then my little "revolution" was complete. Whatever its faults, the 1960s did shake up the college curricula into creating new courses in contemporary problems, passing with fast-lane speed my modest aims. Some of these courses are parodies of college education. But my yearning for the contemporary was achieved. And the journalism side also almost disappeared. Television replaced print as the main medium of communication. Newspapers survived almost to the degree they imitated TV. In teaching mass media courses in the 1960s I used to suggest that television was more toy than monster. I now think it's both, and much else besides: Nintendo suggests that toys may be central in our new culture now a-borning, and I long ago saw that constructing models on computers was very like games. But I leave this sort of thing to my juniors, fascinating though I find it.

So I departed from education for journalism with no regrets. Everything has changed and the more it changed the less it looked the same, to straighten out the old proverb. Yet the old saw still holds. Although the changes are enormous the problems of education remain the same. They still should revolve around reading and writing. And I still teach those gladly.

13

THE MAKING OF
MODERN NOTRE DAME

The 1930s, the decade of my twenties, had a bad name. The first reaction to its mention by those who lived through it, and even more those who have studied it, is a shudder at the train of recollection it brings: unemployment, relief and work programs, deflation, demoralization, the whole "Brother, can you spare a dime?" outlook. Even nature seemed to conspire to make things worse. The winters were cold, the summers not only hot but made dismal by drought and the consequent dust storms. Poverty was everywhere, less so in Hollywood where the depression entertainment of radio and movies was being churned out. But it sometimes seemed as if half the country had joined the Joad family of *The Grapes of Wrath* in a trek to California, so that state had its troubles, too.

The brighter side of the thirties is rarely thought of. But there was one, especially for Catholics. The intellectual dimension of Catholic life, dormant since the turn of the century, mysteriously underwent a tremendous and wonderful revival. There was a revival of Protestant theology as well. It was as if the materialism of the roaring twenties had dissolved into a decade-long retreat. The renewal of the "perennial philosophy" of St. Thomas Aquinas, led by Jacques Maritain, poured new vigor into the Catholic institutions of higher learning. That quickening life also flowered in the arts, especially literature. François Mauriac, Paul Claudel, Gertrud von le Fort, Georges Bernanos, Sigrid Undset, Evelyn Waugh, Graham Greene, many other Catholic writers, cradle and convert, made readers conscious of sin and redemption, not, as it sometimes seemed in Henry James, mere indiscretion.

199

In England the move to the Catholic Church in the nineteenth century, so brilliantly dramatized and so forcefully expressed by John Henry Cardinal Newman, was continued almost as brilliantly in the twentieth by G. K. Chesterton. His visit to Notre Dame in 1930 can be seen as an intellectual call to arms for Notre Dame as well as for North American Catholics generally.

For Notre Dame 1933 is a good starting point. That was the year Father Philip S. Moore returned to Notre Dame from graduate studies in Paris. Moore brought to his work to improve graduate studies at Notre Dame a single-minded devotion that greatly influenced a whole generation of Holy Cross Fathers. It was also in 1933 that George Briggs Collins and Edward Coomes joined the physics faculty and began to build the electrostatic generator that so greatly accelerated graduate study in the physical sciences. And it was the year that John Francis O'Hara became Notre Dame president in all but name. For a year President O'Donnell had been in the limbo of illness. Now O'Hara took over and things began to hum. The title came to him when O'Donnell died in 1934.

Under the daily guidance of his friend and mentor Father James Burns, the provincial superior of the Holy Cross Fathers of the United States, O'Hara began to follow up on O'Donnell's Chesterton lectures. He first went again to England. Whether he thought of the Continent at the outset, I don't know. He certainly did later on. But he turned first to Catholic England. Moreover, he wanted to engage visiting scholars for at least a semester and preferably for an entire academic year. Like most great ideas, the cross-fertilization of homegrown Catholic scholarship with European thought unfolded slowly. And, as usual, history played an unforeseeable part.

Welcoming foreign Catholic scholars displaced by the totalitarian regimes of Europe was a brilliant stroke. It is odd that other American Catholic institutions left the field largely to Notre Dame. But it is important to remember that the foreigners found a homegrown faculty alert to the historic moment. It was as if Notre Dame came of age intellectually. The process was slow. The old provincialism lingered on. But the new age envisioned by O'Hara, Burns, and Kenna was not to be denied.

The first foreigner O'Hara engaged to give regular courses throughout an entire semester, the pattern he was to follow for

the future, was well-known to Notre Dame. This was Shane
Leslie, for many years the editor of the *Dublin Review* and a
devoted friend of Father Daniel Hudson, the editor of the *Ave
Maria* magazine. Leslie was a contributor to the *Ave Maria*, but
his chief concern was to get American Catholicism better represented in his own magazine. Himself a poet of some reputation,
Leslie was naturally drawn to Father Charles O'Donnell, whose
verse he admired, and they also corresponded.

I was a student in Leslie's course in Swift—he also offered
one in Shakespeare—that second semester of 1934–35. I found
him a strange person. I read his life of Swift during the course,
and found it, as I have found everything else of Leslie I read,
jerky, eccentric, highly personal. But more: arcane, semimyste-
rious, as if the author had some special understanding, some
key to an inner temple where no one else might enter but from
which there emanated flashes of insight. This masoniclike quality is uneven, of course; perhaps it is less evident in his life
of Manning, which he wrote to refute a previous "life." But it
is always present, to some degree, in all of his works that I've
read—by no means all there is, though his output was not great;
his family tradition cast him for a more active life.

Leslie's father was a rich Irish baronet; the son eventually
succeeded to the title. His mother was one of the famous American Jerome sisters, which made him first cousin to Winston
Churchill. From his early boyhood Leslie moved in these circles of the rich, the famous, and the influential, educated at
Eton and Cambridge, living in France and Russia, meeting and
knowing the great, but that odd mysterious knot somewhere in
his psyche seems to have prevented him from taking full advantage of his position. He became converted to Catholicism in
his midtwenties and almost immediately began to play a partly
political role in Church affairs, as well as those of a member
of Parliament. One such mission, to gain political support for
a free Ireland, led him to the United States in 1911. Here he
married a sister of Mrs. Bourke Cochran, whose husband was
a New York senator, a famous orator and congressional leader.
He was Notre Dame's Laetare medalist in 1901 and gave the
dedication address of the new library in 1917. These early visits
to the United States brought him sympathetic and interesting
friends. Scott Fitzgerald dedicated his second novel to Leslie.

Leslie wrote warmly and affectionately of his stay at Notre Dame in the winter and spring of 1935. He lived in the northwest corner room of the first floor of Dillon Hall and just before he left wrote a Latin inscription in big black letters on the wall, saying here for a little while there lived happily Shane Leslie.

While Leslie was here Father O'Hara went to England and there recruited Christopher Hollis, then a master at the Jesuit Stonyhurst School. This came about in an odd way. O'Hara had become friends with Orlando Weber, the rather mysterious and reticent chairman of Allied Chemical, who wished to sponsor at Notre Dame research in economics that would defend capitalism and attack communism. Hollis had just published a book on money, and apparently O'Hara thought he was the right man for the job. But Hollis, once he arrived at Notre Dame with his family in the fall of 1935, soon found his ideas incompatible with those of Weber and taught only in the history department. Edward Keller, a Holy Cross priest, took up the Weber position, and his subsequent publications made a great stir of controversy in American Catholic circles. Actually, it seems to me he was just a bit ahead of his time; what he wrote sounds like a rather unsophisticated version of what the editors of *Fortune*, the French Father Raymond Bruckberger, and many others were saying after World War II, when victory and prosperity renewed confidence in the American way.

Hollis came from an English family of modest distinction. His father was an Anglican parson who eventually became a bishop. Christopher went to Eton and Balliol College, Oxford, both of which he loved. They loved him back and filled him with popularity and honors; he came twice to America on tour with the Oxford debate team. He was converted to Catholicism just as he finished his university career.

Hollis was a prime favorite of the English literary set of the 1920s and 30s. He was intimate with Evelyn Waugh, Anthony Powell, George Orwell, Harold Acton, and others; his name occurs frequently in their memoirs. In them, filled with petty jealousies, squabbles, and snobberies, Hollis comes through as he did with us at Notre Dame: intelligent, wise, high-minded, good-hearted, detached, lovable, flexible, above all sane. He taught at Notre Dame about every other semester till World War II kept him at home. Following the war he made a successful career as a publisher (Hollis & Carter) and became a member of Parliament of a rather detached sort, as was his wont. He wrote with accurate insight and warmth about his stay at Notre Dame in his autobiographical *Along the Way to Frome*. He married happily and fathered a son who is now an English Catholic bishop, bowing across the years to his Anglican grandfather bishop.

In all Christopher Hollis wrote forty or so books of all sorts, biography, history, religious studies, social and political comment. In these I feel he was at once the beneficiary and the victim of the English generalist system of education. He did what he did well but without mastery of any subject. Like so many English writers from Carlyle to Muggeridge, especially Hilaire Belloc, who had a considerable influence on him, he would tackle just about any subject that took his fancy. What resulted is a very superior kind of journalism rather than (for however brief a period) the last word. Hollis was a rather extreme example of the breed. His friend Robert Speaight, who taught in Notre Dame's English department during the summer of 1940, when he produced his memorable outdoors *Twelfth Night*, was also something of a generalist, but more firmly anchored in drama, as actor and critic. A close friend of Sister Madeleva of St. Mary's, Speaight returned there to lecture and direct plays again and again, almost until his death in 1975. Hollis died in 1977.

O'Hara also recruited from Ireland the wildly picturesque Desmond Fitzgerald to teach in the political science department. Actually, Fitzgerald was a rather conservative person, in politics and elsewhere, but his history is romantic in the extreme. To quote from a speech he made in 1938 in Washington Hall, "The British had twice ordered me shot. They jailed me three times, the last for a year; and when I was free I was either in rebellion or planning rebellion against them." His role in the formation of the Irish Free State was considerable; he served as minister of defence and external affairs in the cabinet, and was a member of the Dail and the Senate. He also wrote poetry, had a play produced by the Abbey Theater, and edited the *Catholic Bulletin* for some years.

Fitzgerald's Notre Dame career roughly parallels that of Hollis. He came with him in 1935, and returned off and on till

World War II kept him home. He died in 1950. He was a delightful talker and public speaker, and fitted into the life of the university with easy grace. But he was not a scholar in political theory. He was a literary man at heart who was turned to politics by accident.

The career man-of-letters par excellence was Charles DuBos, the French literary critic, who came midway in the fall semester of 1937 to teach at St. Mary's and Notre Dame. Of all the Europeans who came here, he was the best known. He arrived in some state, with a secretary as well as wife and daughter; their arrival was signaled by a shipboard photograph in the *New York Times*. He had written eleven volumes of literary criticism, much of it on English and American writers, and had translated the American novelist Edith Wharton into French. With François Mauriac, the French Catholic novelist, he edited the short-lived magazine *Vigile* (1930–35) devoted largely to Catholic intellectual renewal.

DuBos was a courtly and elegant gentleman. He rented a house in South Bend's Harter Heights, just south of the Notre Dame golf course, and there kept a Sunday afternoon salon. While still a member of the Notre Dame and St. Mary's faculties he died in Paris in 1939, at the age of fifty-seven. I judge his work to be like that of his American contemporary Paul Elmer More, humanistic, deeply sincere, learned, tasteful. A deeply felt religious sense made DuBos rather more than More, I think. But as with More, his reputation has faded.

Arnold Lunn was a very differently colored horse. The son of Sir Henry Lunn, the man who invented Switzerland as far as the middle-class British traveler is concerned, he was a well-known Alpine climber till an injury slowed him down. He kept his interest and connections with mountaineering, however, and while at Notre Dame was still captain of the British ski team. He brought the same vigor and forthrightness into his intellectual concerns. His family was a devout dissenter evangelical one; Sir Henry got his start in Switzerland arranging religious conferences for faithful Methodists, following a stint as a medical missionary in India. What a family! Another son was the well-known literary figure Hugh Kingsmill, who dropped the family name the more to make his own reputation, which he did emphatically, but with scant worldly success.

Arnold Lunn, like Hollis, seems to have become converted to Catholicism largely on his own. His was a rationalist approach to religion, and for that reason, I am sure, appealed greatly to Father O'Hara, who brought him to Notre Dame to be the centerpiece in one of O'Hara's pet projects, a graduate program in apologetics. He was indeed its mainstay for the four years of its operation. How successful he was with American students is hard to say. Lunn was a man of many gifts and abounding energy. He wrote well many books on mountaineering and as many about the truth and rightness of the Catholic Church. But he was English to the bone, as DuBos was French. With the best of wills their students felt alien to their message.

I had some slight acquaintance with all of them and felt that knowing them, and seeing them working here, was rather like foreign travel: interesting, often fascinating, charming, as travel is, in finding interestingly different companions; but like travel, superficial, evanescent, broadening but not deepening to the stuff of education. Yet these were all men of genuine distinction, esteemed by their fellow professionals, and zealous for Catholic education. It is strange.

The next batch of the foreign legion did make a tremendous impression on the life and work of Notre Dame. That was partly because they came to stay, as the first group did not. But it was mostly because American higher education is modeled on that of Germany, with its rigorous specialist Ph.D., rather than on the generalist English model.

What they did at Notre Dame was to enable the university, under the enthusiastic direction of Father Moore, to set up graduate programs leading to the Ph.D. These came with a rush: philosophy in 1936, physics and mathematics in 1938, political science in 1939. In each instance, the "foreign legion" capped and stimulated the work of our homegrown professors. It was the fusion that counted, the mixture, the opening up of horizons. This is what made the period uniquely exciting in Notre Dame's academic history.

This second contingent of the foreign legion all were refugees, one way or another, from the Hitler blight, but they were Catholic rather than Jewish. Some had a remote Jewish connection, some had none (only one, Eugene Guth, was thoroughly Jewish). They were extremely various and able.

The first to come was the most devout Catholic. He was Arthur Haas, who brought with him a distinguished reputation as a theoretical physicist. As an internationally known professor at the University of Vienna, Haas was well-connected in the U.S. and came, in 1935, to be visiting professor at Bowdoin. He lectured at Notre Dame, liked what he saw and whom he met, and applied for a job.

Such was the modesty of Notre Dame at this time that Father O'Hara responded by saying that we didn't have graduate students advanced enough for Haas, but Haas said he didn't mind teaching undergraduates (which, like nearly all the others, he did with indifferent success). Haas came to the faculty in the fall of 1936. He was a rather formal, old-fashioned gentleman and worked somewhat edgily with his colleagues to establish a graduate program in physics.

Mathematics was galvanized by the acquisition of Karl Menger the following year. Menger belonged to an almost legendary academic family of Vienna. His father was a famous economist, duly immortalized by a bust in the court of the University of Vienna. Menger was a dynamo, organizing meetings and symposia, arguing, explaining, expostulating, gesturing, prodding. He became chairman of the mathematics department the year after he came, and the following year brought to the campus the now very famous Kurt Gödel as visiting professor. Gödel was a shy and reserved scholar, almost the archetype of the species. He was supposed to lead a weekly symposium in mathematics, but if Menger was there, as he usually was, Gödel would scarcely broach the matter at hand before Karl would dart in and take over.

As chairman, Menger organized graduate work in mathematics, and Emil Artin, who, like Gödel, has an assured place in the history of mathematics, came to help on the recommendation of Solomon Lefschetz, research professor of mathematics at Princeton, who wrote Father O'Hara on January 12, 1938: "I permit myself to name for your strong consideration [an] absolutely first-rate man, the algebraist E. Artin, at the present time professor at the University of Hamburg. He is an Austrian Aryan, but his wife is one-half Jewish. . . . With two such stars [as Menger and Artin] in your firmament you would outclass in this branch of learning all but a small number of the oldest universities."

Artin stayed at Notre Dame only one year, though he re-turned frequently during his years at Indiana University before going on to Princeton. All who knew him thought him brilliant, including Notre Dame's current provost, Timothy O'Meara, who was his student. I knew him only through music, to which (like most mathematicians) he was devoted, though he cared only for the baroque style. He traveled with his own harpsi-chord.

Menger and Artin helped make Notre Dame better known in science circles. One of Menger's first acts was to organize a mathematics symposium in February 1938, with participants from Harvard, Yale, and Princeton. But his great symposium took place in May of that year, on "The Physics of the Universe and the Nature of Primordial Particles." Its sparkplug was a visiting professor, Canon Georges LeMaitre, the celebrated Bel-gian astronomer, and it included such luminaries as Chicago's Arthur Compton, Cal Tech's Carl Anderson and Harvard's Har-low Shapley. Its papers made a real splash in the world of physics and astronomy. LeMaitre's theories are being approv-ingly revived by some astronomers today.

What is so striking about all this is that it happened at a Catholic university. The typical American scientist or mathe-matician, especially in the O'Hara years, was a solid positivist: indifferent to religion, entrenched in the belief that science is all that matters, and expectant that its devoted pursuit would set all things right.

That was not so among Europeans, as this account shows. Haas was a devout Catholic, Menger a traditional one, LeMaitre an ordained priest. Once, in a discussion of the usefulness of mathematics to liberal education, Menger listened impatiently until he could exclaim, "But it's so beautiful!" Gödel once shocked the American Mathematical Society by telling its mem-bers that the whole number system could only be understood completely by the divine mind.

This sense of science as a reflection of the divine mind was a cliché of Catholic education. What was needed to underpin it was science well done, and that is what Notre Dame was cultivating.

And not only science, but philosophy as well. The two great French Thomists of the time, Etienne Gilson and Jacques

Maritain, lectured frequently at Notre Dame. Maritain especially was enormously influential, not only in philosophy but
esthetics and political theory as well. (Characteristically, Father
O'Hara had some reservations about Maritain's orthodoxy, especially vis-à-vis Franco's Spanish revolution. Characteristically
also he supported Father Moore's bringing Maritain here as
often as possible. In this tension between orthodoxy and its various antonyms O'Hara was by no means alone among Catholic
clergymen in high office.)

Maritain remained a visitor, but his friend Yves Simon came
to stay, the star of philosophy's graduate program in 1938 until
1948, when he left for the University of Chicago. Like Maritain,
Simon was Thomist to the bone. He was a bold and original
thinker whose work stands up well to this day, in some respects
better than Maritain's. Simon had spent his intellectual life in
Catholic circles, first at the Catholic Institute of Paris, later at
the Catholic University of Lille. That was rare, partially because
Catholic universities are rare in Europe.

Simon welcomed the opportunity to come to a Catholic University in the United States. He saw clearly what was brewing in
Europe and foresaw that he might be useful here while he was
almost certain to be useless there, since he was physically crip-
pled since childhood. In manner and chosen role Simon lived
like an ordinary workman; he dressed like one, and he kept his
discourse plain and direct. But it was not simple; it was complex
and considered. Simon could endow words like "faith," "law,"
and "love" with meanings that restored them to their original
honor. He was rapidly and lovingly absorbed into the Notre
Dame community.

But the most famous, the most picturesque, the most colorful,
and in some ways the most influential of the refugee scholars
was Waldemar Gurian. He was born in St. Petersburg in 1902.
But when he was nine the family broke up, and his mother took
him and his sister to Berlin, where she became a Catholic and led
her children into the Church. During World War I young Waldemar, as an alien in Germany, was excluded from the Berlin
gymnasium. His mother sent him to a Dominican school in the
Netherlands for a couple of years. Here he may have imbibed
some of his feeling for Thomist philosophy. But by 1920 he was
back making the rounds of the German universities, where he

rapidly acquired a reputation as a prodigy. In Berlin he came under the spell of the celebrated philosopher Max Scheler and did his doctoral dissertation under him. Scheler was at that time a Catholic, and a Catholic apologist of sorts. His phenomenology was easily assimilated into a Catholic point of view and proved an ideal personal style for humanistic Gurian. To the end of his life he revered Scheler as a genius.

Like most of the refugees Gurian was an indifferent teacher of undergraduates and in his case of graduate students as well. From his earliest days at Notre Dame he set his heart on founding a journal of Catholic intellectual opinion on the models he had known in Europe. These were *Hochland*, edited from Munich by Carl Muth, and *Schildgenossen*, edited from Cologne by Romano Guardini. In addition there was the French *L'Esprit*, edited by Emmanuel Mounier. Gurian had written for the German ones, as well as for German newspapers. He was as much journalist as scholar, on the European model of Bertrand de Jouvenel, Raymond Aron, G. K. Chesterton, Josef Pieper, and Guardini himself.

In his writings Gurian was inevitably antifascist and therefore anti-Hitler. Even though he sometimes wrote under pseudonyms it was becoming clear that his name was mud in the Hitler circles, and he managed to get his wife and daughter to Lucerne in Switzerland, where he spent two years before coming to Notre Dame, befriended there by the well-known Jesuit intellectual Otto Kerrer. He was suggested to Notre Dame by Jacques Maritain.

From the time of his arrival, then, in 1937, Gurian planned his journal. He was assisted in this by Ferdinand A. Hermens, a cradle Catholic from Westphalia. Hermens had become a strong proponent of democracy and had written a book, published in the United States in 1940, which remains to this day the standard attack on proportional representation. Alas, *Democracy or Anarchy*, for all its good sense, has failed to convince the democratic countries and they have indeed invited upon themselves the anarchy the book predicted.

Hermens began his academic career as an economist, but his deep belief in democracy and concern for its successful establishment everywhere led him into political theory. He left Germany because he could see he'd get nowhere in these pursuits under Hitler. He came first to the Catholic University, but Gurian helped persuade him to shift to Notre Dame to assist him in floating his new journal. It was he who worked up the prospectus, and Father L. R. Ward took it to President O'Hara for approval in August 1938.

I suspect Gurian was lurking in the wings because, in his deep pessimism, he feared O'Hara wouldn't approve. But O'Hara did, and the first issue of the *Review of Politics* appeared in 1939 with a lead article by Jacques Maritain. My long connection with the *Review* makes me suspect as its critic, but I still maintain it did more for the intellectual reputation of Notre Dame, especially abroad, than any other single agent, valuable as some were. Like most such enterprises it has been undervalued at home. Its success was Gurian's work. An editor's most important job is attracting good writers and good manuscripts. Gurian brought to the *Review* contributions from Oscar Halecki, Fritz Morstein Marx, Melchior Palyi, Hans Barth, Goetz Briefs, Hans Kohn, Sigmund Neumann, Heinrich Rommen, Hannah Arendt, Hans Morgenthau, Peter Drucker, Eric Voegelin, Don Luigi Sturzo, Stephen Possony, Mario Einaudi, Yves Simon, Jean Daniélou, and Etienne DeGreef among the foreign-born. The Americans were equally distinguished: Jerome Kerwin, Clinton Rossiter, William Yandall Elliott, Francis Wilson, John A. Ryan, Harley McNair, Mortimer Adler, Kenneth Thompson, Edward Shils, Talcott Parsons, and John Kenneth Galbraith. It's a list any learned publication in the humanities would be proud of.

Some of the foreign legion did not arrive till after World War II. Among these was a notable helper on the *Review*, Stephen D. Kertesz. Kertesz had been a distinguished diplomat in his native Hungary, holding various high posts till the Nazis overran his country and snapped short his career—which otherwise would surely have led him to the top. His story is well told in his books, *Democracy in a Whirlpool* and *Between Russian and the West*. Kertesz developed a graduate program in international relations with great success at Notre Dame. He also was easily the best classroom teacher of the lot. And his courtly, charming, and generous personality made him a beloved favorite on the faculty. Along with George Brinkley and John Kennedy he helped develop the faculty of the Department of Government and International Relations.

Matthew A. Fitzsimons succeeded Gurian as editor of the *Review* upon the latter's early death in 1954. Fitzsimons had worked with Gurian from the start. He was perhaps the star of the excellent faculty in history Father T. T. McAvoy built up, most of whom were helpers on the *Review* as well—Aaron Abell, William O. Shanahan, Marshall Smelser, Fredrick Pike. These two departments were the natural allies of Gurian's journal. The *Review* could not last an issue without the intelligent and devoted help of the Notre Dame faculties in the humanities.

The development, in the post–World War II period, of all the faculties in the arts and sciences is the real story of modern Notre Dame. It has been to me, as participant and spectator, an inspiring story.

14

PRESIDENT HESBURGH

Thirty-five of my fifty years as a member of the Notre Dame faculty have been spent in the presidency of Theodore Martin Hesburgh. In this account of his life and work I have tried to distance myself a little from the pride and admiration I have for him. He may well be the American Catholic priest who has caught and kept public interest for longer than any other. His tenure as president of the university whose image he changed is the longest in contemporary American higher education. Some older university presidents have had longer ones, notably Charles Eliot of Harvard (1869–1909) and Nicholas Murray Butler of Columbia (1902–1945). Eliot was fond of saying that a college president's name is writ in water, but Hesburgh's seems graven in more durable stuff.

Hesburgh's influence begins at home, with the university he headed for so long. His accomplishments there are formidable. Under his leadership Notre Dame's endowment has risen from ten million to more than $450 million, from nowhere to twenty-first among the nation's private universities. Under him the Notre Dame campus has spread eastward in a cascade of new buildings, creating a campus almost as large as the original one, and enlarging and renovating the old campus without changing its unique character. Average faculty salaries have soared from $5,400 to $50,000, well past inflation and student tuition. Enrollment has nearly doubled, from 5,000 to 9,600. The yearly operating budget zoomed from nine to 200 million, as Notre Dame went coed and changed over to lay governance from control by its founding religious community of Holy Cross.

But the main Hesburgh achievement lies in the new prestige he has brought to Notre Dame. Whatever its merits—and they were considerable—the Notre Dame Hesburgh took over in 1952

213

simply did not have the prestige of the Notre Dame of 1987, when he retired. Hesburgh inherited a college which had just turned the corner to university status. He left it a full-fledged university, on its way to the top. Hesburgh's own prestige advanced with Notre Dame's. Notre Dame, already well known for its football splendors, gradually became well known for its academic ones, and Hesburgh, in an era when college presidents came and went like professional baseball managers, became the best-known college president in the United States. He had something to start with, to be sure; Notre Dame had two other great presidents in the period between the two World Wars. There had been vision and promise before Hesburgh. But now the circumstances were ripe. By 1952 Notre Dame was ready, and Hesburgh was its prophet.

As if this were not career enough, Hesburgh has played a significant role in national affairs. This story is well told in the late Kingman Brewster's introduction to the printed version of Hesburgh's Terry Lectures, delivered at Yale when Brewster was its president and published in 1974 under the title *The Humane Imperative*.

> In international conciliation he has raised his colleagues out of the ruts of self-interest—in the international control of the peaceful uses of atomic energy, and in the mobilization to help poorer nations and peoples, especially in Africa and Latin America. Father Hesburgh's contribution to the continuing and unfinished effort to make the Declaration of Independence and the Bill of Rights a living reality for all Americans is so widely appreciated that it needs no embellishment. This ideal of equality has been kept alive, and its achievement is still a realistic hope, in considerable part because of Father Hesburgh's strenuous, stalwart championship of the cause of human dignity and equality. This reached a new and critical importance when the tide of the civil rights struggle began to ebb; hope for millions would be more forlorn if it were not for his steadfastness.... This quality [of] spirituality is Father Hesburgh's very special gift to those over whom he presides, those to whom he ministers, and those for whom he writes and speaks. There is no passivity in his contemplation, since the realization of God's will demands that the person throw all of himself into the cause. There is no gloom in his dedication, since it is sustained by a confidence

that the Holy Spirit is at work in us all, in the world, and in the cosmos.

This extraordinary language reflects the high esteem the academic community in the United States has for Hesburgh, which has earned him a record high 121 honorary degrees (Herbert Hoover is second with 89). Responsible American journalism echoes its sentiments. The *Nation* magazine called Hesburgh "the most influential cleric in America." Hesburgh has been on a *Time* magazine cover, and the subject of an admiring magazine article by Fred Hechinger, the longtime education editor of the *New York Times*. On the whole, without trying but with a keen sense of its usefulness to his enterprises, Hesburgh has had an excellent press, particularly in television. He was a natural, with his handsome countenance, his broad smile and easy manner. Even student journalism, ordinarily the worst ordeal a university president has to endure, has been nearly always respectful and often proud and cheering. As for Hesburgh himself, he has said that he was troubled early on by the requests made for his services to the national weal, but as soon as he realized that his educational and civil goals were basically the same he welcomed public service. But he was no ordinary public servant. Outspoken, insistent, hardworking, he seemed indifferent to praise or blame. He often seemed to court trouble, at Notre Dame and in Washington, but he nearly always came through unscathed, the smiling survivor, a Daniel among the tractable lions.

The well-named Theodore ("gift of God") Hesburgh was born in Syracuse, New York, on May 25, 1917, into a family not quite typical in American Catholicism but by no means unusual. His father was of German descent, his mother, Anne Marie Murphy, Irish. But she was schooled in New York City by nuns mostly of German descent and so was no Irish ghetto product. A lovely and intelligent lady, she made a happy home for her husband and five children.

Hesburgh's father and paternal grandfather were both named Theodore. Grandfather Theodore Bernard was a schoolteacher and journalist, presaging the career of his famous grandson. As Father Ted himself might have done, Grandfather Theodore, writing for the *New York World*, Joseph Pulitzer's paper, opposed

Archbishop Michael Corrigan, New York's testy Catholic leader, for suspending the ardent supporter of Henry George, Father Edward McGlynn, from his priestly duties. Journalist Hesburgh argued not so much for the righteousness of the George single-tax program as for the freedom of clerics to take part in political life: a clear anticipation of Father Ted's passionate defense of academic freedom.

Hesburgh's father had a much different sort of life. When he was three years old the flu epidemic of 1891 carried off his mother, brother, and sister. His distracted father brought him to live with some distant relations on a farm in Iowa, but seven years later he was rescued by an aunt who brought him back to New York. But life was never easy for the second Theodore Bernard. He worked at all sorts of odd jobs to help earn his keep and managed somehow to graduate from high school, which was by no means taken for granted in his day. He then started to work for the Pittsburgh Plate Glass Company, where he remained for the rest of his business life, gradually climbing up the ladder till he became manager of its warehouse in Syracuse. His children remember him as a hard worker as well as a sincere and deeply religious man, devoted to his job and his family. In later life he and his wife contributed to the redecoration of the crypt of Sacred Heart Church at Notre Dame, where Father Ted celebrated mass every day he was at the university.

Father Ted was the second of the five Hesburgh children. A younger brother, James, is a Notre Dame graduate and a successful businessman in California. One sister, Mrs. Robert O'Neill, lives in Cazenovia, New York, and another, Mrs. John Jackson, in Syracuse. A third died young, in 1957. The Hesburgh family was normal American middle-class. Young Ted grew up an altar boy, a Boy Scout, a builder of model airplanes, a typical American boy. He was a good student and, with the rest of his family, devoted to the Church and its pious practices. Very early on, at about age twelve, he determined to become a priest and was attracted to the religious orders. At first he thought about becoming a Jesuit, but then he met and admired a Holy Cross Father, Thomas Duffy, and, influenced by Duffy, decided to join the Fathers of the Holy Cross.

The Congregation of Holy Cross is named after the little town of St. Croix, near LeMans, France, where it was founded in

1837. It is a community of priests, brothers, and nuns, one of many such begun in the early nineteenth century in the wake of the French Revolution. This spiritual movement is one of the most striking events in recent Catholic Church history. In the first decade of the century the French Revolution attacked the Church, confiscated her property, closed her houses of study, and established a new regime based on atheism and a passionate anticlericalism. But in little more than a generation a tremendous revival of religion took place in France. Many new religious orders were formed, many older ones rejuvenated. The focus for much of this renewal was the foreign missions. In 1822 the French Societé de la Propagation de la Foi was founded. It eventually underwrote a good portion of missionary support in foreign lands. It was during this period that the French missionaries earned their reputation for being the first and best of Catholics bearing the gospel to lands that knew it not. France once again became "the eldest daughter of the Church," a soubriquet she acquired in the Middle Ages.

Holy Cross was not founded as a missionary enterprise. It was from the beginning a loose organization—an ecclesiastic "congregation," known at the outset of its history as "auxiliary priests." These lived together and helped out in parishes, schools, and the general work of a diocese, so that its members, priests, brothers, and eventually nuns, stayed close to ordinary Catholic lay people and bore little resemblance to the traditional orders with their long traditions and loyalties. But the French missionary spirit was strong in them, and an early recruit, Father Edward Frederick Sorin, ordained in 1838, headed for the wilds of northern Indiana. Indeed, at that time, Indians still traversed the land in greater numbers than the white men. But that was rapidly changing, and Sorin's school, named for Our Lady, superbly located near the burgeoning cities along the southern edges of the Great Lakes, steadily grew. The freewheeling style of the young Congregation of Holy Cross found ready acceptance in freewheeling America.

It was a style which exactly suited Theodore Hesburgh when he arrived at Notre Dame in the fall of 1934, although his initial reception was a frosty one. His father, mistrustful of his own old jalopy, had borrowed a car from a friend to drive his son to Notre Dame. Arriving at the seminary on Saturday, they were told to come back on Monday, when registration began officially. But once over this little mix-up, young Hesburgh throve. He spent a year in the "little" seminary at Notre Dame, getting his studies in order, and then got through the severities of his year in the novitiate. Once in the philosophy department of the seminary he quickly caught the attention of his teachers, who decided to send him to Rome to give him the best education it was then thought a priest could have. It was the custom of the Holy Cross community to send their best and brightest there.

Hesburgh landed in Rome in 1937, as Europe was bracing itself for war. He was lucky in the setup Holy Cross afforded him. The residence was run by the French wing of the community, and French was its normal lingua franca. His lectures and texts at the Gregorian University were in Latin. On the streets he heard Italian, and vacations were spent at a German spa. Thus the young Hesburgh was schooled in many tongues and acquired some facility in all of them, plus the Spanish he picked up later at Notre Dame. Three years of this gave him a cosmopolitan polish and introduced him to the urbanites of the capital of the Catholic world. Then came the war, and all the Americans came home.

To young Ted this meant finishing his studies at the Catholic University in Washington. The Holy Cross theology seminary had been established there, as part of the movement to make the university a center of Catholic studies. Theology was at this time in the United States gradually being disinterred from under the avalanche of secular positivism, which had nearly buried it between 1870 and 1930. But the impact of the depression and Hitler, and above all the new thinking in physics and mathematics which shattered the assurance of the physical sciences, coupled with the distinguished new thinking in theology itself, made way for its renewal, respect, and influence. Theologians like Catholic Jacques Maritain and Protestant Reinhold Niebuhr became as well known as Hemingway and the atom smashers. In this atmosphere young Theodore Hesburgh was ordained a priest in 1943 and took his doctorate in theology two years later. Characteristically his thesis was on the practical rather than the speculative, entitled when published by the Notre Dame Press *The Theology of Catholic Action*.

And throughout his life he was to remain the activist, the doer, the cut-the-gaff-and-let's-get-going type. Although he respected intellectual speculation, the bone and sinew of a university, his temperament was its opposite. It was not until he became immersed in the civil rights movement that he reached the positions he has since held steadfastly. These are basically two: the dignity of the person and academic freedom.

These twin principles inform and help to shape all he has done, in Notre Dame and out of it. They are to him no empty rhetoric. He puts them to work on all occasions and tests their meaning constantly, in encounters with exigent faculty, naive students, and self-seeking careerists in public life. If this is to be liberal, Hesburgh is a pure-bred one, though by no means doctrinaire. He has never revealed how he votes and has served both Republican and Democratic administrations. He does not pop off about anything and everything. Always and above all he is a priest, careful, measured, spiritual.

His position is best expressed in his book *The Humane Imperative*, whose inspired title encapsules the Hesburgh credo. Its key signature is sounded early on, at the beginning of the prelude: "that theological and philosophical principles can become operative in a wide variety [of human affairs]; and that, as a result, the world will become better, more human, even somewhat divine and . . . godly." This cautious optimism is characteristic of Hesburgh's entire career. It is not a rational conclusion, nor, like his devotion to human dignity and academic freedom, rules for action. It is more a prayer than a principle, an expression of faith "that the Holy Spirit is at work in the world." In the book Hesburgh hopes that the United States, with its mixed racial heritage and its history of freedom, can lead the world to ecumenism and to respect for the human person. In spite of the problems of increasing population, the growth of swollen cities, and the poverty of the Third World, the author remains optimistic, seeing in the green revolution and other technology hopeful signs of coping. The book ends with a plea for two citizenships, one's own country, and that of the whole world.

Hesburgh's hopes are noble. They stamp him as a man of God, deeply spiritual and compassionate, trusting that "somehow good will be the final goal of ill" beyond reason's ken and the implications of knowledge. His favorite metaphor for his own work is "mediator": between God and man, between religion and the secular world, between man and man. He is hopeful for education, for unselfishness, for decency, for a world emptying itself of self-indulgence, cruelty, deprivation, and want. This is his liberalism. It is neither sweeping nor dogmatic. It is built on freedom and autonomy.

After his ordination Hesburgh wanted to become a military chaplain, but his superiors told him to "get his ticket," as the Ph.D. is generally known in the trade. It was necessary to his career. When he came to teach theology at Notre Dame in 1946 he was the only Ph.D. in the department. He taught with great success and wrote a widely used textbook.

He also became, in a roundabout way, the military chaplain he yearned to be. After the war Notre Dame was flooded with veterans getting their education on the G.I. Bill of Rights. For married vets, the university built a little village on the campus, by a happy coincidence where the Hesburgh Library now stands. In this odd ambiance of tight quarters, steamy kitchens, drying diapers, and hard study—teaching the vets was a golden time for the faculty—Hesburgh flourished. He became confessor, baby-sitter, confidant, and friend to hundreds of these young people, and they in turn helped to form him into a warm, compassionate, tolerant, and sympathetic person. Because of them Hesburgh identified with the students rather than the administration at Notre Dame. When, after only three years of "Vetville," the then president, Father John J. Cavanaugh, approached him to join administration as his executive vice president, the Hesburgh hackles bristled. He wanted no part of official discipline and officious policing.

But President Cavanaugh knew what he was doing. More than Hesburgh, he was the originator of modern Notre Dame. He set up the Notre Dame Foundation to raise money on a year-round basis, the forerunner of Hesburgh's remarkable organization. He reorganized the structure of the administration and filled it with the ablest men he could find. But most of all Cavanaugh brought Notre Dame into the mainstream of the new world that was being born in the wake of World War II. He realized that Hesburgh's vets required a new approach. They were mature men, not callow boys. Between them, Cavanaugh and Hesburgh created a new tone. Gradually the old boarding-school regulations began to be ignored, then repealed. It was a trying time for the new leadership, for the Holy Cross community, like all such, was full of men who believed that nothing should ever be done for the first time.

Not until Hesburgh became president himself, succeeding Cavanaugh in 1952, did the old regime collapse. The students who followed the vets, rejoicing in their new freedom, wanted, of course, to repeal all regulations, but they found a firm Hesburgh drawing the line where he deemed it essential. In letters to students and their parents he made it plain that he stood for law and order, not anarchy. But at the same time he established rewarding liaison with student leaders and worked with them as best he could. Something in him appealed to the students. College students are a curious lot. Individually generous and idealistic, collectively they can be barbarous as well as foolish. Hesburgh dealt with them with a hand as adroit as it was sensitive. He was ready to talk to them, visit them in their dorms, reason with them, and above all be candid with them. Yet he never got down on all fours with them. Always he kept a certain distance—with Hesburgh a valuable natural trait, for he treated the faculty and staff with the same combination of invitation and reserve. With all he supported the instruments of freedom, a Faculty Senate, student government with some real authority, several varieties of journalism free for civil dissent. Occasionally he slipped into an attitude which could be called overbearing, and he was lucky that no incident of it became magnified or distorted.

Although Notre Dame was not as riddled with student rioting in the stormy 1960s as many other private schools, it had its share of troubles. Drugs, pornography, and outrageous student behavior—some, like the sit-ins, fairly civil; others coarse and nasty, frequently abetted by the anarchists usually latent in any faculty—became the undergraduate's occupation rather than study. Hesburgh bore it with patience until, in the climatic year 1968–69, he tackled the anarchists head-on. The heart of his message was this ultimatum:

> Anyone or any group that substitutes force for rational persuasion, be it violent or non-violent, will be given fifteen minutes of meditation to cease and desist. They will be told that they are, by their

actions, going counter to the overwhelming conviction of this community as to what is proper here. If they do not within that time cease and desist, they will be asked for their identity cards. Those who produce these will be suspended from this community as not understanding what this community is. Those who do not have or will not produce identity cards will be assumed not to be members of this community and will be charged with trespassing and disturbing the peace on private property and treated accordingly by the law.

Bold words. And the rest of the message was just as bold.

Without the law, the university is a sitting duck for any small group from outside or inside that wishes to destroy it, to terrorize it at whim. . . . The last thing in the world a shaken society needs is more shaking. The last thing a noisy, turbulent and disintegrating community needs is more noise, turbulence, and disintegration. . . . Complicated social mechanisms, out of joint, are not adjusted with sledge hammers. . . . I have no intention of presiding over such a spectacle. . . . Without being melodramatic, if this conviction makes this my last will and testament to Notre Dame, let it be so.

The tone of the message, especially the ending, shows that Hesburgh realized he was sticking his neck out. But it also shows he was fed up to the neck. He must have known the message would make the national news headlines in this apprehensive February of 1969. It did, and it provoked an avalanche of response. Some of it was anti-. The student newspaper predictably urged him to resign. Others, equally sophomoric, made the equally predictable noises about Church authoritarianism, hauling the much-maligned Inquisition out of the sixteenth century grotesquely into the twentieth.

But the bulk of the response was a sigh of relief from the vast majority of Americans bewilderingly repelled by the antics of their juniors. Someone, said newspapers and magazines and broadcasts, has at last had the courage to tell these twerps off. Most of these never knew that Hesburgh was almost as troubled by the conservative response as by the protesters. It was his intervention with President Nixon and some members of the Congress that helped prevent the president from sending troops onto college campuses on a national scale, compounding the mischief done earlier at university after university, and later tragically at Kent State. Nor did most students even know that Hesburgh had quietly let it be known that any student wishing to absent himself from classes in order to take part in a civil protest was to be excused.

Some of his fellow university presidents said that Hesburgh's ultimatum had no meaning for them—that only Notre Dame's homogeneous, largely Catholic student body would put up with such a ukase. Said the president of a California state college, "If we tried that, our students would burn the place down." He may well have been right. But, as the chancellor of UCLA noted, Hesburgh's example had a good deal of influence on other university administrators. Along with his civil rights crusade, his courage and example in getting the country through the turmoil of the 1960s may stand as his outstanding accomplishment for the nation at large.

One reason Hesburgh got away with his stand was the trust the Notre Dame students had in him. Even the student journalist who called for his resignation knew that Hesburgh stood for freedom and dignity. He did not hesitate later to call on Hesburgh to get him out of the clutches of the Khmer Rouge when he was working for *Time* in Cambodia—and Hesburgh did not hesitate to use his influence to help secure his release. This undercurrent of trust, this link between Hesburgh and his students never failed him. Moreover, it was based in part on Hesburgh's sympathy with some student causes, much as he deplored their lawless pursuit of them. One of the main student causes was participation in making decisions which affected their welfare. Hesburgh, especially in the 70s and 80s, insisted on student representation on almost every university committee. One of the foremost student concerns was the draft. Hesburgh called for its replacement with a national service system, allowing young men to opt for the Peace Corps and such like. He roundly condemned the shooting of the students at Kent State. But his greatest scorn was reserved for the continued prosecution of the Vietnam War. "Mental midgets" was his contemptuous term for the responsible federal officials.

Surrounding all this, going both forward and backward in time, was Hesburgh's concern for raising the Notre Dame standards of academic excellence. This was his text, endlessly repeated, from the day he took office to the day he resigned it.

A university, he insisted, was first of all an intellectual enterprise. Bolstered by training of character and underpinned by religious faith, it would be a better intellectual enterprise, but neither character nor religion came first. This is a major theme in *The Hesburgh Papers*, subtitled *Higher Values in Higher Education*, published in 1979. Here he reprinted a portion of a 1967 statement issued by a number of Catholic university presidents meeting at Land-O-Lakes, Wisconsin: "In a Catholic university all recognized university areas of study are frankly and fully accepted and their internal autonomy affirmed and guaranteed. There must be no theological or philosophical imperialism." On the opposite page he adds: "Academic freedom, like all freedom, is grounded ultimately in the nature of man and of society and of the development of knowledge and intelligence." His annual addresses to the Notre Dame faculty stressed the twin theme of dedication to becoming the best.

But Hesburgh did not neglect the moral dimension. "While the community is primarily academic, I submit that its basis of unity must be of the heart as well as of the head. It was not merely intellectual problems that recently unravelled great institutions of learning across the world [referring to the disruptions of the 1960s], but rather the dissipation of moral consensus, community, and concern," This theme runs concurrently with that of academic primacy in *The Hesburgh Papers*. Hesburgh emphasizes that in its warm acceptance of the world of the spiritual, Catholic education adds a dimension largely avoided in secular education. "Have no fear of commitment," he says, "as long as it is intelligent and deeply believes on real evidence the truth of those great Christian values to which *we* [my italics] are committed."

With this in mind Hesburgh labored to improve matters academic at Notre Dame. In this he had no instant success, no spectacular turnaround, no national news story. Although he found the going rough, he bore down. One of his earliest plans was the restructuring of academic departments into divisions. Like so many other college presidents, he found the traditional departments inflexible. Another red herring was his investment in television, which he thought would come to be an important, perhaps a major, force for change in university teaching. He wasn't the only one, of course; one of the enduring chimeras of American education has been the substitution of pictures for teachers. Only a live teacher can adjust the pace of comprehension by a class; a film can't know and the class can't tell it. President Hesburgh was on surer ground when he began beating the bushes for superior scholars for the faculty. With the help of George N. Shuster—a Notre Dame graduate and former professor, just resigned as president of Hunter College in New York City—he projected institutes and programs to lure distinguished scholars to Notre Dame.

But the best lure, Hesburgh soon came to know, is money. This meant fund-raising, and in this he made his greatest success. He had a bonanza of good luck fairly early on, in 1960. The recently established Ford Foundation decided, as one of its top priorities, to help substantially some leading private universities. It picked six to help them achieve regional excellence: Johns Hopkins, Stanford, Vanderbilt, Denver, Brown, and Notre Dame. The choice of Notre Dame in such good academic company was itself a ringing affirmation of what Hesburgh had come to stand for in his eight years as president. Gone were the humiliating days of only a few years ago, when his press conferences were attended largely by sports writers. Welcome to the new day of national recognition as the director of a leading educational institution. Hesburgh immediately, with the help of his staff at the Notre Dame Foundation, began a drive to raise twelve million dollars to qualify for the Ford grant of six million. It was an instant success: Twenty-four million in all was raised. Its focus was the new library, now appropriately the Theodore M. Hesburgh Library, dedicated in 1964. Its location changed the face and character of the campus, and its facilities heightened the quality of Notre Dame education. The collection is still far from ideal, but the faculty offices and the study spaces for students created a new ambience for scholarly work.

The focus of the next drive, launched in 1963, was the huge Athletic and Convocation Center, named in 1987 for Hesburgh's executive vice-president and right-hand man during all his term of office, Reverend Edmund P. Joyce, C.S.C. Joyce was an amicable southerner, a native of South Carolina, of conservative instincts and tastes. He masterminded the actual building of the Hesburgh era, forty-eight new structures, six major renovations, three large additions and steady renovation. Joyce's architect of choice for most of these was the Ellerbe organization of St. Paul. Joyce preferred to work with the Ellerbe people, more engineers than artists, who gave the university good value for the cost. This was the sort of thing Ned Joyce did best—quietly working with Hesburgh behind the scenes to use wisely the money Hesburgh was bringing in. Hesburgh has praised Joyce's work again and again. Noting their marked differences—Hesburgh liberal, Joyce conservative, Joyce as clever with figures as Hesburgh with words, northern Hesburgh and southern Joyce—Hesburgh says, "He brought to Notre Dame everything I couldn't bring to it. I include our national reputation for an athletic program with integrity."

During Hesburgh's first year in office Notre Dame's phenomenally successful football coach, Frank Leahy, resigned, ironically driven from the job by the very intensity that made him good at it. Hesburgh's predecessor, Father Cavanaugh, was close to Leahy and spurred his decision to retire, afraid that he would explode if he didn't. Faced with the problem of choosing his successor, Hesburgh and Joyce picked young Terry Brennan, a former Notre Dame star and a successful high school coach in Chicago since his graduation.

It was an engaging idea: young Hesburgh and young Brennan, energetic, ardent, idealistic, confronting the wolves of the college football world together. Terry did pretty well, but not well enough for Notre Dame. After this Hesburgh left athletics largely to Joyce. But he did not, as so often accused, wash his hands of the Notre Dame athletic traditions. One of his most adroit achievements was the shift of Notre Dame's image away from football and toward academic excellence without losing football preeminence. This is an amazing feat. Some universities, on the road to academic preeminence, like Chicago, abandoned football. Others, the Ivy League notably, abandoned big-time football. Hesburgh wanted Notre Dame to be best in both. Of the original Ford Foundation grantees, only Stanford can, and does, play football with Notre Dame.

By the time the Joyce Center was dedicated, in 1968, Hesburgh and his alter ego in money raising, James W. Frick, had perfected their organization and settled down for the long run. Frick, raised in an orphanage and befriended by Holy Cross in his nonage, had a touch of genius in raising money. First came organization, no doubt of that. But along with organization Frick tackled the problem head-on. He simply asked for money. And insisted, and demanded. There was such earnestness in him and in his finisher, Hesburgh, such sincerity, such conviction, that they generally prevailed. Their third campaign, begun in 1967, raised sixty-two million, and their fourth, ending in 1982, 180 million. As with the campaign just being concluded, which is aimed at raising 300 million, these had may foci. Perhaps closest to Hesburgh's heart were the two aimed at faculty improvement, the superb Decio Faculty Office Building, and the endowment of nearly one hundred faculty chairs. The chair salaries are tops, but the average faculty salary compares well with any university in the land, around $50,000, the proud achievement of Provost Timothy O'Meara and his chief.

There is no doubt that the bedrock of Notre Dame's successful money raising was the improved status of American Catholics. In 1920, when Notre Dame's President James A. Burns, tried to raise another million dollars, in addition to the million he had previously raised with the help of grants from the Carnegie and Rockefeller Foundations, he didn't make it. No doubt his failure owed something to weak organization; little was known then about money raising. But, looking back, a social historian might well conclude that the Catholic body simply did not have the money, just as, looking at Hesburgh's career, it's plain that they did. But of course there's more to it than that. It's like mining: getting the stuff out of the ground is just as important as knowing it's there, and takes a great deal more talent and energy. Our social historian may well wonder if there is any private fund-raising in American history as remarkable as Notre Dame's, collegiate or otherwise.

The success at money raising also owed a good deal to Hesburgh's own image. As president he became increasingly prominent. His invitations to serve on boards and committees were far more numerous than the ones he accepted. By the early 1970s he had become the foremost Catholic, cleric or lay, in the United States. He was acknowledged as such by the well-known Father Andrew Greeley, who said that he ought to be a Cardinal. Others said he ought to be a bishop. Both were wrong. The plain fact is that the president of Notre Dame has the best Catholic position in the United States. If he can bring to the post, as

Hesburgh did, charismatic qualities of mind and personality, he will be the first thought of those who turn to the Catholic Church for authority, prestige, and opinion. And the post is best filled by a plain priest. Bishop, Cardinal, layman, all are wrong for the job. There is a priestly dignity natural to it which makes recognition and accomplishment easier. Hesburgh's dignity, ease, and candor brought him wide acceptance especially among non-Catholics.

His first two appointments to positions of national importance came from the president of his early years in office, Dwight D. Eisenhower. The earlier, to the National Science Board, stimulated his deep interest in technology—Hesburgh has an amateur interest in almost anything scientific. The second, however, changed his life.

This was his appointment as a charter member of the first Civil Rights Commission in 1957. Eisenhower had asked the Congress to create this commission in 1956 and was eager to people it with the best he could persuade—partially, no doubt, to take some of the heat off himself. Besides Hesburgh the members were Chairman John Hannah, the former president of Michigan State; John Battle, former governor of Virginia; Ernest Wilkins, a black who was assistant secretary of labor; Doyle Carlton, former governor of Florida; and Robert Storey, former dean of the law school at Southern Methodist. Since there were no precedents, the committee members themselves did work that would normally have been entrusted to a staff—interviews with plaintiffs, searching conversations with officials, all sorts of reports and journalism. During these Hesburgh was deeply touched by the stories of poor people deprived of their rights, especially the right to vote. Then and there he became the passionate advocate of full citizenship for all. In 1961 he was moved to add a long addendum to the commission's report, a special plea for racial justice.

In 1969 President Nixon made him chairman of the commission. Fred Hechinger, the longtime education editor of the *New York Times*, says that Nixon thought of Hesburgh as a "pillar of the establishment, to be used by the White House for its own purposes." If so, never was an estimation wider of the mark. The Nixon administration, bent on braking the black revolution, was constantly under fire from Hesburgh. The climax

came in 1972, when Nixon proposed antibusing legislation entitled the Equal Opportunities Educational Act. Testifying before
the House Committee on Education and Labor, Hesburgh de-
nounced the bill: "If this measure is designed to implement the
1954 decision requiring desegregation of schools, it fails. If it is
designed to provide equal education opportunities, it fails. If
it is designed to move the nation towards justice, it fails. But
if it was designed to fractionalize the nation along racial lines,
it succeeds." He added, "This bill burns the last bridge out of
the ghetto." As John Lundgren notes, it burned Hesburgh's last
bridge to the Nixon administration. By the end of the year Hesburgh was forced to resign, occasioning his famous remark, "I
suppose they will appoint some rabbit."

Partly because it solidified and confirmed his stand on racial
justice, Hesburgh regards his service on the Civil Rights Commission as the most important of his fourteen presidential appointments. He was especially simpatico with President Jimmy
Carter, who named him to head a delegation of eighty Americans to a United Nations Conference on Science and Technology
for Developing Nations in Vienna in 1977, carrying the rank of
ambassador. In 1979 Hesburgh accepted from Carter the chair
of the Select Committee on Immigration and Refugee Policy,
whose report advocated closing the back door a little on illegal
immigration and opening the front door a little on legal admissions. Earlier, as a member of President Gerald Ford's Clemency
Board, his leniency was objected to by a board member. "I'm in
the pardoning business," Hesburgh replied, memorably.

Besides government service, Hesburgh has also been active
in many private service organizations, both religious and secular. For many years he was on the board of the Rockefeller
Foundation, serving as its chairman for a time. Here he devoted himself to the "Green Revolution," which brought greatly
improved agricultural production to the populous have-not nations. Hesburgh has long maintained that the abortion–birth
control controversies, which have so racked both the public and
religious sectors, largely miss the point. Developed or developing countries control their populations, he says, while the
less developed countries do not, irrespective of whether they
are Catholic or not. Italy, he points out, has the same low rate
of population growth as Sweden, and Spain the same rate as

Russia. "I am not arguing the moral implications of these situations," he adds, "although I would welcome some new inspirational, spiritual and moral approaches to human sexuality, which has been largely taken over by the hucksters." Characteristically, Hesburgh threw his energy and talent to work on a practical help toward solving the population problem, while realizing that it is far more complex than what is covered through the Green Revolution.

The great global preoccupation for Hesburgh, one that continues into his retirement unabated, is his concern for the proper use of atomic energy, emphatically not weaponry. As permanent Vatican representative to the International Atomic Energy Agency in Vienna, (1957–70), he searched for ways to switch using atomic energy for weapons to better civilize the world, especially the underdeveloped nations. Harnessing atomic power to green revolution aims is one way, and there are others. As chairman of the Overseas Development Council, Hesburgh sought to influence American foreign policy toward intelligent uses of American power and money in the Third and Fourth Worlds. Always practical, he does not rule out working with nondemocratic regimes. Universal social and economic justice must be realized bit by bit, piece by piece, working steadily upward. It won't come with a wave of ideological wands or revolutionary backlashes. Hesburgh's influence in these matters has campus implications. The new Institute for Peace Studies, financed by Mrs. Joan Kroc of MacDonald's fame, is an ongoing Hesburgh concern, while the established Kellogg Institute for International Relations stresses Latin American conditions.

The interactions of all his extracampus activities with the campus and with education is a special satisfaction to Hesburgh. Moving hesitantly at first, he gradually became convinced that the world and national concerns he devoted himself to were intimately tied to his goals for Notre Dame. Graduate work in government and international relations, history, theology, the sciences, both physical and biological, and much else is deeply and richly connected to government and private philanthropic service. The interplay in the United States between government and science, as reflected in the National Science Foundation, has helped make the Notre Dame of Hesburgh's dreams possible. More and more the Notre Dame faculty participate in the

National Endowment for the Humanities as well. These are the stuff of the modern university. The lonely scholar, typified by Goethe's Dr. Faustus, is as passé as Faustus's esoteric learning. The new university lies in the land where many strands converge: state, nation, world, government, religions, and a hundred other things meet and mingle in the great university. This is new and the convergencies are often difficult and the projects ill-starred. But the vitality of this mix is what counts.

The old Notre Dame was deeply provincial, by contrast. It aimed to inculcate manners and morals. The learning was conventional and perfunctory—some Latin tags for the boys, debating and public speaking rather than scholarship for the serious, character building for all. Religion was not in the curriculum; there were no courses in religion or theology at Notre Dame until the 1920s. But moralizing was everywhere, in all the classes, in all the numerous church and chapel services, in every daily act.

Hesburgh took two important steps to open up Notre Dame for the twenty-first century. Both left old Notre Damers aghast. The first was autonomy. The enlightened and high-minded Father Howard Kenna, the provincial superior of the Indiana Province of the Holy Cross Congregation from 1962 to 1970, working with Hesburgh, developed a plan to remove Notre Dame from the ownership of the Holy Cross community and transfer it to the Notre Dame Board of Trustees, enlarged and reorganized for the purpose. In 1967 this was done.

This historic change—commonplace among American private universities for nearly a century—made concrete the concept of academic freedom Hesburgh thinks so essential to a modern university. Of all the innumerable honors he has received, he most cherishes the Alexander Meiklejohn Award bestowed on him by the American Association of University Professors in 1970. In his response, Hesburgh repeated his exhortation to academic freedom and added, "Each year brings a new crisis. When the battle seems newly won, hostilities break out on another front. Freedom will always be a problem. But, long live academic freedom."

The second change was the admission of women, beginning in 1972. Hesburgh has long been that rare creature, a celibate cleric who loves, admires, and is at ease with women. Where are the wives?, he used to inquire loudly, when the stags gathered on the old pattern. After a false start trying to amalgamate with neighboring St. Mary's College for women, Notre Dame acted unilaterally. The change was not without problems, but nearly all concerned are happy with it. An all-male Notre Dame is inconceivable in the twenty-first-century terms Hesburgh thinks of. The world has indeed two sexes. Ted Hesburgh knew it all along.

Practically all the Hesburgh accomplishments involve skill with words, and Hesburgh can be very good at that. He writes with uncommon ability, perhaps a heritage from his religious order, which has a long tradition of good English prose. When he prepares, he is an excellent speaker; when he doesn't, he often rambles. He is gifted with extraordinary presence, and, as the many examples already quoted show, sharp and telling repartee. Perhaps the best example of his skill at turning things his way with a phrase occurred in the spring of 1975 during a visit to the campus by President Gerald Ford. The mostly student audience for Ford's honorary degree was restive; some radical faculty had proposed a giant walkout to express disapproval of Ford's Vietnam policy. As the tension mounted, it came time for Hesburgh to introduce Ford. He was brief, but his timing was perfect. "Mr. President," he said, "I want you to meet the greatest student body in the world." The place went wild. The tension was lifted, the walkout, if any, was inconspicuous.

The Hesburgh appearance is a help in such situations. Remarkably handsome in youth, he has retained his good looks through greying hair and facial crinkles. Indeed, he is more impressive as time goes on. Although of only average, or less, height, his carriage is graceful. His dress is severely clerical but well-tailored and immaculate; he is one of those people who looked dressed up even in a rowboat.

His physical appearance is a help to his steady poise. He runs a meeting with dispatch, his benign smile easing the hurt of those committee bores who want to prolong every meeting into weariness. In one-on-one encounters he is immensely effective: how and why are mysteries, for he is not in the usual sense of the word charming. But he can talk most people into doing what he wants; there is something about him that makes one want to please him. He does not inspire envy or jealousy. It is doubtful if he has many enemies, always excepting the Notre Dame people who want to capture him and can't, and the extremists on both sides of the religious and social spectrums. For Hesburgh is above all not extremist. One of his favorite phrases is "civil discourse." Within that canon, he is the most tolerant of administrators, the patron of the opposition. He was host to two of the most controversial speeches of recent times: Jimmy Carter on American foreign policy and Mario Cuomo on the Catholic public official and abortion. He has encouraged discussion on both sides of just about everything. This abstention from partisanship inspires, of course, few disciples. If Hesburgh has few enemies, he also has few intimates. He does not wear his heart on his sleeve and rarely indulges in small talk beyond the usual civilities, which he does brilliantly. His memory for everything, especially names and faces, is phenomenal.

He is, in short, nearly an ideal public figure and, like most ideals, lacking in the little human eccentricities and quirks which often endear idols to their public. He is compassionate, he is not amusing, he is not mercurial, he is obstinate, he is not mean, he is not intemperate, he is not avaricious. He is also not artistic. In an age of vulgarity he is never vulgar. He turns the same face to all, for he has only one. He is totally punctilious, answering every letter, noting every accomplishment, thanking every kindness. He is blessed with great good health, a free play of abundant energy, and sturdy independence. He is very manly.

Like his client students, he is a night owl. He loves the midnight hours, often working through them till dawn. He prefers mornings for sleep, saying his daily mass, which he has missed only once since ordination, preferably around noon. At Notre Dame he lives very simply, sleeping in a bare little room in the priests' residence hall and taking with them his abstemious diet. He likes a Manhattan before dinner but rarely takes more than one, even on festive occasions. He reads constantly, history, biography, science, and lots of sci-fi and mystery fiction. He is *sui generis*; one is hard put to think of anyone like him outside his own community. Inside it there are obvious parallels with Fathers Zahm, Burns, and Kenna, but he is not really like any of them.

Nor is he really like the man who has seized his imagination, the founder of Notre Dame, Father Edward Sorin. Hesburgh claims no kinship with Sorin, but he has a keen sense of history, and he often refers to the founder. His final address to the faculty was a mini-biography of Sorin. While he did not draw them, there are some intriguing similarities. Both were possessed, even obsessed, with a vision of a great Notre Dame. Both were wilful and obstinate in pursuit of their visions. Both wished to be missionaries as young priests and retained all their lives something of the missionary spirit. Both were priests above all. And both loved Notre Dame.

Sorin's shadow still hangs over Notre Dame, above all in the place itself. The campus is uniquely beautiful, especially the old parts that Sorin personally designed, whether he had an architect or not. Much of it recalls Sorin's memories of his native Sarthe Department in France, just north of the valley of the Loire. But the spacing of the old buildings, and the planting in the Main Quad, largely Sorin's work, is superb. Few American colleges can rival its layout, none its trees. Many besides Sorin and Hesburgh have loved the place, but none has left a mark on it so powerful and so inimitable as theirs.

EPILOGUE

Of all the things to look at around Notre Dame I think I like the trees best. We've been losing some of my favorites lately. The big ailanthus, the "tree that grows in Brooklyn," died. Ailanthuses are rank trees, growing wild all over Indiana, along the back roads and in the hedges. But ours, on the Main Quad just off the road that curves by the Student Center, was a nobler specimen, tall and slender. I was more surprised to see it flourish than to see it die; these softwood trees don't live long. Our grounds crew labored mightily to save its rare neighbor, a yellowwood across the road toward the east. But it, too, finally died. It was first identified by the elder Michaux, André. François, who followed in the footsteps of his famous father in botany, brought one to Paris. I saw its decendant once in the Jardin des Plantes there, plainly labeled. I wonder if it's still there.

Most of the big trees at Notre Dame are maples of one sort or another; there are many varieties. They are so glorious in the fall I can forgive their often bulging girth and crowding branches. They are the best of the American shade trees—perhaps the best all-round, too. But, except in the fall, they are less interesting to me than the black walnuts. I rather think there was a big virgin grove of these stretching from behind Lyons to the river. Many of them still remain, of later growth, on both sides of St. Mary's Lake, great tall majestic trees, the aristocrats of our woods. They have been sadly pillaged recently by midnight vandals who quickly saw away the long, branchless, valuable trunks. Better security has checked this lately, and one of my favorite sites for the house I can't build, the tongue of land just beyond the island in the southwest part of St. Mary's Lake, is still ringed with them. I seldom look at that island without thinking of how lovely its redbud trees look from the Grotto lawn in the spring. Our redbuds grow to no great height. They are like the Russian olive trees, with the almost-white undersides of their leaves dappling in the wind. They make a pleasant contrast to the huge walnuts and cottonwoods.

The walnuts live longer, I think, than do our oaks. Coming from middle Tennessee, where oaks have protean shapes and leaf patterns, I find these red and white oaks are not prominent on the landscape, handsome though they are. I like better the native sweet gums, even though they can grow scrawny, like the one in front of the east wing of the Main Building. When one grows just right, as on the west side of the Moreau chapel, it is, summer and fall, of elegant beauty. But the great sight of the Notre Dame fall are the dozen or so sour gums in front of the Post Office and Kellogg.

I am not a tree snob. I love the rank old rows of osage orange, now disappearing. I even enjoy the mulberries for their leaves of different shapes, along with the sassafras the only such trees on the campus. And I love the oddball katsura trees east of the Morrissey chapel and the twin hornbeams facing each other across the Library reflecting pool.

They help the planting which makes Hesburgh Library look better than it is. As many trees as possible were spared while it was building, and when the Radiation building went up quite a few large trees were transplanted. It's the planting which gives the Library quad its charm. The buildings are mostly uninteresting. The Library itself is so poorly designed that the stone-and-mural exterior fails by miles to make up for it. It's foolish to do a library tower. A library building should spread out, and go up only as far as necessary. Even so, the building has more character than its satellites, Radiation, Math, and the somewhat better Galvin. But look across from Galvin to the best of the recent buildings at Notre Dame, the Decio Faculty Office Building. It's all the Library isn't, superbly designed. The problem it presented its designer, the avoidance of prison cell monotony, is brilliantly solved in its staggered grouping. Faced with a similar problem, the designers of O'Shaughnessy simply confessed failure with its classroom cell blocks. Only the great hall and the art galleries are good. The Snite Museum, by contrast, is handsomely designed and neatly integrated with the O'Shaughnessy galleries by a charming sculpture courtyard.

Northward from the Library it's the same story. Although the Pasquerilla dorms are well designed, the exteriors look like prison additions. Siegfried and Knott are some better, well designed for female occupancy, but squat and a little gauche in appearance. The tower dorms are also well designed and, to my eye, handsome, but foolish in conception—why towers on an empty prairie?

I roam around these buildings sparingly. My work plops me among them, and I am deeply grateful for my library office and the other amenities. I do find the new landscaping interesting, though I don't much like the artificial rises or the flower beds and borders, here and elsewhere on the campus. I think flower beds out of place in the sweep of a campus. These small riots of color belong in smaller settings—little courtyards and gardens, like that enclosed by Brownson's wings or the charming one between Hurley and Hayes-Healey. But the broad sweep of campus vistas are better served by breaks of greenery. I groan at the flowers on our beautiful Main Quad. The larger planting here is so imaginative and effective that I never tire of strolling through it. As I descend from the Main Building I am almost at once surrounded by the Japanese magnolias and the spreading beeches. In the spring especially I feel almost suffocated by the rich growth and delicate color. But a few steps to my left opens a small vista framed by a tremendous maple on the north and the beautiful white birch to the south. Next to the birch is my favorite young tree on the campus, a European linden, the lime tree so beloved of English writers. It makes me recall sadly the big splendid one that died a few years ago, on the satellite small quad ringed by St. Edward's, Zahm, and Cavanaugh. On this small quad the flowers look good, but in the still smaller little area between Cavanaugh and Washington Hall, the bald cypresses have grown so big it seems almost crowded, like the mini-quad between Nieuwland and Crowley. I like to look from here down to the memorial fountain designed by John Burgee, whose rugged contours mirror the library's large forms and soften its impact. Yet I return to the fanciful Victorian architecture of the Main Quad with renewed pleasure at its contrast with the steel structure severities of the east side. I laugh with pleasure at Architect Willoughby Edbrooke's eyebrows over the windows of the Main Building and the masterful intricacies of the tower of Washington Hall. How well they go with Sorin's curving road, and his evocation of French formality in the design of the quad. I especially love the little eccentricities, the twisted pines, the dwarf beech and the camperdown elm. Oh, this is the place to stroll! Even the nineteenth century convent architecture of Walsh can't spoil the effect, and on the other side Crowley's modest classicism is a neat echo of LaFortune's simple elegance, so immensely enhanced by the recent tasteful reproduction on its east side.

But the only bold note of classicism in the campus architecture is the old Library, now the School of Architecture. This white stone structure, to me pleasingly at variance with the prevailing buff brick, was built to celebrate the diamond jubilee of Notre Dame. There is about this quasi-quad, defined by Corby and the back of the Bookstore, an air of the unfinished. The row of ash trees never grew well, but there ought to be some sort of green barrier to close off the basketball courts, a good spot for these, from the rather interesting planting to the north. Here are two rare cucumber magnolias and the best dogwood on the campus. I wish the architects would think up some effective stroke.

The new dorms planned for this area happily never were built. They came a little later complete with new thinking. Enter Francis Wynn Kervick, the head since 1913 of the Notre Dame Department of Architecture, who, more than anyone since Sorin, influenced Notre Dame architecture until the advent of the Ellerbes in the 1950s.

Kervick seemed a quiet mousey person, but under his reserved exterior he was thoroughly opinionated. He hated modern architecture and shrugged off the plans Frank Lloyd Wright drew up for Notre Dame's expansion in 1923. He adored the Gothic style. He was, of course, in the swim: Yale, Princeton, and West Point led the 1920s in an outpouring of collegiate Gothic building in the United States.

However, Kervick was no slavish copier. His Howard-Morrissey-Lyons group, easily the best of the Notre Dame dormitories, is playful Gothic, a loving adaption of largely English models. Gothic does well as a dormitory style. It also does well for refectories. Notre Dame's best building is its South Dining Hall, designed by the high priest of American Gothic, Ralph

Adams Cram, a Kervick hero. Gothic for gymnasiums or laboratories is questionable, as witness the false fronts of the Rockne Building and Kervick's own Cushing Hall of Engineering.

Kervick's main contribution to Notre Dame was his master plan, which swung building away from Notre Dame avenue to a new east-west mall. Father John W. Cavanaugh had, in the last days of his presidency, commissioned this plan. Kervick submitted it to President Burns, who did no building. It was left for Father Walsh to implement it. The plan has suffered many a sea change, of course. Its main flaw in the long run is, it seems to me, that it is so long that it has too little definition at its west end (Rockne) or its east one (O'Shaughnessy). A bad loss to this one is that of Kervick's imposing entrance building. Notre Dame still suffers from having no main gate. The sorry mound at the northwest corner of Angela and Notre Dame is a child's burlesque of one.

I walk this mall steadily, along with the many students who are ducking into its classroom buildings and dorms, or playing on its long stretches of lawn. I love its feeling of college, of youth and laughter and generosity. It was originally planted with long rows of American elms along its sides, many now lost to the Dutch elm disease, though there remains, happily just west of the junction with the Main Quad, one that is, I often think, the finest big tree on the campus. I also often happily go beyond this mall, through the Lyons arch and around the lakes. I've been doing this since 1930. Basically, thank the Lord, it is mostly the same; the only big difference is that you encounter more people. Yet even among so many I still have a sense of rurality, of woodland and field and wet and wildness. Not much, it's true, but enough to give me a satisfying sense of continuity.

So far the new campus to the east, designed mostly by the Ellerbe Organization of St. Paul, has not proved an inviting place to stroll. The new recreation buildings repeat, sensibly and handsomely, the keynote first struck by the stadium, of straightforward functionalism. This sort of unpretentious structure often slips into genuine esthetic pleasure, as with our Eck Tennis Center—although it may be the only sports spectator building in the world with no public restrooms. But on the east campus I never feel I am part of the college, the community of scholars and dreamers who set the tone. I feel I am among busy, single-minded people who come to exercise, to build muscle, to drill, to practice the piccolo, and to count the number of times they do what they do. No time or place for strolling, for dally-ing, for staring, strutting, drifting, all the things people like to do away from work and purpose. I keep thinking that, espe-cially compared to my own college days, these are too much with us.

And yet I have little nostalgia for the old days, small piety for the lost days of youth. As Evelyn Waugh puts it in *Brideshead Revisited*, "the zest, the generous affections, the illusions, the despair, all the traditional attributes of youth come and go with us through life. Again and again in riper years we experience, under a new stimulus, what we thought had been finally left behind, the authentic impulse to action, the renewal of power and its concentration on a new object; again and again a new truth is revealed to us in whose light all our previous knowledge must be rearranged. But languor—the relaxation of yet unwea-ried sinews, the mind sequestered and self-regarding, the sun standing still in the heavens and the earth throbbing to our own pulse—that belongs to youth and to youth alone."

I beg to differ. It belongs to college, not youth; and something of it stays with us old collegers, I have to think. I'd like to think I'll leave it as joyfully as I entered it, sixty years ago.

INDEX OF NAMES

Unless otherwise indicated all names listed as Rev. here are from the Congregation of Holy Cross (CSC).

Ackerman, Frank, 114
Ackerman, Jacob, 150
Anderson, Carl, 207
Anson, Robert Sam, 195
Anthony, Wilfrid, 76
Apodaca, Joseph, 46
Arendt, Hannah, 79
Artin, Emil, 27, 206
Asselta, Sal, 184

Badin, Rev. Stephen (diocesan), 68
Bain, Reginald, 132
Barrymore, John, 131
Bartholomew, Paul, 46
Becker, John, 23, 153 ff.
Belloc, Hilaire, 121
Bender, Wesley, 66
Benson, Msgr. Robert Hugh, 58
Birder, Cecil, 130
Bird, Otto, 188
Bolger, Rev. William, 46
Bosworth, Henry, 183
Bott, Herbert, 66
Braschi Art Collection, 158
Brennan, Terry, 226
Brewster, Kingman, 214
Brinkley, George, 210
Bromberg, Gertrude, 172
Broughal, Rev. Lawrence, 49–50, 76
Browne, J. Lewis, 154
Brundage, Avery, 144
Buchwald, Art, 124
Buckley, William, 124
Buehr, George and Margo, 159
Burgee, John, 237
Burns, Rev. James, 14, 17 ff., 66, 227

Butterworth, Charles, 130
Byrne, Paul, 160

Callahan, Charles, 140
Campbell, T. Bowyer, 117, 184
Carrico, Rev. J. Leonard, 53, 54, 100
Carroll, Joseph, 34 ff., 121
Carroll, Rev. Patrick, 57
Carter, President Jimmy, 229
Casasanta, Joseph, 156
Cassidy, Claudia, 172–173
Cavanaugh, Rev. John J., 14, 28–30,
   87–88, 220
Cavanaugh, Rev. John W., 14 ff., 28,
   123, 159
Chapin, Francis, 159
Chartrand, Bishop Joseph, 69
Cheney, Brainard and Frances, 174,
   176
Chesterton, G. K., 25, 121 ff.
Chizek, Cletus, 66
Churchill, Winston, 201
Clarke, Isabel, 58
Cochran, Bourke, 201
Collins, Rev. Austin, 149
Collins, George, 200
Compton, Arthur, 207
Confrey, Augustin, 117
Confrey, Burton, 117
Confrey, Zez, 118
Connerton, Rev. James, 23
Coomes, Edward, 200
Cooney, John M., 57, 185
Corbett, James, 46
Corby, Rev. William, 13

Cornell, Katherine, 172
Corrigan, Archbishop Michael, 216
Cram, Ralph Adams, 24
Crawford, F. Marion, 58
Crosson, Fred, 49
Crumley, Rev. Thomas, 52
Cuomo, Mario, 233

Davidson, Donald, 66
Day, Dorothy, 79
DeCicco, Mike, 144
DeValera, Eamon, 124
deVere, Aubrey, 57
Doyle, Gerry, 96
DuBos, Charles, 204
Duffy, Rev. Thomas, 216
Dwan, Allen, 130

Earl, Homer, 66
Edbrooke, Willoughby, 127
Edwards, James, 113
Egan, Maurice Francis, 49, 56, 57
Eisenhower, President Dwight D.,
  228
Engels, Norbert, 65
Evans, Joseph, 107 ff., 194

Fagan, Vincent, 24
Fallon, Tom, 144
Farley, Rev. "Pop," 87
Farrelly, Bishop John, 179
Fenlon, Paul, 77, 119 ff., 133, 135
Fields, William, 172
Finn, Rev. Francis, S.J., 48, 58
Fischer, Edward, 19, 196
Fisher, Mrs. Fred, 159
Fitzgerald, Desmond, 27, 203 ff.
Fitzgerald, "Honey Fitz," 124
Fitzgerald, Robert, 75, 175
Fitzgerald, Sally, 176
Fitzgerald, Scott, 201
Fitzsimons, M. A., 46, 211
Flanigan, Rev. James, 149
Flatley, Lee, 66

Flynn, Charles, 165
Ford, President Gerald, 232
Français, Rev. Gilbert, 18
Frederick, Esther Paulus, 60
Frederick, John T., 49, 59, 175, 189
Frick, James, 226
Frong, Jake, 168, 169

Gasquet, Dom Aidan, 124
Gerrer, Dom Gregory, 158 ff.
Gilson, Etienne, 207
Girac, Max, 115
Gleason, Philip, 180
Gödel, Kurt, 27, 206
Goldblatt, Maurice, 158
Gompers, Samuel, 124
Gordon, Caroline, 176
Greeley, Rev. Andrew (diocesan),
  227
Greene, Edward Lee, 51
Gregori, Luigi, 150 ff.
Groom, Willard, 77, 156
Gurian, Waldemar, 27, 56, 208 ff.
Guth, Eugene, 27, 205

Haas, Arthur, 27, 206
Hager, Rev. Carl, 156
Haley, J. Arthur, 135
Hartke, Rev. Gilbert, O.P., 129
Harvey, Rev. Arthur, 62, 127,
  130 ff.
Hasley, Louis, 193
Hebert, Rev. Peter, 43, 45, 51–52
Hermens, F. A., 27, 189, 209–210
Herrington, Joseph, 184
Hesburgh, Theodore Bernard,
  215–216
Hesburgh, Rev. Theodore M., 1, 10,
  30, 156, 213–234
Hirsch, Sidney Mttron, 40, 173
Hollis, Christopher, 27, 119, 202 ff.
Hope, Rev. Arthur, 126
Howard, Timothy, 115
Howett, John, 161
Hoynes, Col. William, 114

Hudson, Rev. Daniel, 32, 56
Hughes, Msgr. Philip, 180
Hull, Daniel, 65
Huneker, James, 57
Hurok, Sol, 172
Hutchins, Robert Maynard, 29
Huxley, Thomas Henry, 124

Ives, Charles, 155

James, Henry, 124
Johansen, Barry, 195
Jones, Herbert, 135
Joyce, Rev. Edmund, 225–226

Kaczmarek, Regidius, 65
Kahn, Max, 159
Kearns, James, 96, 101
Keeley, Patrick, 76
Kelly, Frank, 130
Kenna, Rev. Howard, 30, 231
Kennedy, John J., 210
Keogan, George, 143
Kerr, Walter, 129–130
Kertesz, Stephen D., 210
Kervick, Francis, 23, 115–116, 238–239
Kilmer, Joyce, 124
Kilmer, Richard, 172, 184
Kingsmill, Hugh, 204
Klein, Abbé Felix, 124
Kline, Jake, 144
Kormendi, Eugene, 150
Krause, Edward, 84
Kroc, Joan, 230

Landis, K. M., 146
Lange, Rev. Bernard, 85
Langford, Walter, 144
Lauck, Rev. Anthony, 149, 160
Layden, Elmer, 138
Leader, Robert, 77
Leahy, Frank, 137–138, 226

Lefschetz, Solomon, 206
LeMaitre, Canon Georges, 27, 207
Lemonnier, Rev. August, 149
Leslie, Shane, 27, 100, 201–202
Levanoux, Maurice, 75
Lunn, Arnold, 27, 204
Lyons, Joseph, 114

McAvoy, Rev. Thomas T., 46
McCarthy, James E., 64
McCue, Martin, 114
McDonald, Rev. James, 100
McGaw, Robert and Elizabeth, 184
McGill, Ralph, 169
McGinn, Rev. John, 46
McKeon, Rev. Frederick, 50
McKinnin, Thomas, 115
Madden, Thomas, 116, 184
Maginnis and Walsh, Architects, 77
Manion, Clarence (Pat), 65, 87, 119
Marconi, Guglielmo, 124
Maritain, Jacques, 27, 62, 105, 109, 126, 208
Maurin, Peter, 79
Maurus, Edward, 65, 115
Meaney, John, 105
Menger, Karl, 27, 206
Mestrovic, Ivan, 149, 160
Michael, C. Everett, 166
Miltner, Rev. Charles, 53–55
Mongan, Agnes, 16
Montgomery, Marion and Dot, 175
Moore, Rev. Philip, 27, 62, 200
Moran, Florence, 65
Moran, Frank, 65
Morrissey, Rev. Andrew, 14, 19, 68
Mott, Frank Luther, 66
Muldoon, John, 160
Muller-Thyme, Bernard, 182
Mundelein, George Cardinal, 124
Murphy, Pat, 144
Murray, Rev. Raymond, 46
Myers, Fred, 65

Napolitano, Dominic, 144

Nicholson, John, 144 ff.
Neville, Paul, 178
Nieuwland, Rev. Julius, 18, 50
Nims, John Frederick and Bonnie,
　61, 175, 193
Nixon, President Richard, 222, 228
Nutting, Willis, 189

O'Connell, Rev. Marvin (diocesan),
　180
O'Connor, Flannery, 80, 175 ff.
O'Donnell, Rev. Charles, 14, 24 ff.
　31, 68, 100, 121, 135
O'Donnell, Rev. Hugh, 14, 28 ff.
O'Grady, Daniel, 118
O'Keefe, Walter, 130
O'Hara, John Cardinal, 23, 68 ff. 100
O'Malley, Austin, 164
O'Malley, Frank, 27, 64 ff., 104 ff.
O'Meara, Timothy, 227
O'Neill, James, Jim, and Gene, 128
Otto, Waldemar, 149

Pall, Augustin, 150
Parseghian, Ara, 138
Payton, Gene, 66
Peat, Wilbur, 161
Pedtke, Daniel, 156
Phillips, Charles, 57, 188
Phillips-Matz, Mary Jane, 172
Pike, Fredrick, 172, 180, 184
Powers, John J., 178
Price, Don K., 39, 177
Price, Stanley, 66

Rauch, Rufus, 65, 105
Reilly, Peter C., 159
Reyniers, Arthur, 47
Rice, Grantland, 133
Rice, Greg, 142
Richter, Eldon, 66
Robinson, Francis, 170 ff.
Rocheleau, George, 159
Rockne, Knute, 16, 25, 129, 135 ff.

Rogers, Will, 124
Roosevelt, President Franklin D., 124
Rubin, Louis, 40
Russell, Fred, 134, 169
Ruth, Babe, 133, 134
Ryan, Msgr. John A., 39
Ryan, Joseph, 116

Sandeen, Ernest, 61, 189
Sandusky, Arthur, 96, 158
Scannell, John, 65
Schlereth, Thomas J., 11
Schumacher, Rev. Matthew, 20, 68,
　152–154
Schurz, Franklin D., 178
Scott, John A., 177–178
Shanahan, William, 46, 184
Shapiro, Mr. and Mrs. Joseph
　Randall, 159–160
Shapley, Harlow, 207
Shaughnessy, Clark, 138
Sheed, Frank, 79
Sheed, Maisie Ward, 79
Sheedy, Rev. Charles, 160
Sheil, Bishop Bernard, 39
Shuster, George, 75, 119, 225
Simon, Yves, 27, 63, 208
Smith, Al, 124
Smith, Red, 143
Smithberger, Andrew, 65
Sorin, Rev. Edward F., 10, 13 ff., 42,
　43, 56, 68, 76, 157, 217, 238, 254
Speaight, Robert, 62, 203
Stace, Arthur Joseph, 114
Stack, Rev. James, 87
Stark, Dennis, 144
Starr, Elizabeth, 183
Staunton, Henry, 58
Steiner, George, 146
Stoddard, Charles Warren, 48, 56,
　113, 149, 164
Stritch, Samuel Cardinal, 14, 15, 31
Stukart, Henry James, 165
Sullivan, Frank, 34 ff.
Sullivan, Gene and Marilyn, 184
Sullivan, Richard, 61, 161 ff.

Syburg, Fred, 130, 132
Sylvester, Harry, 162

Taft, President William Howard, 124
Tate, Allen, 175
Thomas, Ivo, 179
Thompson, Ernest, 23, 149
Tietze, Erica and Hans, 159
Turley, John, 45

Voegelin, Eric, 45, 56

Walker, John, 160
Walker, T. Dart, 152
Walsh, James J., 126
Walsh, Rev. Matthew, 14, 21 ff., 57
Walsh, Rev. Thomas, 14, 120, 123
Walsh, Tom, 182
Walton, James, 166
Walton, W. R., 177
Ward, Rev. Leo L., 59, 64 ff., 100,
    105, 130

Ward, Rev. Leo R., 27, 59 ff.
Ward, Wilfrid, 124
Weber, Ronald, 193, 196
Wenninger, Rev. Francis, 55
Wenzke, Herman, 119
West, Conn Harris, 174, 176
West, Dr. Olin, 169
West, Olin, Jr., 96, 169–170
West, Robert, 40, 169 ff.
Wickett, Mrs. Frederick, 158
Whitman, John, 65
Wightman Art Collection, 157, 158
Withey, James, 23, 54, 75, 100 ff., 185,
    190, 191, 196
Wolfe, Tom, 124
Wood, Paul, 151
Worden, John, 152

Yeats, William Butler, 35, 126

Zahm, Albert, 17, 18, 125
Zahm, Rev. John, 2, 14, 17 ff., 53, 125